3D Graphics
Programming
for Windows 95

Nigel Thompson

PUBLISHED BY
Microsoft Press
A Division of Microsoft Corporation
One Microsoft Way
Redmond, Washington 98052-6399

Library of Congress Cataloging-in-Publication Data
Thompson, Nigel, 1955–
    3D graphics programming for Windows / Nigel Thompson.
        p.   cm.
    Includes bibliographical references and index.
    ISBN 1-57231-345-5
    1. Computer graphics.   2. Three-dimensional display systems.
3. Microsoft Windows (Computer file)   I. Title.
T385.T495397 1996
006.6--dc20   96-32537
                                                     CIP

Printed and bound in the United States of America.
1 2 3 4 5 6 7 8 9 MLML 1 0 9 8 7 6

Distributed to the book trade in Canada by Macmillan of Canada, a division of
Canada Publishing Corporation.

A CIP catalogue record for this book is available from the British Library.

Microsoft Press books are available through booksellers and distributors worldwide.
For further information about international editions, contact your local Microsoft
Corporation office. Or contact Microsoft Press International directly at fax (206)
936-7329.

Macintosh is a registered trademark of Apple Computer, Inc. Autodesk is a registered
trademark of Autodesk, Inc. Dell is a registered trademark and OptiPlex is a trademark
of Dell Computer Corporation. Pentium is a registered trademark of Intel Corporation.
Microsoft, Visual C++, Windows, and Windows NT are registered trademarks and
Direct3D, DirectDraw, DirectInput, DirectPlay, DirectSound, and DirectX are trademarks
of Microsoft Corporation. OpenGL is a registered trademark of Silicon Graphics, Inc.

Acquisitions Editor: Eric Stroo
Project Editors: Averill Curdy and Victoria Thulman
Technical Editor: Jean Ross

To my wife, Tammy, who persuaded me to write this book

Table of Contents

Foreword

Who'd a thunk it: real-time 3D rendering with texture mapping on a $1000 PC. That this is possible is a combination of incredible advances in CPU power, increasingly clever programming on the part of the rendering engine coders, and perhaps even a bit of cheap 3D hardware (though you can get decent results with a plain vanilla CPU). Now the only trick is getting at this capability. In addition to a wide variety of available software rendering engines, a snowstorm of 3D hardware cards is available for the PC. The poor old game designers, who were already buckling under the strain of maintaining compatibility with every two-dimensional graphics hardware card in the known universe, will face Doom in trying to keep up with the fiendish creativity of 3D hardware designers.

Enter Direct3D. Acting as a sort of capabilities broker, it serves as a common ground for accessing similar capabilities of different hardware with a single API. And it contains a not-too-shabby software-only rendering engine of its own. Now you, the game designer (or CAD modeler or Sunday programmer) need to call only a few simple routines to make 3D shapes dance magically on your screen.

But there's a hitch—raw Direct3D has been designed for use with icky old C, and true believers would much rather use the object-oriented stylings of highly desirable C++. In fact, the first urge of dedicated C++ acolytes is to write a C++ wrapper around any C APIs they find.

We have two outstanding problems: Programming nowadays is less a matter of writing code that does something than it is of figuring out which system routine to call next, and programmers want to wrap the C API in cotton wool called C++. Enter Nigel Thompson. He's solved these problems for you. Using his C++ wrapper library, you can easily generate images that would otherwise require intimidating amounts of C code calling raw Direct3D.

So you, the reader of this book, win big. You get a nice introduction to 3D graphics, and you get to access it with C++. And Direct3D makes pictures happen no matter what 3D hardware/software combination you have installed this week. Now you can concentrate more on *what* to draw rather than on *how* to draw it. And Nigel wins big, since you bought his book. And I win big, too. I like games, and now I expect to play with a lot more good ones. So get busy.

—Jim Blinn
Microsoft Graphics Fellow

Acknowledgments

In creating this book, I received small amounts of help from a large number of people and huge amounts of help from a small number of people. Thanks to all of you for the time and effort that you contributed—I hope I've done your efforts justice:

Eric Stroo of Microsoft Press, for taking me to see a demonstration of Direct3D given by Kate Seekings, which inspired me to write the book.

Doug Rabson, Steve Lacey, Giles Burgess, and Servan Keondjian, of the Direct3D programming team, for technical support for the rendering engine. Thanks are especially due to Doug Rabson for answering hundreds of my e-mail questions even while in the middle of doing various beta releases.

Michael Victor, for creating many of the 3D objects used in the samples and for converting my sketches into useful diagrams.

My editors, Averill Curdy, Jean Ross, and Victoria Thulman, and all the other fine folks at Microsoft Press who helped with this book.

Dale Rogerson, for taking time out from writing his own book to review mine.

Special thanks to Nancy Cluts, who took time out from her own writing to build and test some of the sample code as well as thoroughly review all the chapters.

Extra special thanks to Richard Noren for reviewing every chapter in great detail.

Thanks to the many other people who helped review this book, including Don Speray, Eric Berridge, Greg Binkerd, Hung H. Nguyen, Jeff W. Stone, Jim Blinn, Mark Gendron, Michael Malone, Paul David, Steve Lacey, and Sue Ledoux. Thanks to you all!

Thanks to Richard Granshaw for help with some particularly onerous problems I had with my Direct3D sample.

Thanks to Spacetec IMC Corporation for donating a Spaceball Avenger.

Thanks to Dennis Crain, who provided an ear for me to whine in about my troubles and woes of life in general while writing the book.

Final thanks go to my wife, Tammy, who convinced me that I could write this book in my nonexistent spare time and who supported me through the process by keeping our three children, Ron, Nell, and Mark, busy; by pushing food under the door at regular intervals; and by not complaining too much despite getting pregnant again along the way. I love you.

Introduction

I would buy this book because

- it contains lots of practical code examples.
- the code is written in C++.
- it comes with a code library I can experiment with easily.
- the code samples were developed with Microsoft Visual C++ 4.0.
- it has a pretty picture section in the middle.
- it was written by someone who has actually met members of the software development team.
- it contains the full DirectX™ 2 Software Development Kit (SDK).
- it has ideas I could turn into 3D games.
- it has examples that aren't just games.
- I have nothing else to spend my money on.

I wouldn't buy it because

- it has no assembly language code in it.
- it isn't written as a scientific reference text.
- it's not quite thin enough to fix the wobble in my dining room table.
- it doesn't have a set of 3D glasses in the back.
- I already have a copy.

What You Should Get from This Book

My goal for this book is to get you up and running with your first Microsoft Windows 95 3D application. I can't possibly provide all the code examples or library functions you might one day want. Instead I want to teach you enough so that you can create that functionality for yourself by using the DirectX 2 SDK documents and other Windows programming reference material. The C++ class library and code samples included on the companion CD provide everything you need to get your first 3D Windows application written today.

A Little History

Until quite recently it was known that the world was flat. This was very convenient for mapmakers and sailors alike. The mapmakers could draw an accurate representation of the world on a single sheet of paper—being sure to add warnings about the edges. The sailors had no trouble understanding the flat maps of the flat world and always tried to keep the edge in sight in case the maps weren't too accurate. As personal computers evolved, the sailors had their maps digitized to store in computers. Although the computers of Christopher Columbus's time didn't have high-resolution screens and required at least two car batteries to power them, he could still navigate with ease and accuracy, and it was because of these factors that he managed to discover America.

Now we have learned that the world is not flat at all. (Really, I'm not making this up.) In fact, the world is made up of hundreds of small triangles tessellated to form a giant egg shape. This discovery spurred a whole new area of computer graphics as programmers everywhere tried to represent the new egg-shaped world on their flat computer screens. Much of this early work was done by a man named Ray Tracing, after whom one of the techniques is named. Thanks to Ray's work, we can now represent the egg-shaped world on our flat computer screens. (In case you're not familiar with the term, *ray tracing* is simply a method of producing high-quality computer graphics.)

Ray's technology was a little slow on your average Cray II, so other techniques were developed. These weren't quite as stunning, but they were a lot faster. A British company called RenderMorphics created some fine software that could draw solid-looking images in real time on a computer everyone could afford. And so it became possible to see a view of our world actually rotating in space on a humble PC.

3D GRAPHICS PROGRAMMING FOR WINDOWS 95

Until *Star Trek*'s holodeck design becomes generally available on the personal computer (rumor has it that a prototype for the Macintosh has already been built), we will have to make do with representing the egg-shaped world on flat computer screens.

In February 1995 Microsoft bought RenderMorphics and set about tuning RenderMorphics' Reality Lab software for use with Microsoft's operating systems. DirectX 2 was first ported to Microsoft Windows 95, with plans to also include it in Microsoft Windows NT as soon as possible. So now we have a fast three-dimensional (3D) rendering engine built into the operating system. The stage is set for us to create Windows applications that use 3D objects, and all we have to do is figure out how to do it. Creating those applications is what this book is about.

Developing 3D Applications

I developed the samples for this book on a Dell OptiPlex GXM 5120 with 32 MB of RAM, running Microsoft Windows 95 and using Microsoft Visual C++ 4.0 and the DirectX 2 SDK. I wrote all my code in C++ and used the Microsoft Foundation Classes (MFC) to build the applications. Using the combination of C++ and MFC allowed me to quickly build application frameworks in which I could experiment. I developed a set of C++ classes that encapsulate the 3D rendering engine functions and make them a bit easier to use. During the course of the book, we'll explore the C++ classes I created, and you'll learn how to use them and extend them for your own needs.

If you're a C programmer who hasn't moved to C++ yet—this might be a great time to start! My own use of the C++ language isn't very advanced, and my samples can be followed by any C programmer with just a few weeks of C++ experience. If you're not a C programmer, my advice is to skip learning C altogether and jump straight into C++.

I created my applications and C++ classes from a practical point of view. In other words, I tried to create tools that solve problems I have rather than create endless examples that show off features. So you won't find any CDog, CLabrador, or CAardvark classes in my examples. This doesn't mean that we won't explore many of the features the rendering engine has to offer, but we'll use those features as we need them to create the applications we want to build.

If you're new to the entire concept of 3D graphics, you might like to read one of the many excellent works that discuss this topic in detail. I like *Computer Graphics Principles and Practice* by Foley, vanDam, Feiner, and Hughes (Addison-Wesley, 1991) as a reference text, but there are many others to choose from—for example, *3D Computer Graphics* by Glassner (Lyon & Burford, 1989). It's not necessary to read these reference books—you can still have a lot of fun without them.

The DirectX 2 SDK contains support for the Direct3D, DirectInput, DirectSound, Direct3DSound, DirectDraw, and DirectPlay application programming interfaces. We'll be using the Direct3D, DirectDraw, and DirectInput interfaces but not the interfaces for DirectSound and DirectPlay. Some of the applications do use sound, so if you have a sound card, you'll be in for a surprise occasionally. The Direct3D interface actually consists of several parts of which the highest level is called Retained Mode. The level below that is called Immediate Mode, and below that are device drivers. I sometimes refer to the "rendering engine" in the text. I'm using this term to mean the entire Direct 3D engine from the Retained Mode level on down to the drivers and not just the rasterizer in the Immediate Mode layer.

Code Style

Don't worry, I'm not about to embark on a tirade about how to indent your code or where the curly braces should be placed, but I do want to mention some points about the samples. In particular, it's important to remember that the sample code is exactly that—*sample* code—and it's not intended to be production code. In many cases, I have shortened the code by eliminating some of the error handling and instead used *ASSERT* statements to make run-time checks in the debug version. This technique traps silly programming errors quickly and also serves to highlight code where you might be able to use a better error-handling technique. You should also be aware that I do not handle run-time exceptions at all. The most common place where an exception might be raised is when memory is allocated, and this can happen during the construction of many different C++ objects. As a minor note, it is pointless to place *ASSERT* statements on pointers created by the *new* operator because the implementation of *new* in the MFC libraries raises an exception if the memory is not available to allocate the object. So as far as you're concerned, *new* always succeeds.

I use a simple variable tagging scheme that has its roots in the so-called "Hungarian notation" used by Microsoft for its own development projects. My own version is somewhat simpler. The following table shows the prefixes I use and the types they represent. You might come across other prefixes occasionally, but this table represents the common ones.

Prefix	Type
i	int
d	double
p	pointer
pI	pointer to a COM interface
m_	A data member of a C++ class

If you're a veteran Windows programmer, you'll remember the hateful days of *NEAR* and *FAR* pointer types before we moved to 32-bit systems. Many of the

Windows data structures and function prototypes include elements with the prefix *lp*, meaning long (far) pointer. All pointers in my code are just pointers and hence I use only one prefix: *p*. I generally put numbers in integer values (type *int*) and avoid long integer types and so on. If I need a floating-point value I always use a *double*. This uses more data storage than a *float* but avoids compiler-generated conversions when math functions are called.

So I have a somewhat simplistic approach to my data types, which I find serves me well and helps to reduce the complexity of my programs. You are welcome to do whatever you want, of course. I'm not out to convert you to my way of working, I just want you to be able to follow my code.

The 3dPlus Library

There are several ways to create samples that evolve as a book progresses. One approach is for each sample to contain only the code it needs at that point in the evolution of the reader's knowledge. The entire code from one sample is then copied to the next sample before being added to. I like this approach, which I used in my previous book *Animation Techniques in Win32*, because you can see exactly what is required to implement the sample at any point.

For this book, however, I've decided to handle the code samples differently by having more or less all the code available at the start and pointing out only the bits you need for any given sample. I chose to show the samples this way because the amount of code required to create the first sample is quite large. Although it all needs to be there, you really don't need to know how it all works right from the outset. (Also, by developing a common body of code used by all the samples, I reduce the chance of propagating small bugs through all the samples.) I have created a library to contain all the common code for my samples: the 3dPlus library.

If you're concerned about the performance of an application that depends on a lot of C++ code, let me reassure you that the C++ code layer is very thin. In many cases, a call made to a member function in a C++ class maps directly to a call made to a Direct3D COM interface member, and if you want, you can easily bypass the C++ code layer and call the Direct3D interfaces directly. In fact, as your application progresses, you're bound to find that I haven't implemented all the functionality that you might like in the library. At that point, you can either extend the library software yourself or call the underlying Direct3D interfaces directly.

The Direct3D Interface

The Direct3D system is built using the Component Object Model (COM), which is the technology Microsoft is using to build its next generation operating system, code-named Cairo. Direct3D is one of the first add-ons to Windows outside of object linking and embedding (OLE) to use this technology. COM objects are to C++ what dynamic-link libraries (DLLs) are to C programming in Windows. That's not to say that COM objects can be used only by C++ applications but rather that COM objects provide a great framework for creating system components. They are also very easy to use from C++ code.

COM objects use a table of pointers to their member functions commonly called a *vtable*. This same mechanism is used in C++ to implement virtual member functions in a C++ class. Just as you can call C++ functions from C code with a bit of extra effort, you can also call COM object interfaces from C code. Calling COM object interfaces from C++ is easier because it looks just like calling member functions in any C++ class. Here's an example of a piece of C code calling a COM object interface:

```
pInterface->lpVtbl->Member(pInterface, arg1);
```

Here's the same call as it would typically appear in C++ code:

```
pInterface->Member(arg1);
```

COM objects use reference counting to determine how long they should live. When there are no more references to a COM object it destroys itself. This simple mechanism makes sharing COM objects very easy and frees the programmer from all sorts of data management tasks. It does, however, mean that you need to be aware of how the reference counting system works so that you can use the objects correctly.

Essentially, every time a COM object gives you a pointer to one of its interfaces it increments its own reference count. If you copy the interface pointer, you must increment the object's reference count by calling its *AddRef* member function. When you're finished with the pointer you call the interface's *Release* function, which decrements the COM object's reference count again. There's a bit more to it than that but that's most of the story. Here's an example of a piece of C++ code getting a pointer to a COM object interface, calling a member function, and then releasing the interface:

```
pInterface = GetSomeCOMInterface();
pInterface->CallMember();
pInterface->Release();
```

Note that once you have called *Release*, the pointer is no longer valid because the object it was addressing might now be destroyed (if you released the final or only copy of the object). After calling *Release*, I typically assign NULL to the pointer to help track programming errors such as attempting to use an invalid interface pointer. If you're a fan of macros (I'm not), you can always create a *RELEASE* macro that calls the *Release* function and assigns NULL to the pointer for you:

```
#define RELEASE(p) ((p)->Release(); (p)=NULL;)
```

I thought that learning how to use 3D techniques would be enough of a task, so I've hidden the Direct3D COM interfaces inside the C++ classes in the 3dPlus library. If you stick to calling the 3dPlus library functions, you do not need to know anything about the underlying COM interfaces. But if you want to extend the library or you want to program without calling the library functions, you should review how COM objects work. Along the way we'll be looking at many of the Direct3D interfaces, so by the end of the book you should be quite familiar with how they operate, whether you intend to use them directly or not.

If you want to know more about COM objects, read Kraig Brockschmidt's book *Inside OLE* (second edition) or the many articles available on the Microsoft Developer Library.

Some Final Notes

When you're reading through the code examples in the text, you can usually determine whether calls are being made to 3dPlus library objects or to the rendering engine by looking at the names of the objects involved. If you see a *C3d<name>*, then it's a C++ class object and is a member of the 3dPlus library. If you see *C<name>*, then there's a chance it came from the 3dPlus library—or maybe it's an MFC class object—but more likely it's a C++ object created just for that one example. If you see *I<name>*, then it's an interface and belongs to the Direct3D engine in some way. Any pointer that begins with *pI<name>* is a pointer to a Direct3D interface.

When you run the sample applications, you'll notice that many of them have black backgrounds. These backgrounds have been changed to white in the text for the sake of clarity.

Using the Companion CD

The CD attached to the inside back cover of this book contains sample applications that demonstrate the concepts discussed throughout the book. You can access the files for the applications directly from the CD, but I would recommend you run the Setup program to copy the files to your hard disk so that you can practice with them, modify them, and use them to create your own applications. (This will require approximately 45 MB of hard disk space.) Run Setup.exe and follow the on-screen instructions. All the sample applications will be copied to your hard disk in the \3D directory (unless you choose to change the default). Included will be the directory structure for the samples, all the required files to make and run the samples, the executable files, and the project workspace (MDP) files.

Also included on the companion CD is the DirectX 2 SDK in the \MSDX2SDK directory, and a \Tools directory with some utilities that might be useful to you in your 3D programming activities. The SDK has its own Setup program you must run, and you can manually copy the utilities from the Tools directory when you need them.

The Small Print

My own code is never perfect, and my approach to solving a problem might not be quite what you had in mind. Also, despite my best efforts there might be technical errors in the text. If you find errors or have suggestions, please let me know. I can't offer to fix all your problems for you, but I do try to respond constructively to all the mail I receive.

You can e-mail me at: nigel-t@msn.combusy.

—Nigel
1996

CHAPTER 1

Your First 3D Application

any years ago I taught a Microsoft Windows programming course that took C programmers from ground zero to Windows programmer in four days. The best part for me was at the start of the first day when I'd tell them that by the end of the day they would all have created a Windows application. Not many thought this was possible, but nobody failed. By the end of the day, I had a lot of pumped up apprentice Windows programmers who didn't want to go home. I hope that's how you'll feel by the end of this chapter.

In this chapter you'll learn how to create a Windows application that shows a few 3D objects in a window. We'll use Microsoft Visual C++ and the Microsoft Foundation Classes (MFC) to create the application framework. Then we have to add only about 50 lines of code to call functions in the 3dPlus library and we'll be done. If you want to see what we're going to create, try running the Basic sample from the companion CD. Figure 1-1 shows a screen shot of the Basic sample.

NOTE

Before you can run any of the samples from this book or from the DirectX 2 SDK, you must install the DirectX run-time libraries on your computer. To do this, read the installation instructions in the DirectX 2 SDK or run the DirectX Setup program from the companion CD and select the option to install only the run-time components.

Figure 1-1. *The Basic sample application.*

The Basic sample creates a window that shows a scene containing three spherical objects of different colors. The spheres are lit by two different light sources. The objects are set in motion so that the two smaller spheres appear to orbit around the large sphere.

This might not seem like much to achieve, and, as you'll see in a moment, the guts of the application turn out to be quite simple, which is the important point. There's a lot of code behind the scenes in the MFC libraries, the DirectX libraries, and the 3dPlus library, but you don't need to know how any of that works to build your first application. All you need is a little guidance to get you started. The rest is just a matter of finding out exactly which calls you need to make to achieve the effects you want. We'll spend the rest of the book looking at how the 3dPlus library is built and the reasoning behind all the code you're about to see. So say good-bye to the dog, take a big breath, and let's jump off the dock and see if we can swim.

Building an Application from Scratch

There are two kinds of programmers in the world, and I think the balance is about 50:50. Half of us like to take some existing code and munge it around until it does what we want. The other half like to start from scratch and type everything in for ourselves. I belong to the second category. I hate to use someone else's code because I might not know how it works, which could mean that debugging it later will be a nightmare. So just in case you don't want to take the Basic sample and play with it, I'll describe how I built it. (Of course, you're going to have to use my 3dPlus library for now, but by the end of the book you'll be able to rewrite that, too.) If you don't care right now how the application got built, skip this section and come back later when you need to.

Here are the steps I followed to create the Basic sample:

1.   Use the Visual C++ MFC AppWizard (EXE) to create an SDI (Single Document Interface) application with no database support and no OLE support. You can also leave out the toolbar, status bar, printing, and 3D features. This is the simplest Windows application you can create. I named my project *Basic*. I chose to use the MFC As A Shared DLL option, but you can link it statically if you want.

2.   Remove the document and view class files from the project. Mine were called BasicDoc.h, BasicDoc.cpp, BasicView.h, and BasicView.cpp. Delete the files from your directory and from your project.

3.   Remove the main window files (usually MainFrm.h and MainFrm.cpp) in the same way. This leaves you with two C++ files: Basic.cpp and StdAfx.cpp.

4.   Edit the source files to remove any reference to the header files for the document, view, or main frame classes. I usually clean up some of the resources, like the About dialog box, any unused menus, the string table, and so on at this point, but a lot of this cleanup can also be done later.

5. In StdAfx.h, add lines to include <mmsystem.h> and <d3drmwin.h>. The Mmsystem header is used for joystick functions we'll need later, and the d3drmwin header defines all the Direct3D functions.

6. Include <3dplus.h> in either StdAfx.h or Basic.h. I put mine in Basic.h so that when I modify the library I don't need to rebuild all the files in an application I'm working on.

7. Modify the *InitInstance* function in Basic.cpp so that it looks like the *InitInstance* function that begins on page 5. I also removed the About Box code (*CAboutDlg*).

8. Use ClassWizard to add an *OnIdle* function stub to Basic.cpp.

9. Edit the *OnIdle* function so that it looks like the code segment on page 6.

10. Choose Settings from the Build menu, and add the DirectX libraries and the 3dPlus library to the link list in the dialog box. My samples all have 3dPlusd.lib, d3drm40f.lib, ddraw.lib, and winmm.lib. Note that the 3dPlus library project allows you to build either a debug version (3dPlusd.lib) or a release version (3dPlus.lib). For the samples, I use the debug build so that you get all the library symbols and you can trace into the library code if you want. The directories for the necessary libraries and the include files must be specified in the Options dialog box. See page 14 for more information.

11. Update all dependencies and build the application. Your application should look just like the sample.

You might find the idea of ripping out files from a project that AppWizard created rather scary. This is where you have to trust me! If you're familiar with using AppWizard and the MFC library, then I'm sure this is no big deal to you. If you're new to MFC, you might want to use AppWizard to create a new project and explore the files for a while to see what the files contain before you set about dismembering them. The Scribble tutorial that comes with the Visual C++ samples provides some excellent insight into what all the files are for. Once you've acquainted yourself with the document/view architecture, you'll perhaps see more clearly why we want to remove it.

The Code

Let's look at the code required to create the spheres and set them spinning in the window. If you don't follow everything you're about to see, just take in what you can for now and trust that, as you read on, more and more of this will become clear. For now I want to show you how little you need to do, not explain why it's all in there. Here are the two functions from the Basic.cpp file that set up the scene and make it run:

```cpp
BOOL CBasicApp::InitInstance()
{
    // Create main window
    C3dWnd* pWnd = new C3dWnd;
    pWnd->Create("3D Basics",
                 WS_OVERLAPPEDWINDOW | WS_VISIBLE,
                 50, 50,
                 400, 350);
    m_pMainWnd = pWnd;
    pWnd->UpdateWindow();

    // Create an initial scene we can add objects to
    static C3dScene scene;
    scene.Create();

    // Set ambient light level
    scene.SetAmbientLight(0.4, 0.4, 0.4);

    // Add directional light to create highlights
    static C3dDirLight dl;
    dl.Create(0.8, 0.8, 0.8);
    scene.AddChild(&dl);
    dl.SetPosition(-2, 2, -5);
    dl.SetDirection(1, -1, 1);

    // Create big white sphere
    static C3dShape sh1;
    sh1.CreateSphere(1);

    // Add big white sphere to scene
    scene.AddChild(&sh1);

    // Create small blue sphere
    static C3dShape sh2;
    sh2.CreateSphere(0.3);
    sh2.SetColor(0, 0, 1);

    // Attach blue sphere to white one
    sh1.AddChild(&sh2);
```

(continued)

```
        // Set blue sphere's position relative
        // to white sphere
        sh2.SetPosition(0, 0, -2);

        // Create small red sphere
        static C3dShape sh3;
        sh3.CreateSphere(0.15);
        sh3.SetColor(1, 0, 0);

        // Attach red sphere to white one
        sh1.AddChild(&sh3);

        // Set red sphere's position relative
        // to white sphere
        sh3.SetPosition(0, 0, 5);

        // Start rotating big sphere slowly around
        // the 1, 1, 0 axis
        sh1.SetRotation(1, 1, 0, 0.015);

        // Attach entire scene to the stage
        pWnd->SetScene(&scene);

        return TRUE;
}

BOOL CBasicApp::OnIdle(LONG lCount)
{
        BOOL bMore = CWinApp::OnIdle(lCount);

    if (m_pMainWnd) {
            C3dWnd* pWnd = (C3dWnd*) m_pMainWnd;

            // Tell 3D window to move scene one unit,
            // and redraw window
            if (pWnd->Update(1)) {
                bMore = TRUE;
            }
        }
        return bMore;
}
```

CBasicApp::InitInstance creates the window and the objects that form the scene, and *CBasicApp::OnIdle* updates the positions of the objects in the scene when the application is idle. The *CBasicApp* class was generated by AppWizard when the application was first built. *CBasicApp* is derived from the MFC class *CWinApp*, which provides the essential framework for a Windows application. Let's look at what the two functions do, step by step.

The first thing *InitInstance* does is create the window that will display the 3D scene. A window of the *C3dWnd* class is created as the application's main window. The *C3dWnd* class comes from the 3dPlus library as do all of the other classes we'll look at here that begin with the *C3d* prefix. (The source code for the 3dPlus library is on the companion CD with the other samples.) A pointer to the main window is stored in *m_pMainWnd*, which is a member of the MFC *CWinApp* base class. This window pointer is used by the MFC code in implementing the application's message handling and so on. The final step in creating the window is to call *UpdateWindow* to paint the window onto the screen.

A *C3dScene* object is then created. The scene object is used to contain all the elements of one scene that we might want to display in our 3D window, such as lights, 3D objects, and so on.

The next step is to set up the lighting in the scene. We use two different lights: an ambient light and a directional light. The ambient light illuminates all objects evenly and on its own gives a flat appearance to the objects. The directional light behaves more like a spotlight. (Directional light alone gives a very harsh contrast, making the darker parts hard to see.) When an object is illuminated by a directional light, the intensity of the object's colors varies in a way that suggests a light shining on it from one direction. By using both kinds of light, we get a reasonable 3D impression and we can still see all the bits of an object even if they are in the shadow of the directional light. The *C3dScene* class has a built-in ambient light, so all we need to do here is set the level. The stage is roughly equivalent to the application window that the current scene is being viewed in. Here's how the ambient light level is set:

```
scene.SetAmbientLight(0.4, 0.4, 0.4);
```

Lights are made up of different levels of red, green, and blue. In this case, we set the red, green, and blue values to produce white light so that the colors of the objects look correct. Color values for lights can vary from zero to unity (0.0 through 1.0); in Windows programming we are used to integer color values that vary from 0 through 255. Using a floating-point value (a *double*) might seem a bit of overkill, but bear in mind that the colors you set here are used to mathematically determine the exact colors of the faces of the objects in a scene. There's a lot of trigonometry and so on required to do the calculations, so using floating-point values for color components isn't so strange really. For those of you with a passion for C++, you can of course define a color class for yourself and redo some of the 3dPlus library functions to make them take your color object as an argument rather than as individual RGB values. I didn't do that simply because I wanted it to be quite obvious what the RGB levels were in some cases in the code.

Unlike the ambient light that just needs to be set, the directional light needs to be created and added to the scene, and then the position and direction of the directional light can be set. The position coordinates are *x*-, *y*-, and *z*-axis values. The direction is set by defining a vector that points the way we want the light to look. Let's not worry about coordinates and vectors at the moment, but take it for granted that the light is positioned so that it appears to come from the top left side of the scene.

I chose to set the directional light at the top left because this is the lighting direction Windows uses for its own 3D controls.

Figure 1-2 shows the scene with the directional light in place and also shows the *x*-coordinate, *y*-coordinate, and *z*-coordinate axes.

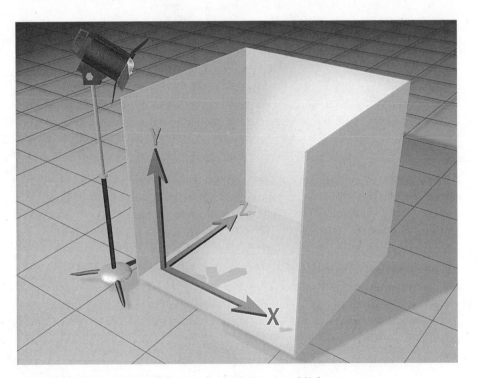

Figure 1-2. *The stage, coordinate axes, and directional light.*

Having created the lighting setup, we are ready to add some objects. We create three spheres and add them to the scene by calling the *AddChild* method. You can think of the *AddChild* function as attaching a child object to a parent object. In the case of the first object we create, the scene is the parent, but as we'll see later, the hierarchy can be much more complex than that. We set the colors of the spheres using red, green, and blue values in the same way we specified the colors of the lights. White is the default color for objects.

The white sphere remains in its default position of 0, 0, 0. The red and blue spheres are set some distance away from the white one by calling *SetPosition*. The dimensions given as parameters to *SetPosition* are "model units," which are rather arbitrary. You'll learn how object sizes get determined later.

The last steps are to apply a rotation value to the large sphere and then attach the entire scene, consisting of the lights and the spheres, to the 3D window. The arguments to *C3dShape::SetRotation* define an axis as a vector of *x*-, *y*-, and *z*-coordinates to rotate around and a rate at which the rotation should take place. Rotating an object is actually quite complicated, but the *SetRotation* function makes it very easy to apply the simple rotational effects we're using here. In Chapters 5 and 6 we'll be looking at the subject of rotating objects in a lot more detail.

The *CBasicApp::OnIdle* function is called by the MFC framework code when the application is idle—that is, when the application has no messages to process and no other applications are busy, which actually turns out to be most of the time. We use this idle time to move the scene to its next position and draw it into the window. All of this happens when the *C3dWnd::Update* function is called (*pWnd->Update(1)*). The argument to *C3dWnd::Update* is used to determine how far along the scene should be advanced. We'll use this argument later to keep movement in the scene at a fixed rate even though the idle time might vary. For now, we'll use the default value of *1* to advance the scene one (somewhat arbitrary) unit.

As you can see, we didn't use too many lines of code, but we did skate over a few of the points. You get a special prize if you spotted my use of a few static variables back there—sorry about that. I used them here to keep the code as short as possible. As we progress, we'll add some support that makes using static variables unnecessary.

At the risk of repeating myself, let me remind you not to worry if everything wasn't clear the first time around. We'll be looking at it all again as we progress through the book. Let's look at some of the details next.

Performance, Shadows, Frames, and Coordinates

If you run the Basic sample on a decent machine with a good video card that supports hardware bit block transfers (bitblts), you should be impressed by the performance. By a "decent" machine, I'm talking about at least a 50-MHz 486 or, preferably, a more recent Pentium machine with PCI video. The most critical element is the video card. If your card has lots of video memory (more than required for the display resolution you're using) and hardware that implements functions for moving video memory around, the DirectX libraries can take advantage of that memory and hardware. This greatly increases performance over older video cards that require the system processor to move the video memory around. In fact, supporting the hardware features of the latest generation of video cards is really what the Direct3D interface is all about—letting you get the most from your host.

To return to the sample: Each sphere has 256 faces that have to be painted. For each face there are three or four coordinates that need to have their positions computed. The color of each face has to be altered according to the position of the face and the sum of all the effects of the lights in the scene. That's quite a lot of math to do, and the smooth movement you see is the result of all the calculations being done pretty quickly. The Direct3D rendering engine really is quite an impressive piece of code that has been optimized to get absolutely the best possible performance.

OK, so you're sold on the engine, but can you tell that I'm leading up to something? Of course, with such terrific performance, some trade-offs were made along the way. For example, there are no shadows or reflections. Perhaps you didn't notice? Run the sample again and watch as the spheres revolve. Look at where the light is coming from; the red and blue spheres both pass between the white sphere and the directional light source, but no shadows appear on the white sphere. You don't see any reflections of the small spheres on the big one either.

Our rendering engine does not do ray tracing, so it doesn't generate shadows and reflections. The benefit we get from this is a massive increase in performance. If you didn't notice that the shadows were missing until I told you, you can see that effective 3D animations don't rely on having shadows and reflections. As you'll learn later, we can actually generate some shadows, and even the appearance of reflections, by using a technique called a *chrome wrap,* discussed in Chapter 8—so keep reading.

If you look back at the code on page 6, you'll see that a call was made to *SetRotation* to make the big white sphere revolve in the scene. When you run the sample you might see that the white sphere is revolving—the shading is so good it's quite hard to tell. However, you can certainly see that the two small spheres are rotating around the bigger one. But where is the code that told them to rotate? The secret lies in how they were added to the scene. You'll notice that the big sphere was added to the scene directly,

```
scene.AddChild(&sh1);
```

but the small spheres were added to the big sphere instead.

```
sh1.AddChild(&sh2);
sh1.AddChild(&sh3);
```

By attaching the small spheres to the big sphere, we are able to rotate the small spheres when we set the big sphere in motion. The ability to attach objects in a hierarchy is a popular idea in 3D rendering systems.

Each object in the scene we created has an associated *frame*. The frame is really just a description of the mathematical *transform* (the position, size, or nature of an object) that needs to be applied to all the objects and frames attached to that frame before they are rendered. A frame can have other frames attached to it as child frames, and the transforms for any child frames get applied after the parent transform. The result is that the child frames move with the parent and can also have their own motions relative to the parent. To picture this, think about walking around inside an office in a big building. Your frame is the office you're in. The office's frame might be the entire floor, and the floor's frame might be the entire building. Although you see yourself as moving only in the room, you're also moving relative to the floor you're on and the building you're in. You'll learn more about these topics in Chapter 5 when we look at transforms and in Chapter 6 where we see how objects are moved.

In implementing the 3dPlus library of objects, I chose to give each scene a frame. Each shape and light also has its own frame. So you can group together any collection of objects and attach them to a frame or each other in any way you want.

Why do you want to do this? Well, apart from orbiting spheres, there are quite a lot of effects that are very simple to implement using an object (frame) hierarchy. Consider the Mark VII Interplanetary Battle Tank, which, as we all know, has an X-Band Doppler Radar for ranging its guns. If we want to model this tank in our 3D application, we can create a shape for the radar, attach it to the body of the tank, and set the radar rotating about its support axis. In frame terms: The radar frame becomes a child of the tank's frame. Then we can concentrate on moving the tank and not have to worry about the radar—it will always be in the right place and rotating correctly. Figure 1-3 shows a Mark VII tank in action.

Figure 1-3. The Mark VII Interplanetary Battle Tank with its X-Band Doppler Radar.

The last point that I'd like to cover here is the coordinate system. Because we're working in three dimensions, any point requires three values to represent its position. We have three axes—x, y, and z—arranged in what is known as a left-handed set. Let's do a little audience participation here. (If you're reading this in bed, you might want to warn your significant other that you are about to make weird hand gestures, which are not to be taken as some form of communication on your part.) Stick your left hand out in front of you, extending your fingers away from you with the palm of your hand facing right. Your thumb should be on top. Put your thumb up. Now curl your third and fourth fingers into your palm and bend your second finger to the right. Your hand should look something like Figure 1-4; your thumb is the y-axis, your first finger is the z-axis, and your second finger is the x-axis.

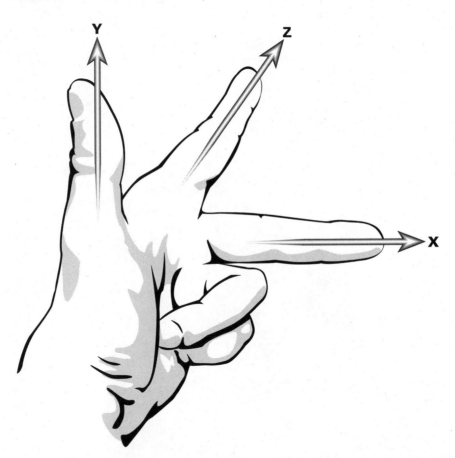

Figure 1-4. *A left hand showing the left-handed coordinate axes.*

In the left-handed 3D world, the y-axis is up, the x-axis is to the right, and the z-axis is into the screen (away from the user). Of course, it's not called left-handed just because you can make your left hand into this strange shape, but because if you had a threaded rod and rotated it from the x-axis to the y-axis, it

3D GRAPHICS PROGRAMMING FOR WINDOWS 95

would move in the direction of the z-axis. You can see we'd need a rod with a left-hand thread to make this work for our set of left-handed axes.

Many 3D environments are based on right-handed coordinate sets, but ours is not, so get used to sticking out that left hand when you want to sort out which way things will be pointing. If you really hate the left-handed system and want passionately to use right-handed coordinates, then go right ahead. Adding a simple transform to your right-handed coordinates will convert them to the left-handed system that the rendering engine uses. Transforms are covered in Chapter 5.

The coordinates of points in 3D space are specified in two ways in code that uses the DirectX engine. Sometimes coordinates are supplied as three *doubles* representing the x-, y-, and z-axis values, and sometimes they are supplied as a *D3DVECTOR*, which internally is a structure with member variables for the x, y, and z values. In either case, the axis values are floating-point numbers. The scale used is totally arbitrary, but I chose to set the camera position and other stage parameters so that a one-unit cube looks like a reasonable-sized object when placed at point 0, 0, 0 in the scene. We'll look at coordinates and so on again later.

NOTE

The 3dPlus library includes the *C3dVector* class, which is derived from *D3DVECTOR*. Anywhere that a *D3DVECTOR* type is specified as a function argument, you can also use a *C3dVector* object as the argument. I created the *C3dVector* class because I can make a C++ class more useful in the code than a simple data structure. You might also note that the Direct3D functions take float arguments—not doubles. I use doubles in my code because they offer more precision, convert more easily, and are what all the C run-time math routines need as arguments.

Want to Start Playing Yet?

You've probably had enough of reading and hand exercises by now and want to crank up Visual C++, copy the Basic project from the companion CD (or run the Setup program), and start modifying the application to do a few different things. You can try changing the colors of the shapes, the color of the lights, the rotation parameters, or even add a few more objects, such as cubes, cones, or tubes. The *C3dShape* class has functions to create all of these simple shapes. Just before you leap into action, however, you should know a little bit about the samples and the development environment you need to set up.

Before you can compile any of the sample code, you need to set up your development environment correctly by doing the following:

1. Run the DirectX 2 SDK Setup program and install the DirectX 2 SDK development tools. This will add the DirectX 2 SDK include files, libraries, and so on to your hard disk. It will also install the DirectX 2 SDK run-time libraries if you didn't install them earlier.

2. Run Visual C++ and choose Options from the Tools menu; click the Directories tab in the Options dialog box.

3. Add the path to the DirectX 2 SDK include files to the Include Files list and the path to the DirectX 2 SDK libraries to the Library Files list. If you don't do this, your applications won't compile or link.

> **NOTE**
>
> The Direct3D headers have references to two files, subwtype.h and d3dcom.h, which are not actually used when building a Windows application and consequently are not shipped in the SDK. Unfortunately, the Visual C++ dependency checker notices that these files might be needed and complains that it can't find them. To fix this problem I created two dummy files: subwtype.h and d3dcom.h. You'll find these files in the 3dPlus library Include directory. The files are empty except for a short comment.

All the samples use the 3dPlus library, and you need to copy at least the include files and libraries to your hard disk before you can build the samples. It's simplest to copy the entire tree of the 3dPlus sample directory. That way you can compile the entire thing for yourself as a confidence test and be sure that everything is in place before you start work on the other samples. If you choose to run the Setup program on the companion CD, you will not need to manually copy the 3dPlus directory structure. You will, however, need to include the 3dPlus\Include directory in your Include Files list and the 3dPlus\Lib directory in your Library Files list. Using the default Setup, your entries for the include and library lists should look like this:

```
C:\MSDEV\INCLUDE
C:\MSDEV\MFC\INCLUDE
C:\DXSDK\SDK\INC
C:\3D\3DPLUS\INCLUDE

C:\MSDEV\LIB
C:\MSDEV\MFC\LIB
C:\DXSDK\SDK\LIB
C:\3D\3DPLUS\LIB
```

Of course, you can do whatever you like with your files and set your compiler paths to find them. I set it up this way to cause the least amount of pain. The directory tree on your development machine should look something like the following:

```
C:\
    3D
        3dPlus
            Include
            Lib
            Source
```

```
        Basic
        Color
        :(The other samples)
    Dxsdk (The DirectX 2 SDK)
        sdk
            inc
            lib
            ⋮

    ⋮
    Msdev (Visual C++ installation)
    ⋮
```

Once your environment is set up and you're ready to start on a project, don't forget to choose Update All Dependencies from the Build menu in Visual C++ to make sure the compiler can find all your header files.

So What Did We Learn Today?

If you said "Not much," then I guess you weren't impressed! I was hoping for more like "Creating my first 3D application was really easy" or "I always wanted to make some colored spheres float around in a window and now I've done it." Each to his or her own, I guess. Of course, now you have thousands of questions about where we go from here and how all this works and how we get an elephant into the scene and how we fly through the planets with majestic music playing as a large bone floats up into space from the planet below and how to get a picture of President Nixon texture-mapped to a cube and what exactly is the armament complement of a Mark VII Interplanetary Battle Tank? All this and more will be revealed in the following chapters. Well, most of it will—I couldn't find a picture of Nixon and the tank is currently in the shop.

In the next chapter we're going to start building a slightly more complete application framework, to which we'll add features as we progress through the rest of the book. We'll also look at how the underlying rendering engine is configured and start to explain how it works.

CHAPTER **2**

Setting the Stage

n the last chapter we created a simple application to show how little code was required to get up and running. In this chapter we're going to build a slightly more complex application framework that we can expand on in the following chapters. The new framework is similar to what you created in Chapter 1 except that it has a menu bar and toolbar and creates the 3D window a little differently.

I'm also going to cover a good deal of conceptual information you should find useful. I'll go through the details of how this framework was built so that you understand how to add menu items of your own and so on. We'll look at how the 3D window works in more detail. We will examine the Direct3D device and viewport interfaces, see what they are, how they work, and how we control them. We are also going to look at frames in more detail and see how the stage, camera, scene, and the scene's objects relate. Finally, we'll look at how to load 3D objects from disk files and show them in a window. By the end of this chapter you'll at least have an object file viewer you can modify to test different sample objects.

The sample application, named Stage, that accompanies this chapter is in the Stage directory. You might like to run it now and see what it does before we get into how it was built and how it works.

The Application Framework

The architecture that you start with in a project often greatly influences how the rest of the project grows. A bad framework can mean that your project grows rather more warts than one would ideally like. For example, when I wrote *Animation Techniques for Win32* I was new to C++ and also to using Microsoft Visual C++ and the MFC libraries. I made then what I now consider to be a bad mistake when I started creating the samples: I used Visual C++ to build a single document interface (SDI) framework and just assumed my work would fit in somewhere. I built an SDI application because at the time the only choices were SDI or MDI (multiple document interface), and MDI was the last thing I needed to show off an animated game. With hindsight, I think that my samples would have been simpler if I had avoided the Visual C++ document/view metaphor and stuck to using a simple window with a menu bar.

This time I decided that the application framework for the samples in this book would be simpler and closer to what might be needed to create a game. (That's not to say that you can't use this framework for more complex applications, it's just that I've dispensed with the document/view idea to simplify the sample code, and this happens to also fit into what a game builder might want.)

In fact, as you will see shortly, the window object we use can be used as an application's main window as it was in the Basic sample, or as a child window as it is used in the Stage sample. You can even switch it to full-screen exclusive mode, take over the video display entirely, and run the video in some mode other than the one Microsoft Windows was using before your application was started. On the whole, even though the overall application framework is much simpler than I've used before, there is enough flexibility in the design for many different uses.

I'm not suggesting that you use the sample code here as the basis for a real product. But it can provide a platform on which you can effectively experiment with ideas for a product. The 3dPlus library code was designed as a teaching tool—not as a production library. If you use it as the basis for a real product, you'll have to add a fair bit of code to deal with error handling, exceptions, and so on.

Here are the steps I took to build the framework using Visual C++:

1. Use the Visual C++ MFC AppWizard to create an SDI application with no database support, no OLE support, and no printing support. This is the simplest windowed application you can create. I called my project *Stage*. You can choose to use MFC linked statically or in a DLL. My samples all use the DLL to keep the EXE file size smaller.

2. Remove the document and view class files from the project. Mine were called StageDoc.h, StageDoc.cpp, StageView.h, and StageView.cpp. Delete the files from your directory and remove them from your project. This leaves you with three C++ files: Stage.cpp, MainFrm.cpp, and StdAfx.cpp.

3. Edit the source files to remove any reference to the header files for the document or view classes.

4. In StdAfx.h, add lines to include <mmsystem.h> and <d3drmwin.h>. The Mmsystem header is used for joystick functions we'll need later, and the d3drmwin header defines all the Direct3D functions.

5. Include <3dplus.h> in either StdAfx.h or Stage.h. I put mine in Stage.h so that when I modify the library I don't need to rebuild the precompiled header file in an application I'm working on.

6. In the Project Settings (Build-Settings), add the Direct3D libraries and the 3dPlus library to the Link list. My samples all have 3dPlusd.lib, d3drm40f.lib, ddraw.lib, and winmm.lib. Note that the 3dPlus library project allows you to build either a debug version (3dPlusd.lib) or a release version (3dPlus.lib). For the samples, I use the debug build so that you get all the library symbols and can trace into the library code if you want. The d3drm library provides the 3D functions we'll be calling. The ddraw library provides DirectDraw support; and the Winmm library provides some multimedia functions for playing sounds.

Now you should have the essential bits. There's a lot of code that needs to be added to this framework before we'll have a buildable application, but this is as far as we can go with AppWizard. Figure 2-1 on the next page shows the architecture of the Stage application.

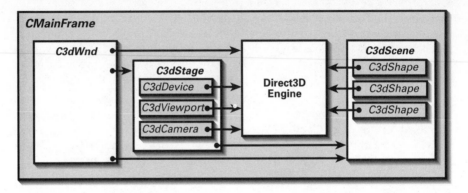

Figure 2-1. *The application architecture.*

The box labeled Direct3D Engine is a bit like Rome—all roads lead there. We'll be looking at what's in the box as we see how each of the *C3d* classes uses the Direct3D engine.

Making the Main Window Visible

The next step is to modify the application's startup code to create the main window. In the Stage.cpp file we'll edit the function *CStageApp::InitInstance*. When AppWizard builds an SDI framework it adds code to the *InitInstance* function to create the first empty document, which in turn creates the main window. Because we threw out the document code, we need to create the main window ourselves. Here's what the new version looks like:

```
BOOL CStageApp::InitInstance()
{
    // Standard initialization
    // If you are not using these features and wish to
    // reduce the size of your final executable, you should
    // remove from the following the specific initialization
    // routines you do not need.

#ifdef _AFXDLL
    Enable3dControls();         // Call this when using
                                // MFC in a shared DLL
#else
    Enable3dControlsStatic();   // Call this when linking
                                // to MFC statically
#endif

    LoadStdProfileSettings();   // Load standard INI file
                                // options (including MRU)

    // Load the main frame window
    CMainFrame* pFrame = new CMainFrame;
    if (!pFrame->LoadFrame(IDR_MAINFRAME,
```

```
                         WS_OVERLAPPEDWINDOW |
                         WS_VISIBLE)) {
        return FALSE;
    }

    // Save the main window pointer
    m_pMainWnd = pFrame;

    return TRUE;
}
```

Two things are important here: calling *LoadFrame* to load and display the frame and saving a pointer to the frame window in *m_pMainWnd*. We save the pointer to the frame because the MFC classes need to know which window is the main window of the application so as to be able to pass messages to the window, enabling the application to function correctly. You'll also have to edit the MainFrm.h file to make the *CMainFrame* constructor public—it's protected by default. While you're in MainFrm.h, you need to add the *C3dWnd m_wnd3d* member variable declaration to the public attributes of *CMainFrame*.

If you were to compile the code now, your application should run and show the main window with its menu and toolbar. Let's go ahead and finish up with Stage.cpp so that we can move on to creating the 3D window.

There are two functions left to add to Stage.cpp: *OnIdle* and *OpenDocumentFile*. The first updates the scene during idle time, and the second deals with one aspect of opening files. The idle time handler is added by using ClassWizard to add an *OnIdle* function to the *CStageApp* class. We then edit the *OnIdle* function to look like the following:

```
BOOL CStageApp::OnIdle(LONG lCount)
{
    BOOL bMore = CWinApp::OnIdle(lCount);

    // Get the main frame window
    CMainFrame* pFrame = (CMainFrame*) m_pMainWnd;
    if (pFrame) {
        // Tell the 3D window to update
        if (pFrame->m_wnd3d.Update(1)) {
            bMore = TRUE;
        }
    }
    return bMore;
}
```

The *OnIdle* function is called when the application is idle. The idea is that if our application has nothing to do, it returns *FALSE* and a different application gets to run for a while. If our application has lots of stuff to do, such as making a 3D scene move, it returns *TRUE* to indicate that it would like more idle cycles. The *C3dWnd::Update* function that is called from the *OnIdle* function returns *TRUE* if it has a scene it can render and *FALSE* if there's nothing to display. This way our application doesn't needlessly request idle cycles when there is nothing to draw.

The second function we need to add to Stage.cpp, *OpenDocumentFile*, handles the most recently used file list in the menu. If you add the code described in the next section, "Modifying the Main Window," but don't add this function, everything works fine until you click an item in the Recent File list. At that point MFC generates an *ASSERT*, and your application stops. It's a little unfortunate that the MFC framework is so closely tied to the document/view architecture, but it is, so we must deal with the problems caused when we stray from what AppWizard creates, as we did when we removed all the *Doc* and *View* files from our project. Fortunately, the fix is simple. All we need to do is override *CWinApp::OpenDocumentFile* (using ClassWizard to add the function to the *CStageApp* class) as follows:

```
CDocument* CStageApp::OpenDocumentFile(LPCTSTR lpszFileName)
{
    // This function is called when the user selects an item
    // from the Recent File list.
    // The return value is not important as long
    // as it's NULL on failure and non-NULL on success

    CMainFrame* pFrame = (CMainFrame*) m_pMainWnd;
    if (pFrame) {
        return (CDocument*) pFrame->OpenFile(lpszFileName);
    } else {
        return NULL;
    }
}
```

When a Recent File list item is clicked, pass the name of the selected file on down to the main frame window to deal with just as if the user had used Open from the File menu.

That's it for the application framework, but we haven't seen the implementation for all the functions yet, such as *OpenFile*, so if you compile at this point you'll get a few errors. Now we're going to configure the main window and add the 3D elements to it.

Modifying the Main Window

We need to do quite a bit of work with the main window to get it to look and behave the way we want. There are lots of small details here, and I'm going to go through them all so that if you're not an MFC expert you'll have some idea of what everything is in there for. After this we'll leave the framework alone and concentrate on the far more interesting issues associated with displaying 3D objects. (If you're so inclined, now is a good time to get another cup of coffee—I just did.)

Creating the 3D Window

AppWizard adds a lot of code to the *OnCreate* function of *CMainFrame*. This code creates the window itself, the toolbar, and the status bar. We need to add some more code to create a 3D window as a child of the main frame window. And just for interest, we'll create an initial scene with an object in place so that we can tell when we've built something that works. There's nothing worse than typing in hundreds of lines of code, compiling, and then running only to see a large black window. (Not the sort of thing to get you jumping up and down with excitement.) Here's the *OnCreate* function with the code that AppWizard generates omitted so that you can see just the bits we need to add (refer to the *Stage* project on the companion CD to see where in the program the code was added):

```
int CMainFrame::OnCreate(LPCREATESTRUCT lpCreateStruct)
{
    ⋮

    // Create the 3D window
    if (!m_wnd3d.Create(this, IDC_3DWND)) {
        return -1;
    }

    ⋮

    NewScene();
    ASSERT(m_pScene);

    // Create a shape to add
    C3dShape sh1;
    sh1.CreateCube(2);
    m_pScene->AddChild(&sh1);
    sh1.SetRotation(1, 1, 1, 0.02);

    return 0;
}
```

This is pretty much the code we used in the Basic sample to get the initial scene displayed. Note that the IDC_3DWND constant needs to be added to the project by using the View-Resource Symbols menu item in Visual C++. The *CMainFrame* class has gained a couple of data members: *m_wnd3d* and *m_pScene*. We added *m_wnd3d* to MainFrm.h earlier after we edited the *CStageApp::InitInstance* function (on page 20). We add *m_pScene* now as shown:

```
class CMainFrame : public CFrameWnd
{
    ⋮
public:
    C3dWnd      m_wnd3d;
    C3dScene*   m_pScene;

    ⋮
};
```

NOTE

C++ purists might not like the fact that I've declared the window and scene objects as public. However, I often do this in sample code to avoid having to declare an access member function such as *GetScene*. It's less cluttered to just provide direct access to the object even if it does break the encapsulation.

Now our main frame window includes a 3D window and a pointer to the current scene. Looking back to the *OnCreate* function on the preceding page, you can see that the 3D window is created, a new scene is created using the *NewScene* function (we'll see how *NewScene* works later), and then a cube is created, added to the scene, and set rotating. If you look at the *C3dWnd::Create* function in the 3dPlus library you'll see that it creates the 3D window as a child window, and the *this* pointer shown in the call on the preceding page is used to identify the 3D window's parent. Not much technology here but important groundwork nonetheless.

Adjusting the Window Size

I run my development machine with a screen resolution of 1280 by 1024. Microsoft Windows has an annoying habit of creating huge windows by default just because I have a big display. When I'm working on applications that don't need large windows I usually fix the initial size by adding a couple lines of code to *CMainFrame::PreCreateWindow*. This example fixes the initial size of the main window at 300 by 350.

```
BOOL CMainFrame::PreCreateWindow(CREATESTRUCT& cs)
{
    // Make the initial window a fixed size
    cs.cx = 300;
    cs.cy = 350;

    return CFrameWnd::PreCreateWindow(cs);
}
```

The *NewScene* Function

We mentioned above that we would look at the *NewScene* function. Let's do that now:

```
BOOL CMainFrame::NewScene()
{
    // Delete any scene we might have
    if (m_pScene) {
        m_wnd3d.SetScene(NULL);
        delete m_pScene;
        m_pScene = NULL;
    }

    // Create an initial scene
    m_pScene = new C3dScene;
    if (!m_pScene->Create()) return FALSE;

    // Set up the lighting
    C3dDirLight dl;
```

```
dl.Create(0.8, 0.8, 0.8);
m_pScene->AddChild(&dl);
dl.SetPosition(-2, 2, -5);
dl.SetDirection(1, -1, 1);
m_pScene->SetAmbientLight(0.4, 0.4, 0.4);

m_wnd3d.SetScene(m_pScene);
return TRUE;
}
```

We add the *NewScene* function to MainFrm.cpp. *NewScene* removes any existing scene and creates a new one with a default lighting arrangement. It then attaches this scene to the stage that is part of the 3D window. When I'm experimenting with creating new objects, I like to be sure they can be destroyed and re-created without problems. This function allows us to destroy everything we've set up in a scene and start again. (It also turns out to be very useful when my young son has grabbed the joystick and moved all the objects off the screen so they can't be selected.)

Repositioning the 3D Window

Because the AppWizard created a toolbar and status bar in the framework that share space in the main window's client area, we need to be able to reposition the 3D window if the user moves or removes the toolbar or hides the status bar. Overriding the *CFrameWnd::RecalcLayout* function by using ClassWizard to create *CMainFrame::RecalcLayout* allows us to control this process:

```
void CMainFrame::RecalcLayout(BOOL bNotify)
{
    // Rearrange control bars and fit 3D window in the
    // middle. Let the frame rearrange the control bars.
    CFrameWnd::RecalcLayout(bNotify);

    // Find the space that's left over
    CRect rc;
    RepositionBars(0,
                   0xFFFF,
                   IDC_3DWND,
                   CWnd::reposQuery,
                   &rc);
    if (IsWindow(m_wnd3d.GetSafeHwnd())) {
        m_wnd3d.MoveWindow(&rc, FALSE);
    }
}
```

Essentially, this code rearranges the control bars, figures out what space is left over, and uses that to position the 3D window. Check out the MFC documentation if this sort of stuff excites you.

Window Destruction

All good things must come to an end, and so do windows. Adding an *OnDestroy* message handler (by using ClassWizard with the WM_Destroy message) allows us to tidy up:

```
void CMainFrame::OnDestroy()
{
    CFrameWnd::OnDestroy();

    // Delete any scene we might have
    m_wnd3d.SetScene(NULL);
    if (m_pScene) {
        delete m_pScene;
    }
}
```

Failing to delete all the objects we create results in memory leaks. Thanks to the MFC memory tracking mechanism in debug builds, these are reported when the application exits, so spotting them is easy. Fixing them can be a bit more demanding, so let's be tidy, folks.

Prepare to Draw the 3D Window

One of the things that's interesting about the Direct3D rendering engine is that it draws directly to the video memory and doesn't use the Windows Graphics Device Interface (GDI). So it's *really* important that the rendering engine knows where the window it's drawing into is positioned on the screen. If it doesn't know the exact position, either it won't draw or, worse, it will draw over other windows. The rendering engine also needs to know whether the application is active or not and whether the application has received any palette messages. If the application becomes inactive, the rendering engine must release the palette so that other applications can use it. All of these requirements are handled by adding functions to process WM_ACTIVATEAPP, WM_PALETTECHANGED, and WM_MOVE messages:

```
void CMainFrame::OnActivateApp(BOOL bActive, HTASK hTask)
{
    CFrameWnd::OnActivateApp(bActive, hTask);

    // Tell 3D window about new state
    m_wnd3d.SendMessage(WM_ACTIVATEAPP,
                        (WPARAM)bActive,
                        (LPARAM)hTask);
}

void CMainFrame::OnPaletteChanged(CWnd* pFocusWnd)
{
    // Let the 3D window know palette has changed
    m_wnd3d.SendMessage(WM_PALETTECHANGED,
                        pFocusWnd ?
                        (WPARAM)pFocusWnd->GetSafeHwnd()
                        : 0);
```

```
}

void CMainFrame::OnMove(int x, int y)
{
    CFrameWnd::OnMove(x, y);

    // Let 3D window know the frame has moved
    m_wnd3d.SendMessage(WM_MOVE,
                        0,
                        MAKELPARAM(0, 0));
}
```

As you can see, all that's required for the rendering engine to draw to the video display is for your application to send the messages to the 3D window, which handles the details of communication with the rendering engine.

The File Menu Options

The final steps are for handling the File-New and File-Open menu items. Since we already wrote a function to delete the scene and start again, handling the File-New menu item is trivial (using the ClassWizard with the ID_FILE_NEW Object ID):

```
void CMainFrame::OnFileNew()
{
    NewScene();
}
```

Handling the File-Open menu item is done with these two functions:

```
BOOL CMainFrame::OpenFile(const char* pszPath)
{
    // Attempt to open a shape file
    C3dShape sh;
    const char* pszFile = sh.Load(pszPath);
    if (!pszFile) return FALSE;

    // Create a new scene
    NewScene();
    ASSERT(m_pScene);

    // Attach new shape to the scene
    m_pScene->AddChild(&sh);
    sh.SetRotation(1, 1, 1, 0.02);

    // Add name to the Recent File list
    AfxGetApp()->AddToRecentFileList(pszFile);
    return TRUE;
}

void CMainFrame::OnFileOpen()
{
    OpenFile(NULL);
}
```

Now let's see how the *OpenFile* function works.

A new *C3dShape* object is created, and its *Load* member function is called. Either this function tries to open the file or, if no filename is supplied, it displays a dialog box asking the user to select a file. Assuming that the file is a valid 3D object file, the *C3dShape* code opens the file and creates a new 3D object from the data in the file. Easy, eh? The new object is added to the scene and set rotating so you can see it in all its glory. The name of the newly opened file is then added to the Recent File list to make it easy to open again later. (Remember that the *OpenDocumentFile* function in Stage.cpp also calls the *OpenFile* function when you select an item from the Recent File list.)

We need to add a few finishing touches before our *Stage* project will compile cleanly and run correctly. First we must initialize *m_pScene* in the *CMainFrame* constructor with the statement *m_pScene = NULL*. Also, since the functions *NewScene* and *OpenFile* were not created by the ClassWizard, you need to manually add declarations for them in MainFrm.h in the *CMainFrame* class constructor.

If you're still awake, you can compile and build the code. You should now have a functional 3D object file viewer. Of course, you haven't any idea how it works, but we'll look at that next, and I think you'll find it a lot more interesting.

Windows, Viewports, and Devices

The word *window* means lots of things: To traditional graphics programmers, it relates to how a scene is projected onto a flat surface; and to many of us, it's an object in an operating system that seems to have a zillion APIs. Any way you look at it (no pun intended), *window* is a vastly overused word, running a close second to *object*. The problem with describing a 3D rendering system is that no matter what words are used to describe the various parts of the system, someone won't understand or will insist that a term is used incorrectly. I subscribe to the idea that even if the usage is grossly wrong, if it's common terminology it's good enough for me. The same applies to documentation. If the documents refer to it as a window, a window is generally what I'll call it. So if you don't like how I'm about to describe the rendering system, don't blame me—I didn't pick the words.

Let's start at the top. The *window* is the Microsoft Windows object that handles messages, and it appears in your application. The *viewport* is a mathematical description of how the appearance of a set of objects in 3D space are drawn into the window. The *device* is software associated with the actual video device that implements the video system in your computer. To create a 3D scene in your application you need a window, a viewport, and a device. In fact, you can have multiple viewports and multiple windows associated with a single device, but we're going to build a system that has one window, one viewport, and one device. You manage the window; the rendering engine manages the viewport and the device.

GDI vs. DirectDraw

Let's look at what having a window open on the desktop really means. Figure 2-2 shows an open window at an arbitrary position on the desktop.

Window

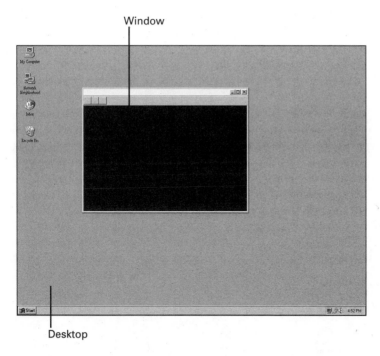

Desktop

Figure 2-2. *A window open on the desktop.*

Now let's drop down to the hardware level and look at a map of the memory on the video adapter card. (See Figure 2-3.)

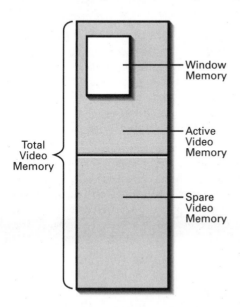

Total Video Memory

Window Memory

Active Video Memory

Spare Video Memory

Figure 2-3. *The video adapter memory map.*

Let's say you have a video adapter with 2 MB of video memory as shown in the memory map diagram in Figure 2-3. You're running your video display at 1024-by-768 resolution with 256 colors, so the video card is actually using only 786,432 bytes (1024 × 768) of your video memory. This is the part shown as the active video memory in Figure 2-2. The open window is about 512 by 400 pixels, which uses 204,800 bytes of the video memory.

Now let's say that you want to show a 3D animation in your open window. You define the window by setting its size and position on the desktop. This determines the area of video memory that will be used to display the contents of the window (shown as window memory in Figure 2-3). If you were to use normal Windows GDI functions to draw to your window, GDI would use the video device driver to set pixels in the video memory that give the effect you asked for. Figure 2-4 shows the software architecture we usually deal with in Windows programming.

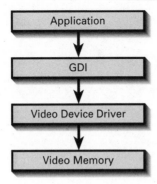

Figure 2-4. *The Windows drawing model.*

In this case, to draw a rectangle, you call the *Rectangle* function. GDI asks the video device driver if it draws rectangles; if not, GDI negotiates with the device driver for some other way to draw the rectangle by using lots of lines or whatever. The device driver then draws the pixels into the video memory or, if we're lucky, uses hardware on the video card to draw the rectangle directly. So, do you think this process is fast or slow? Well, it's not *that* slow, but it's not super speedy either. The problem is that GDI is very general, and there is a price to pay for that.

Wouldn't it be great if you could bypass GDI and the video device driver and just write to the video memory directly? That might be faster, but you'd have to understand how every video card on the planet works. DirectDraw provides a better approach that allows you to ask the device driver for direct access to the video memory, and if it can provide access, you get to party on the pixels directly. If the driver can't provide the access, it provides a mechanism so you *think* you're drawing pixels directly to the video memory even though the device driver is doing some of the work. The application can choose to use either GDI or DirectDraw functions to get the effect and performance it needs. When DirectDraw is installed, the drawing model looks more like Figure 2-5.

DirectDraw also provides bit block transfer (bitblt) functions that you can use, which the video hardware implements if it is capable of doing so. By calling the bitblt functions in DirectDraw, either you get totally awesome bitblt performance implemented directly in the adapter hardware or you get merely stunning performance implemented by the DirectDraw code writing directly to the video memory.

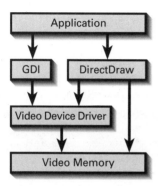

Figure 2-5. *Drawing with DirectDraw.*

There's one other very important feature to DirectDraw. Look back at Figure 2-3 on page 29 for a moment. Less than half the available video memory is actually being used to provide the desktop image you see on screen, and the remainder is wasted. OK, so what could we do with it? Given that the video card in Figure 2-3 has a hardware blitter (a special system built to perform bitblt operations), we could perhaps use some of this spare memory to store sprite images, texture maps, and so on. Then we could use the hardware blitter to quickly move the images in this off-screen video memory area directly to the active video area. By avoiding the need to move data over the computer's data bus, we can potentially speed up our video effects. DirectDraw provides a management scheme for this spare memory and allows you to create surfaces within it for whatever use you can think of. We can even use a chunk of this spare memory as a second page buffer that is the same size as the main window and use this buffer as our animation rendering area. We can compose a new scene in this off-screen video memory and do an extremely fast bitblt to update the active video memory when we want the scene to change.

Video Transfer

To understand why copying memory within the video memory is faster than copying from main memory to video memory, you need to understand the hardware architecture. Figure 2-6 shows a simplified hardware model that illustrates the main components.

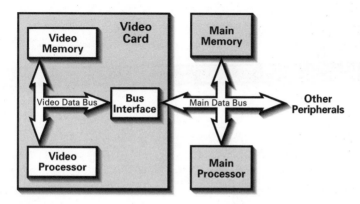

Figure 2-6. *An example of a video hardware architecture.*

The video processor works closely with the video memory and is highly optimized for performance. Transferring data between chunks of video memory means the data moves only across the video data bus. Transferring data from the main memory to the video memory is generally much slower because the block of data in main memory needs to be moved across the computer's main data bus, which is narrower than the video data bus, and then via the video bus interface to the video bus and into the video memory. Transferring data between the two buses involves a negotiation between the main processor and the video processor. This takes time, and the processors might not get anything else done until the transfer is complete. I've really oversimplified the story here, but you can see that video to video bitblts involve fewer bits of hardware than main memory to video bitblts do, which generally means they are faster.

In fact, you can go even further to speed up the video transfer with DirectDraw. If you are willing to run full-screen in Exclusive mode, the video hardware can flip between two pages in the video memory, achieving the kind of animation performance normally associated with DOS games.

So what does all this have to do with the 3D rendering engine? Well, the engine needs to draw very quickly—ideally, straight to the video memory or, better still, by using some nifty piece of 3D rendering hardware on the video card. By the time you read this book there could be hardware-accelerated video cards on the market for about $200. To make all this video transferring work, the rendering engine calls a software layer (in this case, Direct3D Immediate Mode), which notifies the video card to execute a set of 3D primitive operations directly. If the video card can't handle the request, the Direct3D software drivers emulate the function. With all this new software in place, we now have a model (Figure 2-7) that allows any software—not just the rendering engine—to call a set of 3D drawing functions and be assured of the best possible performance.

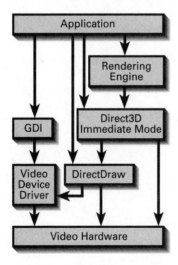

Figure 2-7. *Rendering through the Direct3D layer.*

Can you tell who the winner is here? The application is. Now your applications can take whatever path you need to get the effect and performance you want on the Windows platform.

   3D GRAPHICS PROGRAMMING FOR WINDOWS 95

Creating the Device and
the Viewport in the Stage Sample

Let's return to where the device and viewport fit into this scheme. The device is a chunk of software in the rendering engine that deals with the Direct3D layer (Figure 2-7), and the viewport controls how the device is used to draw into the video memory area defined by the window. So the entire function of the window that you create is simply to define the area of video memory that the device will manage. When we build a 3D window we also create a device, specifying which area of video memory the device gets to run with. There are several ways to do this but we'll look at just two.

It's easiest to call a function that creates the device directly by using a window handle. This is wonderful because you don't need to have any idea about how the Direct3D layer works; you just provide your window handle and the rendering engine figures the rest out. You can also use the DirectDraw functions to allocate the video buffers you'll need and use some of the Direct3D functions to define a Z buffer. (A *Z buffer* is a special video buffer that provides depth information about each pixel in the image.) You can then pass all this information to the rendering engine, which builds a device you can use.

Obviously it's much easier to create the device directly from the window handle than to create it from a bunch of DirectDraw surfaces—but that's not what I did. In my first pass at the 3dPlus library I did indeed create my device from the window handle. Then one weekend I went crazy and decided to play with the DirectDraw functions. As a result, I created a set of classes that act as wrappers for the DirectDraw functions, making it just as easy to create the rendering engine device from DirectDraw surfaces as it is to create the device by using a window handle. I can tell you're not convinced, so here's the code that creates the stage object in the 3D window for the Stage project we've been discussing in this chapter:

```
BOOL C3dWnd::CreateStage()
{

    // Initialize DirectDraw objects
    if (!m_pDD) {
        m_pDD = new CDirectDraw;
    }
    if (!m_pDD->Create()) return FALSE;

    // Set the mode for the window
    if (!m_pDD->SetWindowedMode(GetSafeHwnd(),
                                m_iWidth,
                                m_iHeight)) {
        return FALSE;
    }

    // Create Direct3D object
    if (!m_pD3D) {
        m_pD3D = new CDirect3D;
    }
```

(continued)

```
        if (!m_pD3D->Create(m_pDD)) return FALSE;

        // Set the color model
        if (!m_pD3D->SetMode(D3DCOLOR_MONO)) return FALSE;

        // Create a stage object
        if (!m_pStage) {
            m_pStage = new C3dStage;
        }
        if (!m_pStage->Create(m_pD3D)) return FALSE;

        // Attach any current scene
        m_pStage->SetScene(m_pScene);

        return TRUE;
    }
```

The first half of the *C3dWnd::CreateStage* function deals with creating the DirectDraw and Direct3D objects, which provide the underlying mechanism for drawing 3D objects to the window. The DirectDraw object is set to operate in windowed mode rather than full screen, and the Direct3D object is set to run using what is known as the MONO (monochrome) color model. (We'll look at color models in Chapter 10.) The last few lines create a *C3dStage* object from the DirectDraw object and attach the current scene to the stage object. The *C3dStage* object contains *C3dDevice* and *C3dViewport* objects that communicate with the DirectDraw and Direct3D components. The stage also contains a *C3dCamera* object that we'll take a closer look at a little later. The function that actually creates the stage from the Direct3D object looks like this:

```
    BOOL C3dStage::Create(CDirect3D* pD3D)
    {
        // Remove any existing scene
        SetScene(NULL);

        // Create new device from Direct3D surfaces
        if (!m_Device.Create(pD3D)) return FALSE;

        // Set current quality
        m_Device.SetQuality(m_Quality);


        // Create viewport
        if (!m_Viewport.Create(&m_Device,
                               &m_Camera,
                               0, 0,
                               m_Device.GetWidth(),
                               m_Device.GetHeight())) {
            return FALSE;
        }

        return TRUE;
    }
```

As you can see, the function above consists of creating the *C3dDevice* and *C3dViewport* objects. The creation of the device is done by calling the Direct3D engine and passing it a pointer to the DirectDraw components we want to use:

```
BOOL C3dDevice::Create(CDirect3D* pD3D)
{
    if (m_pIDevice) {
        m_pIDevice->Release();
        m_pIDevice = NULL;
    }
    m_hr = the3dEngine.GetInterface()->CreateDeviceFromD3D(
                pD3D->GetD3DEngine(),
                pD3D->GetD3DDevice(),
                &m_pIDevice);
    if (FAILED(m_hr)) {
        return FALSE;
    }
    ASSERT(m_pIDevice);

    return TRUE;
}
```

If we were creating the device from a window handle instead of from a set of DirectDraw surfaces, this function would be calling *CreateDeviceFromHWND* instead of *CreateDeviceFromD3D*.

Because I'd already written the code using DirectDraw rather than a window handle, I chose to leave it in place as an example of how it is used. At some point, if you're going to do your own thing with the rendering engine rather than use the 3dPlus library, you should look at creating your device from a window handle. Of course, if you use the 3dPlus library classes, you can forget all about how they are implemented and just use them as a set of black box functions if you want. However, knowledge of the underlying engine is essential if you want to extend the 3dPlus library.

The Projection System

Having had a quick look at the hardware to keep the engineers happy, let's move into a more abstract plane and look at how the projection system works. Because objects can float almost anywhere in 3D space, we need a way to define what's going to be visible in our window. In photographic terms, this translates to which way you point your camera and the focal length of the lens you're using. In addition, in the interest of efficiency, we need to define two clipping planes: front and back. Anything behind the back plane isn't rendered, and anything in front of the front plane isn't rendered either. Figure 2-8 on the next page shows the viewing frustum that defines what will be visible in a scene.

NOTE

Frustum is defined by Webster's as "The basal part of a solid cone or pyramid formed by cutting off the top by a plane parallel to the base."

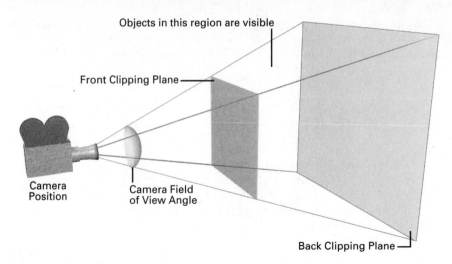

Figure 2-8. *The viewing frustum.*

The front and back plane positions can be set using *IRLViewport::SetFront* and *IRLViewport::SetBack*. *IRLViewport* is a COM interface used to control the viewport. The angle subtended at the camera can be altered using *IRLViewport::SetField*. The creation of the *C3dStage* object sets some of these parameters and leaves others at their default values. If you look at the *C3dStage* class, you'll see that I haven't exposed methods to play with the frustum parameters because the default values work fine for the sample applications. (If you want to, it's very easy to add these additional methods for yourself so that you can experiment with different camera angles and so on, but we are getting ahead of ourselves a bit.)

In order to calculate exactly how a 3D object will appear on the screen, the position of the object's vertices (corners, if you like) have to be manipulated by applying a transform, which maps the 3D coordinates into 2D coordinates on the window. This coordinate transformation process is done using a 4-by-4 matrix that is constructed by combining transforms for perspective, scale, and translation (position). Essentially, each 3D coordinate gets multiplied by the transform matrix to produce a 2D coordinate in the window. If you want to know more about the theory, I suggest you refer to Foley et al. (listed in the bibliography on page 314) or to some other computer graphics text.

In practice the story is a little more complex. (Isn't it always?) In Chapter 1 I mentioned that the rendering engine uses frames to represent a hierarchy of transforms. Objects attached to frames can be moved (transformed) relative to other frames. To compute the 2D coordinates for any given object, the transforms of all the frames in the hierarchy above the object must be combined to get the final transform for the object.

NOTE

I should mention that I'm using a bit of poetic license here. A frame isn't a physical object as I've shown in Figure 2-9 on the next page, but rather a transform that gets applied to all of its children. As such, it has no physical size or shape. Having said that, I like to think of frames as structures made from pipe cleaners and drinking-straws that are glued to each other. This helps me visualize how shapes move when attached to their frames in a scene.

Combining all those transforms sounds lengthy and costly to performance, which it would be if it were done needlessly. The rendering engine is a little more subtle, though. Instead, it keeps a copy of the final transform for each frame (obtained by multiplying all the frame transforms together), so if none of the frames above a particular frame in the hierarchy change, the final transform doesn't need to be recomputed. Therefore, using frames doesn't necessarily reduce performance. In practice, if you have various objects moving in a scene, calculating the location of all those objects has to be done somehow. Having a hierarchy of frames to keep track of relative object positions greatly improves the chances that you won't perform redundant computations in figuring out the final result. We'll look at transforms in more detail in Chapter 5, so if you're feeling a bit lost, hang in there and I'll try to clear things up later.

The *C3dStage* object provides the root frame for our application's projection system. All other frames are in some way child frames attached to the stage frame. A frame for the camera and a frame for the current scene are attached directly to the stage frame. All the frames within a scene are child frames of the scene's frame. By using frames in this way, it's very easy to define the relative positions of the camera and the scene. It's also easy to move the camera on the stage frame to give a feeling of flying through a scene or to fix the camera in one place while moving the scene around—another way to achieve the flying effect.

When the stage frame is created, the camera is placed in front of the stage facing in toward the center. In other words, the camera is placed at a negative value on the z-axis. Figure 2-9 shows the relationship between the camera frame and the stage frame.

We'll be looking at frames and how they affect an object's position in the scene again when we cover transforms in more detail. For now, we'll move on to a quick look at how shapes get loaded from files.

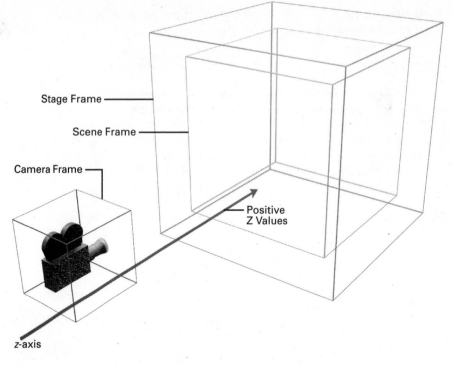

Stage Frame

Scene Frame

Camera Frame

Positive
Z Values

z-axis

Figure 2-9. *The camera frame and the stage frame.*

Creating Shapes

The last piece of code we added to the main frame window on page 27 was to load a *C3dShape* object from a disk file and show it in the current scene. We'll look at shapes in more detail in Chapter 4, but I want to introduce you to what's in a *C3dShape* object and discuss why I created it that way.

The DirectX 2 SDK provides the tools you need to create applications that employ the rendering engine. The SDK doesn't include any tools to create 3D shapes, nor are there many simple functions in the SDK that create shapes, because it is assumed that you have your own tools to create scenery, 3D objects, texture maps, and so on. However, I considered a slightly different scenario. I imagined a small company wanting to evaluate this rendering engine before investing money in the tools required to generate the artwork for a big project. But with no tools to create shapes, how would anyone be able to experiment? In fact, the SDK does have functions that allow you to create shapes: You provide a list of vertex coordinates and a set of face vertex lists for your shape and call a function to create the shape. I thought this implementation was way too low-level for initial tinkering, so I added functions in the 3dPlus library to create common geometric shapes such as cubes, spheres, rods, and cones. I also added some code to make it easy to use Windows bitmaps as images and texture maps, which the SDK was missing at the time of this writing. But before I implemented any of these functions, I discovered a single function that loads a shape from a .X file. So my first implementation of the *C3dShape* class consisted, more or less, of a constructor and the *Load* function. With this minimal piece of code I could get some objects visible on my stage.

If you review the DirectX 2 SDK documentation you will see that a frame can have one or more visuals attached to it. A *visual* is a shape or texture that can be rendered as a visible object. A visual in itself doesn't have a position but needs to be attached to a frame so that it can be transformed in a way that makes it appear where it's supposed to be in the window. To keep things simple, I built my *C3dShape* object so that it always has one frame and one visual associated with it. With both a frame and a visual, the *C3dShape* object has position as well as shape, which makes it a lot more like a real object. The downside to this is that if you want to have 23 trees in a scene and all the trees are exactly the same, you apparently need 23 frames and 23 visuals to create your forest, which isn't very efficient. It would be much better to have only one shape (visual) and to render that one shape in 23 different places. In other words, we would attach one visual to 23 frames, thus saving the vast amount of data required to define the other 22 shapes.

Actually, you *can* attach the same visual element from a *C3dShape* object to several frames, as we'll see later in Chapter 4 when we look at how to clone a shape. Even though this simple design looks a bit inefficient here, it can be used quite efficiently.

Let's look now at how the *C3dShape::Load* function works. This will allow me to introduce you to some of the details of the implementation and to show you some examples of how the rendering engine COM interfaces are used.

Here's the *Load* function in its entirety:

```
const char* C3dShape::Load(const char* pszFileName)
{
    static CString strFile;

    if (!pszFileName || !strlen(pszFileName)) {

        // Show a File Open dialog box
        CFileDialog dlg(TRUE,
                        NULL,
                        NULL,
                        OFN_HIDEREADONLY,
                        "Shape Files (*.x)|*.x|"
                        "All Files (*.*)|*.*||",
                        NULL);
        if (dlg.DoModal() != IDOK) return NULL;

        // Get the file path
        strFile = dlg.m_ofn.lpstrFile;

    } else {

        strFile = pszFileName;

    }
```

(continued)

```
// Remove any existing visual
New();

// Try to load the file
ASSERT(m_pIMeshBld);
m_hr = m_pIMeshBld->Load((void*)(const char*)strFile,
                         NULL,
                         D3DRMLOAD_FROMFILE|
                         D3DRMLOAD_FIRST,
                         C3dLoadTextureCallback,
                         this);
if (FAILED(m_hr)) {
    return NULL;
}

AttachVisual(m_pIMeshBld);

m_strName = "File object: ";
m_strName += pszFileName;

return strFile;
}
```

You can use this function in two ways. If you know the name of a file you want to open, you can call it like this:

```
C3dShape shape;
shape.Load("egg.x");
```

If you need to browse for a file to open, you can call the following:

```
C3dShape shape;
shape.Load(NULL);
```

If no filename is provided, a dialog box appears with the filter string set to "*.x" so that by default the dialog box shows only files the function can open. Having obtained the name of the file to open, the local function *New* is called to remove any existing visual from this shape. Because I always try to create objects that are reusable, you can call *Load* on a *C3dShape* object as many times as you want. I find this much more useful than having to create a new C++ object each time I want to load a shape to play with.

The next bit of the loading code performs the real magic and needs the most explanation:

```
ASSERT(m_pIMeshBld);
m_hr = m_pIMeshBld->Load(strFile);
if (FAILED(m_hr)) {
    return NULL;
}
```

First a test is made to verify that the *m_pIMeshBld* pointer is not NULL. You'll find these *ASSERT* statements throughout the 3dPlus library code. Then a call is made to *IRLMeshBuilder::Load* to load the file and create a mesh from it. *IRLMesh-Builder* is a COM interface that deals with the creation and modification of meshes. A *mesh* is a collection of vertices and faces that define the shape of an object. (Actually, a mesh has a little more to it than that, but that's enough of a description for the moment.) This function, like the majority of COM functions, returns an *HRESULT* that contains a code indicating whether the call was successful. Two macros, *SUCCEEDED* and *FAILED*, are defined to test an *HRESULT* value to see whether a call was successful or not. These are actually defined as a part of the OLE functions and aren't specific to Direct3D. I made it a policy to assign the result of all COM interface calls made in the 3dPlus library to the *m_hr* member variable, which is common to all of my *C3d* classes. This way, if a call fails and the class member function returns *FALSE*, you can interrogate the object's *m_hr* data member to find the cause of the error. It isn't rocket science, but it is handy when debugging.

The *m_pIMeshBld* value is initialized when the *C3dShape* object is constructed:

```
C3dShape::C3dShape()
{
    m_pIVisual = NULL;
    C3dFrame::Create(NULL);
    ASSERT(m_pIFrame);
    m_pIFrame->SetAppData((ULONG)this);
    m_strName = "3D Shape";
    m_pIMeshBld = NULL;
    the3dEngine.CreateMeshBuilder(&m_pIMeshBld);
    ASSERT(m_pIMeshBld);
    AttachVisual(m_pIMeshBld);
}
```

The global object *the3dEngine* uses some of the global Direct3D functions to create various rendering interfaces. Just so you can see that I'm not hiding anything nasty, here's how the *IRLMeshBuilder* interface is obtained:

```
BOOL C3dEngine::CreateMeshBuilder(IDirect3DRMMeshBuilder**
                                  pIBld)
{
    ASSERT(m_pIWRL);
    ASSERT(pIBld);

    m_hr = m_pIWRL->CreateMeshBuilder(pIBld);
    if (FAILED(m_hr)) return FALSE;
    ASSERT(*pIBld);

    return TRUE;
}
```

OK, so I'm still hiding where the *m_pIWRL* value came from, but I'm sure you get the idea: Calling COM interface functions is just like calling the member functions in C++ objects. In fact, it's hard to tell the difference, which is why I use the *pI* prefix for COM object interfaces. To see why there's a difference, look on the next page at what happens to these COM interface pointers when a *C3dShape* is destroyed.

```
C3dShape::~C3dShape()
{
    if (m_pIVisual) m_pIVisual->Release();
    if (m_pIMeshBld) m_pIMeshBld->Release();
}
```

This is very different from disposing of a pointer to a C++ object. Whenever you are finished with a COM interface, you *must* call its *Release* function to decrement the object's usage count. If you don't, the COM object lives in memory forever.

There's just one last point about the code that I want to point out here, which has to do with calling functions inside of a C++ object's constructor. It should be obvious that when the constructor of a *C3dShape* object is attempting to create the mesh builder interface, it might fail—typically, with an out-of-memory condition. As you can see, I don't attempt to detect this in my code. The memory problem should raise an exception, which I'm assuming you'll catch in your code! It's not very nice of me to dump this problem on you, I guess, but it's difficult to write totally robust code without adding a lot more lines, and I've tried to keep this code as simple as possible so that you can follow how it works. As I mentioned in the introduction, this isn't a production quality library but a set of examples. The production version is up to you. If you want to know how to create robust C++ classes that survive exceptions properly, then I'd strongly suggest you look at *More Effective C+++: Thirty-Five More Ways to Improve Your Programs and Designs* (Addison-Wesley, 1996) by Scott Meyers.

What Did We Learn Today?

In this chapter we looked at how the application framework that we're going to use throughout the rest of the book was built. We also learned what DirectDraw is all about and how 3D objects get projected onto a 2D screen. We finished up with a look at how to load a 3D object from an .X file and show it in the current scene. Along the way I've introduced you to some of the workings of the underlying engine. If you're interested in looking at the engine in more detail, now might be a good time to browse through the DirectX 2 SDK documents.

The majority of samples for the rest of the book started out as copies of this application, so if you want a place to start, you might try that approach too. Copy the entire thing, remove the bits you don't need, and you're ready to create your first scene.

If what we've covered in this chapter seems like a lot of work, I'd like to leave you with a short story about what happened to me when I reached this point in my experimenting.

After I had written the code for the sample in this chapter, I was admiring my work as it revolved on the screen when my 8-year-old daughter came in for a visit. Her perception of my work wasn't quite what I expected. She asked, "Why is there just a teapot spinning around there?" to which I had no answer. It did, however, give me a chance to reflect on how far I had gone and how far I had left to go if I was going to create anything even remotely spectacular.

Don't worry, it gets easier from here.

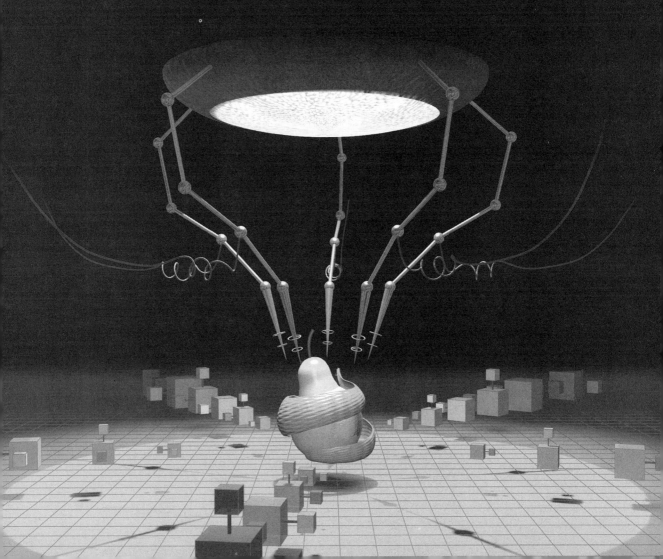

CHAPTER 3

Interfaces and Classes

n this chapter we'll take a brief look at the interfaces provided by the Direct3D rendering engine and the C++ classes in the 3dPlus library that use those interfaces. It won't be a complete discussion of every interface and class we'll be using but rather an introduction to each of them. Each interface and class mentioned here is discussed in more detail in later chapters. By the end of this chapter you should have a good idea of the uses of most of the rendering engine interfaces and how to call them. You should also have an understanding of the 3dPlus library class architecture. If you don't want to dig through all the classes and interfaces in one go, skip this chapter and come back when you need to.

Using COM Object Interfaces

Let's take a brief look at the Component Object Model (COM) and how COM object interfaces work.

An interface is really just a collection of functions that share a common purpose. The interface functions are similar to the member functions of a C++ class except that the interface defines only the interface functions, it doesn't implement them. It's like a design plan for a C++ class you might want to write.

A COM object is a chunk of code that implements one or more interfaces. COM objects can be as simple as statically linked C++ class objects or as complex as a piece of code running on a server on the other side of the world. If you're familiar with dynamic-link libraries (DLLs), "COM objects are to C++ programs what DLLs are to C programs," in the words of my colleague Dale Rogerson.

COM objects are required to support an interface called *IUnknown*, which provides two mechanisms for every COM object: reference counting and the ability to request other interfaces. We can use the *IUnknown* interface to see what other interfaces the object has that we might want to use. Let me give you an example. Suppose that you have just created a 3D object using the rendering engine and now you want to change its position in the scene. Because the *IDirect3DRMFrame* interface provides a function to change position, you can test to see if your new object supports the *IDirect3DRMFrame* interface. If it does, you can call the appropriate *IDirect3DRMFrame* function to change the object's position. You interrogate the object for interfaces by calling the *IUnknown::QueryInterface* function:

```
HRESULT hr;
IDirect3DRMFrame* pIFrame = NULL;
hr = pIUnknown->QueryInterface(IID_IDirect3DRMFrame,
                               (void**)&pIFrame);
```

If the call is successful, the object supports *IDirect3DRMFrame* and you can use the interface:

```
pIFrame->SetPosition(2, 4, 5);
```

When *QueryInterface* returned the *IDirect3DRMFrame* pointer, it also added one to the object's reference count. Therefore, when you are finished with the pointer, you must release it to decrement the object's reference count again:

```
pIFrame->Release();
pIFrame = NULL;
```

Setting the pointer to NULL isn't required. I do this just so that the debugger will catch any attempt to reuse the pointer after I have released the interface it was pointing to. If you like macros (and I don't), you can always write a macro to release the interface and NULL the pointer all in one call:

```
#define RELEASE(p) ((p)->Release(); (p)=NULL;)
```

NOTE

I don't like macros because they hide the implementation. This has caused me more problems when debugging code over the years than is warranted by their convenience, in my opinion.

All COM interfaces are derived from *IUnknown*, so if you have *any* interface pointer, you can call *QueryInterface* on it for any other interface you might want to use. For example, if you already have an *IDirect3DRMFrame* interface pointer *(pIFrame)* and you want to see if the object it points to supports the *IDirect3D-RMMesh* interface, you can make the following test:

```
HRESULT hr;
IDirect3DRMMesh* pIMesh = NULL;
hr = pIFrame->QueryInterface(IID_IDirect3DRMMesh,
                             (void**)&pIMesh);
if (SUCCEEDED(hr)) {

    // Use the mesh interface
    int i = pIMesh->GetGroupCount;
    pIMesh->Release;
    pIMesh = NULL;
}
```

This is a very powerful capability because, if you have *any* interface pointer to *any* COM object, you can find out whether the object supports another interface you might want to use. The only thing you can't do is get a list of all the supported interfaces.

NOTE

I didn't point it out because it's fairly obvious, but just in case it's been mystifying you, all COM interface names begin with the letter *I*, indicating that they are interfaces rather than C classes or some other kind of entity. The *I* prefix is also handy as a reminder to call *Release* when you're finished with an interface.

In addition to the fact that you can call *QueryInterface* to test for supported interfaces, it's possible that any given interface for a COM object might inherit the functions and properties from some other interface or set of interfaces. But you can't tell programmatically; you need to look at how the interface is defined. For example, if you look in the d3drmobj.h header file in the DirectX 2 SDK, you'll see that *IDirect3DRMFrame* is derived from *IDirect3DRMVisual*. So the *IDirect3D-RMFrame* interface supports all of the functions in the *IDirect3DRMVisual* interface as well. *IDirect3DRMVisual* is derived from *IDirect3DRMObject*, which in turn is derived from *IUnknown*. In fact, the *IDirect3DRMFrame* interface supports all of the *IDirect3DRMFrame* functions plus those of the *IDirect3DRMVisual* interface, the *IDirect3DRMObject* interface, and the *IUnknown* interface.

> **NOTE**
>
> All the rendering engine interfaces have an *IDirect3D* prefix. Those interfaces that have the *IDirect3DRM* prefix refer to the higher level 3D interfaces that deal with frames, shapes, lights, and so on. The letters *RM* stand for Retained Mode (as opposed to the Immediate Mode layer below it).

It's not terribly important to know which interface inherits from which other interface because you can always call *QueryInterface* to find out the interfaces that are supported. But if performance is important, knowing the hierarchy helps you avoid making a redundant call.

Let me finish this brief review of COM objects by discussing how the *AddRef* and *Release* functions in *IUnknown* help us share objects. Let's say we want a scene containing several trees. The design for the tree consists of a set of vertices and face descriptions in a *mesh*. The mesh is a visual object that can be attached to a frame to position it in a scene. In fact, one mesh can be attached to many frames. To implement our small forest, we create one mesh for the shape of the tree and several frames to represent the individual tree positions. The single mesh is then attached to each of the frames as a visual using code like this:

```
pIFrame->AddVisual(pIMesh);
```

If you could look at the code for the *AddVisual* function in *IDirect3DRMFrame*, you'd see something like this:

```
HRESULT IDirect3DRMFrame::AddVisual(IDirect3DRMVisual*
                                    pIVisual)
{
    pIVisual->AddRef();
    AddVisualToList(pIVisual);
    ⋮
}
```

The visual interface's *AddRef* member is called to increase the reference count of the object supplying the visual interface. Why? Because while this frame object exists, the object supplying the visual interface to the frame can't be destroyed.

When the frame is destroyed or a call is made to remove this specific visual interface from the frame, the frame's code will release the object supplying the visual interface:

```
pIVisual->Release();
```

So if this frame was the last frame to release the object supplying the visual interface, the reference count for that mesh object would drop to zero and the mesh object would destroy itself.

What does all this mean to you? If you use COM object interfaces correctly with *AddRef* and *Release*, you never need to worry about having to track which objects are alive in memory or whether it's safe to delete an object, because the object's internal reference counting handles these details for you.

Let me give you a couple of final tips when dealing with COM objects. Any function call that returns an interface pointer will call *AddRef* to add a reference to the pointer before returning it to you; you must call *Release* for the pointer when you're done with it to avoid keeping objects needlessly in memory. If you copy an interface pointer, you should call *AddRef* for the copy and *Release* both pointers when they are no longer used. Remember that returning a pointer to an interface from one of your functions is essentially copying the pointer. You should call *AddRef* before returning the pointer.

Now having set the rules, I'm going to break one. If you know what you're doing, you don't absolutely have to call *AddRef* when you copy a pointer, but you do need to be religious about calling *Release* the correct number of times. Calling *Release* once too often will destroy an object while it's still being used; not calling *Release* results in memory leaks. If you look at the 3dPlus library code, you'll see that many of the C++ objects support a *GetInterface* function. This function returns an interface pointer to the rendering engine object for which the C++ class provides a wrapper. I did this for convenience and performance inside the library code. The *GetInterface* function does not add a reference to the pointer, so if you call one of these *GetInterface* functions, do not call *Release* on the pointer it returns.

NOTE

The bibliography at the end of this book lists texts that have more details about COM objects.

The Rendering Interfaces

We are going to look at only the most commonly used interfaces, which I use in the 3dPlus library. All of the rendering engine interfaces are documented in the help files that come with the DirectX 2 SDK, so I'm not going to discuss the details of how every function of each interface is used. Figure 3-1 on the next page shows the hierarchy of the interfaces used in the 3dPlus library. This diagram was created by looking at the individual interface definitions in d3drmobj.h in the DirectX 2 SDK.

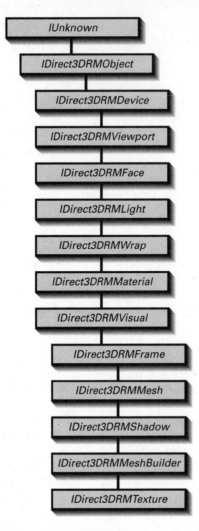

Figure 3-1. *The interface hierarchy of the rendering engine.*

As you can see, there are two major groupings: interfaces derived from *IDirect3DRMObject* and interfaces derived from *IDirect3DRMVisual*. *IDirect3DRMObject* serves as a convenient root for all of the rendering engine interfaces and includes the *SetAppData* function, which allows you to add a 32-bit private data value to any interface. This can be very useful when an interface is encapsulated in a C++ class, for example. The private data value can be a pointer to the C++ class object and, given the interface pointer, you can quickly get at the containing C++ object.

The interfaces derived from *IDirect3DRMVisual* are important because they can be used as an argument to any function that needs an *IDirect3DRMVisual* pointer. (See the *IDirect3DRMFrame::AddVisual* example on the facing page.) On the subject of function arguments, now would be a good time to point out that the actual function prototypes defined in the DirectX 2 SDK don't use the interface type names directly. For example, a function requiring a pointer to an *IDirect3D-RMVisual* interface might be defined like this:

```
HRESULT IDirect3DRMFrame::AddVisual(LPDIRECT3DRMVISUAL
                                    pVisual);
```

As you can see, the type for a pointer to an *IDirect3DRMVisual* interface is LPDIRECT3DRMVISUAL.

NOTE

Using a defined type as a pointer is a common Microsoft Windows practice. I happen to think that in the brave new 32-bit world this practice is obsolete because we no longer need to differentiate between near and far pointers. As you can see from the example above, using special defined pointer types also increases the effort required to figure out exactly what the argument to this function really is. Declaring the type name all in uppercase is another common practice, which in this case also manages to alienate the pointer type from the object type the pointer references. All in all, this is not a practice I find helpful. However, it is how the SDK defines things, as well as being a Windows standard, so we need to be aware of it and deal with it in our code.

In the 3dPlus library, I have defined the pointer type as shown below for the few cases where a function has an interface pointer argument:

```
void AttachVisual(IDirect3DRMVisual* pIVisual);
```

Almost all the interface functions return an *HRESULT* value, and my code will generally test this value like this:

```
ASSERT(SUCCEEDED(m_hr));
```

Or sometimes, my code will test the value like this:

```
return SUCCEEDED(m_hr);
```

You should note that a COM interface can return the value *S_FALSE*, which is not an error but which will pass the *SUCCEEDED* macro successfully. None of the Direct3D interfaces return the *S_FALSE* value, so using the *SUCCEEDED* and *FAILED* macros will always give the correct result.

Let's go through the interfaces derived from *IDirect3DRMObject*, which are shown in Figure 3-1, and take a brief look at the purpose of each.

IDirect3DRMDevice

This interface provides control functions that affect how the scene gets rendered into your window. The functions deal with the Direct3D support layer and, in effect, with aspects of the physical display device. You're most likely to use this interface to alter the rendering quality using the *SetQuality* function. You might also use *IDirect3DRMDevice* to limit the number of color shades used when working on a palletized display by calling the *SetShades* function. As an example, let's look at how the rendering quality is set. Here's the code that implements the *SetQuality* function in the *C3dDevice* class (found in 3dStage.cpp):

```
void C3dDevice::SetQuality(D3DRMRENDERQUALITY quality)
{
    if (!m_pIDevice) return;

    m_hr = m_pIDevice->SetQuality(quality);
    ASSERT(SUCCEEDED(m_hr));
}
```

Here's how the *C3dDevice::SetQuality* function is used when a *C3dStage* object is first created and *m_Quality* has been initialized to D3DRMRENDER_GOURAUD:

```
BOOL C3dStage::Create(CDirect3D* pD3D)
{
    ⋮

    // Set the current default quality
    m_Device.SetQuality(m_Quality);

    ⋮
}
```

The quality can be set to various levels from a simple wire frame to the Gouraud shading model, as shown in Table 3-1. I chose Gouraud shading (one technique for smooth shading) as the default because I think it gives the most realistic effects.

TABLE 3-1
Possible Parameter Values
for the *SetQuality* Function

Quality	Shading	Lighting	Fill
D3DRMRENDER_WIREFRAME	Flat	Off	None (wire frame)
D3DRMRENDER_UNLITFLAT	Flat	Off	Solid
D3DRMRENDER_FLAT	Flat	On	Solid
D3DRMRENDER_GOURAUD	Gouraud	On	Solid
D3DRMRENDER_PHONG	Phong	On	Solid*

* Not supported in Direct3D version 2 (DirectX 2).

Many of the 3dPlus library functions return a *BOOL* indicating either success or failure. However, I decided that for some functions to fail, something had to be catastrophically wrong, so those functions have no return value. Rather, an *ASSERT* statement in the function traps any failure that might actually occur.

IDirect3DRMViewport

This interface controls the projection system, shown in Figure 3-2, employed to convert the 3D coordinates to 2D coordinates on your computer screen. You can use the *SetBack* function to set the location of the back clipping plane on the *z*-axis. You can also use the *SetField* function to alter the focal length of the camera viewing the scene.

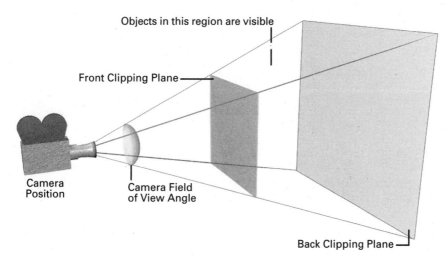

Figure 3-2. *The projection system.*

The *SetProjection* function is used to determine whether perspective correction should be applied or whether objects should be rendered with a simple Orthographic projection type. In most cases we'll want to use the Perspective projection type for realism. We'll look at perspective correction in Chapter 8 when we see how texture maps are applied.

After the initial rendering conditions have been set, the primary use of this interface is in conjunction with the selection of objects in a scene. The *Pick* function is used to determine which object, if any, lies under a given point on the screen. We'll explore the *Pick* function a bit more in Chapter 7 when we look at hit testing.

IDirect3DRMFace

This interface allows you to examine a single face of a 3D object or set the attributes of a face. For example, you can set the color of a given face using *SetColor*, or you can obtain the normal vector to a face by calling *GetNormal*. Getting an *IDirect3D-RMFace* pointer is usually done by asking the *IDirect3DRMMeshBuilder* interface for a list of faces and then asking the face array returned from the mesh builder for the interface to a specific face in the array. Here's how the color of a single face is set in the *C3dShape::SetFaceColor* function:

```
BOOL C3dShape::SetFaceColor(int nFace, double r, double g,
                            double b)
{
    if (nFace >= GetFaceCount()) return FALSE;

    // Get the face list
    IDirect3DRMFaceArray* pIFaces = NULL;
    ASSERT(m_pIMeshBld);
    m_hr = m_pIMeshBld->GetFaces(&pIFaces);
    ASSERT(SUCCEEDED(m_hr));

    // Get the requested face from list
    IDirect3DRMFace* pIFace = NULL;
    m_hr = pIFaces->GetElement(nFace, &pIFace);
    ASSERT(SUCCEEDED(m_hr));

    // Set face color
    m_hr = pIFace->SetColorRGB(r, g, b);
    ASSERT(SUCCEEDED(m_hr));

    // Release the face and list interfaces
    pIFace->Release();
    pIFaces->Release();

    return TRUE;
}
```

IDirect3DRMLight

This interface controls the various kinds of lights supported by the rendering engine. (Lights are examined in some detail in Chapter 10.) A light can have many different properties, ranging from color to how its intensity varies with distance. Here's a simple example of setting the color of a light from *C3dLight::SetColor*:

```
BOOL C3dLight::SetColor(double r, double g, double b)
{
    ASSERT(m_pILight);
    m_hr = m_pILight->SetColorRGB(D3DVAL(r),
                                  D3DVAL(g),
                                  D3DVAL(b));
    return SUCCEEDED(m_hr);
}
```

The *D3DVAL* macro is used to convert values to the floating-point argument format that the rendering engine uses.

IDirect3DRMWrap

A *wrap* determines how a texture is applied to an object. Wraps can be flat, cylindrical, spherical, or chrome. Unless you use chrome wraps, the function you're most likely to use is *Apply*, which applies the wrap to a mesh. If you use a chrome wrap to make an object appear reflective, you'll need to use *ApplyRelative* to apply the wrap to the object so the texture remains oriented relative to a frame other than the object's. This is how the "reflection" stays the right way up, even though the object might be rotating. Wraps are discussed in more detail in Chapter 8.

A wrap can also be applied to a single face of an object. Here's the code (found in 3dImage.cpp) that allows a *C3dWrap* object to be applied to a single face of a *C3dShape* object:

```
BOOL C3dWrap::Apply(C3dShape* pShape, int nFace)
{
    ASSERT(pShape);
    ASSERT(m_pIWrap);
    if (nFace >= pShape->GetFaceCount()) return FALSE;

    // Get the face list
    IDirect3DRMMeshBuilder* pIBld =
                        pShape->GetMeshBuilder();
    ASSERT(pIBld);
    IDirect3DRMFaceArray* pIFaces = NULL;
    m_hr = pIBld->GetFaces(&pIFaces);
    ASSERT(SUCCEEDED(m_hr));

    //Get requested face
    IDirect3DRMFace* pIFace = NULL;
    m_hr = pIFaces->GetElement(nFace, &pIFace);
    ASSERT(SUCCEEDED(m_hr));

    //Apply wrap to face
    m_hr = m_pIWrap->Apply(pIFace);
    ASSERT(SUCCEEDED(m_hr));

    //Release interfaces
    pIFace->Release();
    pIFaces->Release();

    return SUCCEEDED(m_hr);
}
```

IDirect3DRMMaterial

Materials determine the way surfaces reflect light. Using the material properties, you can affect how shiny a surface looks and whether the surface looks more like plastic or metal.

In general, a material has two colors: its normal color and the color it looks when it's illuminated strongly. Take a look at a green apple under a bright white light. The apple looks green all over except for where the light shines directly on it—it looks white there. The colors you see are a result of the object's diffuse and specular reflection properties, and these can be simulated using a material. We'll look at materials more in Chapter 8.

IDirect3DRMVisual

This interface has no member functions of its own. It serves only as a root interface from which any interface that can be used as a visual is derived. You won't find many references to *IDirect3DRMVisual* in the SDK documentation, but you'll find it used as a type for various function arguments, as shown in the *AddVisual* declaration on page 49.

IDirect3DRMFrame

IDirect3DRMFrame is the most commonly used interface and is used to change the properties of a frame. For example, you can set the position of a frame by calling *SetPosition*, and you can set which way the frame points using *SetOrientation*. As another example, you can call *SetTexture* to give the frame a texture of its own so that meshes attached as visuals to the frame can use the frame's texture. This allows a single mesh defining a shape to be used in many places but with different textures. Here's how *C3dFrame::SetPosition* uses the interface to set the position (having declared *IDirect3DRMFrame* * *m_pIFrame*):

```
void C3dFrame::SetPosition(double x, double y, double z,
                           C3dFrame* pRef)
{
    ASSERT(m_pIFrame);
    m_hr = m_pIFrame->SetPosition(_GetRef(pRef),
                                  D3DVAL(x),
                                  D3DVAL(y),
                                  D3DVAL(z));
    ASSERT(SUCCEEDED(m_hr));
}
```

You can also use *SetRotation* and *SetVelocity* to set a frame's rotation around a given vector and the speed at which it rotates. This can be useful if you want some continuous action in a scene and don't want to constantly compute the position.

If the frame is the root frame (it has no parent frame), the background image can be set using *SceneSetBackground* or you can simply set the background color using *SceneSetBackgroundRGB*.

IDirect3DRMMesh

The mesh interface is primarily used to set the attributes of groups within the mesh. A *group* is a set of vertices with common attributes such as color. Grouping common elements can improve rendering performance and is extensively employed by the Direct3D Retained Mode engine.

Two other functions that might be of interest are the *Save* function, which saves the details of a mesh to a disk file, and the *Translate* function, which adds an offset to every vertex in a mesh. This latter function is most useful when adding several meshes to a common frame to build a complex shape.

IDirect3DRMShadow

This interface has no member functions of its own but serves as a data type for shadow objects, which are a kind of visual. Using shadows is discussed more in Chapter 10.

IDirect3DRMMeshBuilder

This is a complex interface used for the creation of 3D objects. The *C3dShape* class uses the *IDirect3DRMMeshBuilder* interface to implement most of its own functionality. The interface includes some very simple functions such as *Load*, which loads a mesh from a disk file, and other more complex functions such as *AddFaces*, which uses a list of vertices, normals (vectors that signify direction), and face descriptions to add a new set of faces to a mesh. (See Chapter 4 for more details of how meshes are used to create 3D objects.)

Given that *m_pIMeshBld* is declared as a pointer to *IDirect3DRMMeshBuilder*, here's the *C3dShape::Create* function that uses the mesh builder interface to construct new objects from vertex and face descriptions:

```
BOOL C3dShape::Create(D3DVECTOR* pVectors, int iVectors,
                      D3DVECTOR* pNormals, int iNormals,
                      int* pFaceData, BOOL bAutoGen)
{
    ASSERT(m_pIMeshBld);

    // Build mesh from vector list
    ASSERT(sizeof(ULONG) == sizeof(int));
    m_hr = m_pIMeshBld->AddFaces(iVectors, pVectors,
                                 iNormals, pNormals,
                                 (ULONG*)pFaceData, NULL);
    ASSERT(SUCCEEDED(m_hr));
    if ((iNormals == 0) && bAutoGen) {
        m_pIMeshBld->GenerateNormals();
    }

    AttachVisual(m_pIMeshBld);

    // Enable perspective correction
    m_pIMeshBld->SetPerspective(TRUE);

    return TRUE;
}
```

The mesh builder interface also has many interrogation functions to allow you to get more information about a mesh. For example, we can find out how many faces there are in a mesh:

```
int C3dShape::GetFaceCount()
{
    ASSERT(m_pIMeshBld);
    int i = (int) m_pIMeshBld->GetFaceCount();
    return i;
}
```

IDirect3DRMTexture

Textures are images that can be applied to faces or entire shapes to make them look more realistic. The interface functions are used most often to control how a texture will be rendered. For example, if it's important to restrict how many colors are used in rendering a texture, you can call the *SetShades* function. Otherwise, one colorful texture can use all of the palette colors and leave none for other shapes and textures to use.

You can call *SetDecalTransparencyColor* to define transparent areas in a texture. Decals are textures that are rendered directly as visuals and are generally used as a kind of sprite object that's flat and always facing the camera. However, the transparency feature of textures doesn't actually rely on the texture being used as a decal. We look at textures in more detail in Chapter 8 and at sprites in Chapter 9.

The 3dPlus Class Library

As I've mentioned in previous chapters, the 3dPlus class library is not intended to be the definitive class library for all of the rendering engine functions. I designed it so that I could explore 3D ideas in a way I found more familiar than using COM object interfaces. You don't need this library to create 3D applications, but using it as a learning tool or as the basis for a real library might get you going a little faster.

The library code uses the *ASSERT* statement to test pointers and various conditions. In many cases, mistakes in your code cause the Visual C++ debugger to stop at the *ASSERT* statement rather than letting your application blow up in the rendering engine core.

Many of the classes are very simple wrappers around a rendering engine interface. Some of the classes provide a higher level of functionality than a single interface. In all cases, I've tried to make it easy for you to figure out how to bypass the class and call the underlying interfaces directly if you want. To this end, most classes have a *GetInterface* function that returns the underlying interface pointer. Note that *AddRef* is *not* called before the pointer to the interface object is passed back to you, so, in these cases, you must not call *Release* on the pointer—just treat it as a C++ class pointer.

Figure 3-3 shows the hierarchy of the classes in the 3dPlus library. I have not included any of the classes that relate directly to the DirectDraw layer. The classes in Figure 3-3 all relate to the Direct3D Retained Mode engine.

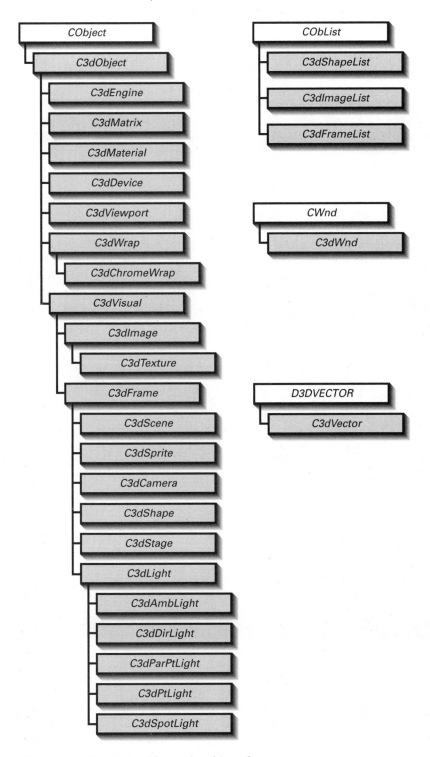

Figure 3-3. *The 3dPlus library class hierarchy.*

The classes fall into three groups: those simply derived from *C3dObject*, those derived from *C3dVisual*, and those derived from *C3dFrame*. If you look at the Direct3D rendering engine hierarchy in Figure 3-1 on page 48, you'll see that the two hierarchies are quite similar. The main difference between the two lies in the fact that I derived several classes from *C3dFrame* so that those classes can have a position and direction as well as being visual components in their own right. So in interface terms, the classes derived from *C3dFrame* are using both *IDirect3DRMFrame* and *IDirect3DRMVisual* in some way. Let's walk through most of the 3dPlus library classes, looking at what the classes do and in some cases how you might use them.

C3dEngine

The *C3dEngine* class collects several global functions from the rendering engine in one place. The 3dPlus class library includes a single global instance of this class called *the3dEngine*. Member functions of this class are typically used to create some other rendering engine object and usually return an interface pointer. You generally won't have a reason to use this class in an application directly, but when you create instances of some of the other classes, their code will use the engine functions. The following function is shown as an example of using the *the3dEngine* object:

```
BOOL C3dFrame::Create(C3dFrame* pParent)
{
    if (m_pIFrame) {
        m_pIFrame->Release();
        m_pIFrame = NULL;
    }
    if (!the3dEngine.CreateFrame(_GetRef(pParent),
                                 &m_pIFrame)) {
        TRACE("Frame create failed\n");
        m_pIFrame = NULL;
        return FALSE;
    }
    ASSERT(m_pIFrame);
    m_piFrame->SetAppData((ULONG)this);

    return TRUE;
}
```

A call is made to the *CreateFrame* member of *the3dEngine*, which actually creates the frame interface and assigns it to the frame's *m_pIFrame* variable.

C3dMatrix

The rendering engine defines its own 4-by-4 matrix for coordinate manipulation, but again I prefer to use a C++ class because it reduces the amount of code I need to write. For example, look at the *C3dPosCtlr::OnUpdate* example on page 64 for the *C3dVector* class and you can see a matrix being used to apply a rotation to two vectors. The code looks ridiculously simple despite the complex math involved in the calculations. Using a C++ class gives me great flexibility in how I use my matrices without cluttering the code.

Of course, you don't have to use *C3dMatrix* or *C3dVector* if you don't want to. But if you're using the other classes in the 3dPlus library, you'll find that the matrix and vector classes make your job a bit easier. We'll look at using matrices in more detail in Chapter 5.

C3dDevice

This class provides a simple wrapper for the *IDirect3DRMDevice* interface. *C3dDevice* is used by *C3dStage* to build an environment for displaying 3D objects. You're not likely to want to create one of these objects yourself unless you redesign the stage concept. You might, however, want to call the *SetQuality* member function to modify how rendering is handled in your particular application. Here's a part of the code that creates a stage that shows how the device class is used:

```
BOOL C3dStage::Create(CDirect3D* pD3D)
{
    ⋮
    // Create a new device from Direct3D surfaces
    if (!m_Device.Create(pD3D)) return FALSE;

    // Set current quality
    m_Device.SetQuality(m_Quality);
    ⋮
}
```

C3dViewport

This class is a simple wrapper for the *IDirect3DRMViewport* interface. Again, you aren't likely to be using this class directly because the *C3dStage* object controls the viewport for you. Here's the rendering function in the stage class, which is called to render the latest view of a scene:

```
void C3dStage::Render()
{
    ASSERT(m_pIFrame);

    // Clear the viewport
    m_Viewport.Clear();

    if (m_pScene) {

        // Render the scene
        m_Viewport.Render(m_pScene);
    }

    // Update the display
    m_Device.Update();
}
```

As you can see, using these classes is very simple. The various member functions hide the underlying COM object interfaces and make the code a little easier to follow.

C3dWrap

This class (defined in 3dImage.cpp) is again primarily just a wrapper for the *IDirect3DRMWrap* interface, but it does have a little added value. The *Apply* member function has two implementations. The first implementation, which is easy to implement and shown below, applies the wrap to the entire object:

```
BOOL C3dWrap::Apply(C3dShape* pShape)
{
    ASSERT(pShape);
    ASSERT(m_pIWrap);
    HRESULT hr;

    hr = m_pIWrap->Apply(pShape->GetVisual());
    return SUCCEEDED(hr);
}
```

The other implementation of the function, which we looked at on page 53, applies a wrap to a single face.

Having a couple of different implementations of the *Apply* method simplifies the code while retaining a lot of flexibility in how the method is implemented. Wraps, including chrome wraps, are explained in more detail in Chapter 8 when we look at texture maps.

C3dVisual

This serves as the base class for all other classes that can be used as visuals in a scene. *C3dVisual* includes a member variable to hold the name of the object. You can use the *SetName* and *GetName* functions to set and retrieve the name. I found attaching names to visual objects useful when implementing mouse selection of objects in a scene. The object's name can be displayed to verify the selection.

C3dImage

This is the only class that does not use any rendering engine interfaces. Its purpose is to load an image from either a disk file or an application resource for use in a texture map or decal. The rendering engine defines a structure for images, named *D3DRMIMAGE*. The *C3dImage* class uses the *D3DRMIMAGE* structure to hold the image data once it has been loaded. Here's an example of how the *C3dImage* class is used to load an image from a disk file for use as a background image in a scene:

```
C3dImage* pImg = new C3dImage;
if (!pImg->Load()) {
    delete pImg;
    return;
}

ASSERT(m_pScene);
m_pScene->m_ImgList.Append(pImg);
m_pScene->SetBackground(pImg);
```

The *C3dImage::Load* function is called here with no arguments, which causes a dialog box to appear. The dialog box allows the user to select a Windows bitmap file to be used as the background image. You can also specify which bitmap to load by providing either a filename or the ID of a bitmap resource as a parameter to the *Load* function. Here's an example where a bitmap resource is loaded and then used to create a texture:

```
// Load the image of the world
C3dImage* pImg1 = new C3dImage;
if (!pImg1->Load(IDB_WORLD)) {
    AfxMessageBox("Failed to load world1.bmp");
    delete pImg1;
    return;
}
m_pScene->m_ImgList.Append(pImg1);

// Create a texture from image
C3dTexture tex1;
tex1.Create(pImg1);
```

C3dTexture

This class (defined in 3dImage.cpp) provides a wrapper for the *IDirect3DRMTexture* interface. Textures are created from images, as shown in the example above. The image used to create a texture must have sides that are integral powers of two in size: 32 by 64, 128 by 128, and 4 by 8 are all valid image sizes for a texture; 32 by 45 and 11 by 16 are invalid sizes. The *C3dTexture::Create* function will fail if the image is not a valid size:

```
BOOL C3dTexture::Create()
{
    if (m_pITexture) {
        m_pITexture->Release();
        m_pITexture = NULL;
    }
    // Validate that image size is in power of 2
    for (int i = 0; (1 << i) < GetWidth(); i++);
    for (int j = 0; (1 << j) < GetHeight(); j++);
    if (GetWidth() != (1 << i) || GetHeight() != (1 << j)) {
        TRACE("This image can't be used as a texture."\
                " Its sides are not exact powers of 2\n");
    }

    if (!the3dEngine.CreateTexture(GetObject(),
                                    &m_pITexture)) {
        TRACE("Texture create failed\n");
        m_pITexture = NULL;
        return FALSE;
    }

    ASSERT(m_pITexture);
    return TRUE;
}
```

Textures are attached to an image and rendered under the control of a wrap. The wrap determines the algorithm used to apply the texture. Here's some code that creates a texture from an image and then applies it to a shape using a cylindrical wrap:

```
C3dImage* pImg1 = new C3dImage;
pImg1->Load(IDB_LEAVES);

C3dTexture tex1;
tex1.Create(pImg1);

C3dWrap wrap;
wrap.Create(D3DRMWRAP_CYLINDER,
            NULL,
            0, 0, 0, // Origin
            0, 0, 1, // Direction
            0, 1, 0, // Up
            0, 0,    // Texture origin
            1, 1);   // Texture scale

pTree->SetTexture(&tex1);
wrap.Apply(pTree);
```

C3dFrame

The frame class is a wrapper for the *IDirect3DRMFrame* interface with some additional member functions to make it easier to use. A frame has several attributes, including position and its orientation in 3D space. Setting the position is done using *SetPosition*. The orientation is set by using the *SetDirection* function, which determines the direction the frame *points*. To determine the orientation exactly, you need to specify two vectors. The first vector describes the *forward* direction, and the second vector describes the *up* direction. Think of setting the direction in which an airplane is flying. The forward vector specifies the direction in which the nose of the plane is pointing. The up vector determines which way the tail fin points—up, down, left, and so on. Some objects don't really need an up vector when you point them. For example, a cone can be used as a pointer in a scene. The tip of the cone is set to point in some direction, using only the forward direction vector. The up vector is irrelevant because the cone can be rotated about its axis any amount and still look the same. To make life easy for you, the *SetDirection* function allows you to specify only the forward direction vector and it supplies the up vector for you. Here's the code that implements it:

```
void C3dFrame::SetDirection(double dx, double dy, double dz,
                            C3dFrame* pRef)
{
    ASSERT(m_pIFrame);

    // Create a vector for the forward direction
    C3dVector d(dx, dy, dz);

    // Generate an arbitrary up vector
    C3dVector u = d.GenerateUp();
```

```
        SetDirection(d.x, d.y, d.z, u.x, u.y, u.z, pRef);
    }
```

The *C3dVector* class includes a member function for generating up vectors, which makes this piece of code look extremely simple. I like that.

All the position and direction functions have a reference frame argument (the *pRef* value shown in the example above). This is very important because a frame can be anywhere in the frame hierarchy and its position is determined by its own transform and also by those of all its parents. It's like running around in your kitchen. If you move your home from Washington to Colorado, you can still run around in your kitchen but your actual position on the planet is different. In other words, all movement is relative to some reference frame. As a convenience, you can pass NULL as the reference frame and the frame's parent will be used as the reference. As an example of how the reference frame is used, here's some code (found in 3dInCtlr.cpp) that positions objects in the scene as the user changes the objects' positions with the keyboard, mouse, or joystick:

```
void C3dPosCtlr::OnUpdate(_3DINPUTSTATE& st,
                          C3dFrame* pFrame)
{
    // Get the stage to use as a reference frame for the
    // positions, etc.
    ASSERT(m_pWnd);
    C3dStage* pStage = m_pWnd->GetStage();
    ASSERT(pStage);

    double x, y, z;
    pFrame->GetPosition(x, y, z, pStage);
    x += st.dX * 0.1;
    y += st.dY * 0.1;
    z += st.dZ * 0.1;
    pFrame->SetPosition(x, y, z, pStage);

    C3dVector d, u;
    pFrame->GetDirection(d, u, pStage);
    // Rotate the direction and up vectors
    double a = 3.0;
    C3dMatrix r;
    r.Rotate(-st.dR * a, -st.dU * a, -st.dV * a);
    d = r * d;
    u = r * u;
    pFrame->SetDirection(d, u, pStage);
}
```

You can see that all the positions are relative to the stage, which is the expected behavior when a user attempts to move an object into place in the scene.

C3dScene

This class holds all the information required for a scene: the lights, the list of shapes, the current background image, and the camera setup. A single *C3dScene*

object is attached to the stage at any one time. The scene has a built-in ambient light that can be set with *SetAmbientLight*. You can add other lights to the scene by calling *AddLight*. The scene is actually the topmost frame in the frame hierarchy, so 3D shapes (which are also frames) are added by calling *AddChild*. The background color of a scene can be set with *SetBackground(r, g, b)*, or an image can be used instead by calling *SetBackground(pImage)*. The *Move* function is used to update the position of any objects in the scene that might be moving and to render the current scene to the application window. The scene must be attached to the stage for the *Move* function to have an effect. *C3dScene* also stores vectors for camera position and direction. These vectors can be set using *SetCameraPosition* and *SetCameraDirection*. Here's a code fragment that creates a new scene and sets the initial lighting arrangement:

```
// Create an initial scene
m_pScene = new C3dScene;
if (!m_pScene->Create()) return FALSE;

// Set up the lighting
C3dDirLight dl;
dl.Create(0.8, 0.8, 0.8);
m_pScene->AddChild(&dl);
dl.SetPosition(-2, 2, -5);
dl.SetDirection(1, -1, 1);
m_pScene->SetAmbientLight(0.4, 0.4, 0.4);
```

In this case, the ambient lighting level is set quite low and a directional light is added that points down from the top left corner to add highlights to any shapes that might be added to the scene.

The *C3dScene* object contains two list objects to help you manage your scenes. Use the *m_ShapeList* member list object to track any *C3dShape* objects you want deleted when the scene is destroyed, and use the *m_ImageList* member list object to track *C3dImage* objects you want deleted when the scene is destroyed. Objects are added to these lists only if you call the *Append* member function of the list object. No objects are ever added on your behalf.

C3dSprite

The *C3dSprite* class provides support for two-dimensional beings in the 3D world. The DirectX 2 SDK documents refer to these sprites as *decals*. Chapter 9 looks at how sprites can be used to implement games where performance is more critical than a real 3D appearance. The *C3dSprite* class is derived from *C3dFrame*, so sprites have the same positional capabilities as the 3D objects.

C3dCamera

The *C3dCamera* class doesn't have any member functions and, in fact, doesn't do much of anything at all. The class is derived from *C3dFrame* so you can set its position and direction, which is all the control that's needed to fly through a scene or simply look in a particular direction.

C3dShape

This class combines the functionality of a frame interface and a visual interface, providing a convenient way to create 3D shapes that can be directly positioned in a scene. One shape can be attached to another as a child, so you can build complex shapes easily. There are several functions that build simple geometric shapes such as spheres, rods, and cones, and a *Load* function allows you to create a *C3dShape* object from an .X file. You can set the color and texture of the entire shape or individual faces of the shape. There are some limitations when you attempt to apply textures to individual faces, and these are covered in Chapter 8. Here's an example of creating a simple geometric shape and adding it to the current scene:

```
C3dShape sh1;
sh1.CreateCube(2);
m_pScene->AddChild(&sh1);
```

Note that the *C3dShape* object is just a container for the underlying frame and visual interfaces. When a shape is added to a scene or another frame in this way, the containing C++ object is no longer required because the interfaces, not the C++ containing object, are used to create the object in the scene. When the visual from one object is used in a second object, the second object calls *AddRef* on the visual's interface pointer. So if the original container is destroyed and releases its own interface pointer, the visual object still stays alive.

Having said that the container doesn't need to be kept around, it's still useful to keep it because the user might select an object to manipulate in a scene, and it's through the containing C++ object that we want to exercise control. Not clear? We'll cover this subject in more detail in Chapter 6 when we look at ways of letting the user manipulate objects in scenes.

C3dStage

The *C3dStage* class is used by the *C3dWnd* class to provide the device and viewport necessary for viewing a 3D scene in a window. The class contains functions for retrieving the camera, setting the rendering quality, and setting the background to the current scene. You're not likely to want to use many of these functions to start with, except perhaps for retrieving the camera. Attaching a scene to the stage can be done through the *C3dWnd* class, which has a *SetScene* member function that passes the request down to the stage:

```
BOOL C3dWnd::SetScene(C3dScene* pScene)
{
    if (!m_pStage) return FALSE;
    m_pScene = pScene;
    m_pStage->SetScene(m_pScene);
    if (m_pScene) {
        // Enable the idle-time rendering
        m_bEnableUpdates = TRUE;
```

(continued)

```
        } else {
            m_bEnableUpdates = FALSE;
        }

        return TRUE;
    }
```

C3dLight

This light serves as a base class for the other light types. Its *Create* function is called by derived classes to construct the underlying light interface:

```
BOOL C3dLight::Create(D3DRMLIGHTTYPE type, double r,
                      double g, double b)
{
    // Create the frame that holds the light
    if (!C3dFrame::Create(NULL)) return FALSE;

    // Create the light object
    ASSERT(m_pILight == NULL);
    if (!the3dEngine.CreateLight(type, r, g, b, &m_pILight))
    {
        return FALSE;
    }
    ASSERT(m_pILight);

    // Add light to its frame
    ASSERT(m_pIFrame);
    m_hr = m_pIFrame->AddLight(m_pILight);
    if (FAILED(m_hr)) return FALSE;

    return TRUE;
}
```

C3dAmbLight

This class is used to implement the ambient light object, which is built into the *C3dScene* object. You can manipulate the ambient light in the scene by using *C3dScene::SetAmbientLight* rather than by calling member functions in this class directly.

C3dDirLight

This class implements a directional light that can be placed in a scene to provide highlights on your scene's objects. An example of a directional light being placed in the top left corner of a scene follows on the facing page:

```
C3dDirLight dl;
dl.Create(0.8, 0.8, 0.8);
m_pScene->AddChild(&dl);
dl.SetPosition(-2, 2, -5);
dl.SetDirection(1, -1, 1);
```

Note that the direction in which the light is shining is set using only the forward direction vector. The up vector is generated automatically, which saves you from having to compute it.

Several other light types are derived from the *C3dLight* class. All the different light types are discussed in Chapter 10.

C3dShapeList, C3dImageList, C3dFrameList

The *C3dShapeList* class provides a way to keep a list of *C3dShape* objects, *C3dImageList* keeps a list of *C3dImage* objects, and *C3dFrameList* keeps a list of *C3dFrame* objects. Each of these classes is derived from the MFC class *CObList*. For details on how *CObList* works, refer to the MFC documentation. The *C3dScene* object contains these list objects to track shapes, images, and frames that need to be deleted when the scene is destroyed.

C3dWnd

This class provides everything you need to create either a pop-up window or a child window containing a 3D scene. It contains a stage object and can support an object movement controller (keyboard, mouse, or joystick) and object selection via the mouse. Using it as a child window is extremely simple, as this code fragment shows:

```
// Create the 3D window
if (!m_wnd3d.Create(this, IDC_3DWND)) {
    return -1;
}
```

The 3D window is created as a child window with a specified parent and child ID value. Once the window is created, you just need to create the scene and attach it to the 3D window's stage to make the scene visible:

```
m_pScene = new C3dScene;
if (!m_pScene->Create()) return FALSE;

// Set up the lighting
C3dDirLight dl;
dl.Create(0.8, 0.8, 0.8);
m_pScene->AddChild(&dl);
dl.SetPosition(-2, 2, -5);
dl.SetDirection(1, -1, 1);
m_pScene->SetAmbientLight(0.4, 0.4, 0.4);

m_wnd3d.SetScene(m_pScene);
```

C3dVector

The rendering engine defines its own 3D vector, *D3DVECTOR*, which is a simple structure, but I prefer to work with C++ vector objects. This way, I can have multiple constructors to simplify how I create the vectors, and of course, I can implement operators such as add and multiply to simplify the code. The *C3dVector* class is derived from the *D3DVECTOR* structure, so anywhere you can use a *D3DVECTOR* structure, you can also use a *C3dVector* object. As an example of how the *C3dVector* class is used, here is a piece of code that updates the position of a 3D object as it is moved about the screen by the user:

```
C3dVector d, u;
pFrame->GetDirection(d, u, pStage);
// Rotate the direction and up vectors
double a = 3.0;
C3dMatrix r;
r.Rotate(-st.dR * a, -st.dU * a, -st.dV * a);
d = r * d;
u = r * u;
pFrame->SetDirection(d, u, pStage);
```

Using the vector class (and the matrix class) here greatly simplifies the code. Mind you—understanding how it works might be a different matter. We'll be looking at this topic again in Chapter 6 when we see how to move objects under user control.

The 3dPlus Library DirectDraw Classes

The 3dPlus library includes a few classes to support the DirectDraw interfaces. These classes are shown in Figure 3-4.

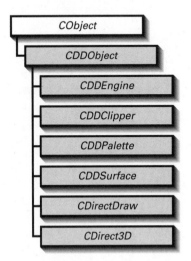

Figure 3-4. *The DirectDraw support classes in the 3dPlus library.*

These classes all provide very simple wrappers around the underlying DirectDraw interfaces. (A more detailed explanation of the DirectDraw interfaces can be found in Chapter 12.) The code that implements these classes can be found in 3dDirDraw.cpp in the 3dPlus library source directory. To create the code for these classes, I used the VIEWER sample application code that is a part of the DirectX 2 SDK as my guide. I implemented only enough support to enable my *C3dDevice* class to work. You are, of course, most welcome to browse the source code and make of it what you will.

Chapter 13 looks in more detail at the Direct3D interfaces for which there are no wrapper classes in the 3dPlus library at all. The sample code for Chapter 13 does include some very thin wrapper classes of its own for these interfaces.

Thanks for Taking the Lightning Tour

We have very briefly touched on all of the interfaces and C++ classes that we'll use to implement the sample applications in the remaining chapters. I'm sure you have many questions about what we just covered, and everything that has been mentioned here is discussed in more detail in later chapters. If you're a bit confused about which bits of the functionality come from the 3dPlus library and which bits come directly from the Direct3D interfaces, remember that all interface pointers in the code have a *pI* prefix to distinguish them from pointers to the 3dPlus library C++ objects, which have just a *p* prefix. Also, remember that the C++ classes are frequently just convenient wrappers for the Direct3D interfaces. Only a few of the classes, such as *C3dShape*, have any real code content of their own, and we'll see what all that's for in the subsequent chapters.

n the previous chapter we waded through the Direct3D rendering engine interfaces and the classes in the 3dPlus library. I'm sure you'll be happy to know that we're back to coding in this chapter as we look at ways to create our own shapes. By the end of this chapter you should have a good handle on how to create the shapes you might need for a real application.

I should warn you, though, that I'm not about to reveal the secrets of how characters are created for Saturday morning cartoons. We'll be working at a slightly lower level than that, looking at cubes and spheres and the like. Nonetheless, the techniques you'll learn here are the basis for more complex shape generation mechanisms.

On a practical note, it's unlikely that in a real 3D application you'd generate more than just a few of your shapes using the direct approach described here. Instead you'd probably have an artist use an application such as Autodesk's 3D Studio to build your shapes. You could then convert this artwork to the .X file format, which your code can load into your application. However, you might want to generate some of your shapes or scenery yourself—so let's look at what's involved.

Geometry

Sorry. I know the book cover doesn't mention offering a geometry class, but we need to cover a little terminology and see how things work in the 3D world before we can start coding our own shapes. Let's start at the beginning with another look at the coordinate system.

The rendering engine uses a left-handed set of axes. (Astute readers will now be thrusting out their left hands, demonstrating which ways X, Y, and Z point.) If you dozed off when we went over that earlier in Chapter 1, Figure 4-1 shows the left-handed axes we'll be using.

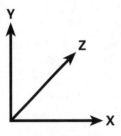

Figure 4-1. *The left-handed system of axes.*

Positive Y is up, positive X is to the right, and positive Z is into the screen away from the user.

Now that we have defined which way the axes point, we need to look at the dimensions we'll use to create objects. Dimensions are somewhat abstract. We could, for example, say that all objects are measured in miles. That might sound silly, but if we put the camera miles back from these huge objects, we'll be able to see them just fine—no air pollution out here in 3D-land to mess up the image.

Just to digress a little more, did you know that one of the problems faced by astronauts during space walks is that they can't judge the size or distance of objects very well? The reason for the problem is that light passes through the vacuum of space without any reduction in intensity or any of the scattering we get in the Earth's air. So objects in space look extremely clear even if they are miles away. Interesting, eh? Almost makes you want to write to NASA and sign up for training.

We encounter similar problems when determining how big to make our 3D shapes, because their final size on your computer screen depends on the size of the objects created from the shapes and their distance from the camera. What we need to do is make an arbitrary choice about the camera position, and then we can determine how big to make our objects. The default camera position in the scenes we'll be creating is ten units out from the origin, so the camera coordinates are 0, 0, –10. Within the default field of view for the camera, objects of one unit in size (a one-unit cube for example) placed at the origin (0, 0, 0) look OK on the screen. So the objects we create will be typically just a few units long, wide, and high.

Because the coordinate values we are using are floating-point, you don't lose any precision by using numerically small units. It's not like working with integer values that can't be endlessly subdivided. Figure 4-2 shows the axes again but with the sort of coordinate values we'll be using.

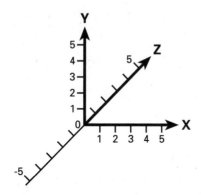

Figure 4-2. *The coordinate axes showing typical scale values.*

Having now seen how far away things are and which way the axes point, we can start to create the points in space that define what an object looks like.

One Vertex, Many Vertices, One Dog

Let's draw a dog. Get a pencil and connect the dots in Figure 4-3 on the next page, starting at dot 1 and following them in sequence.

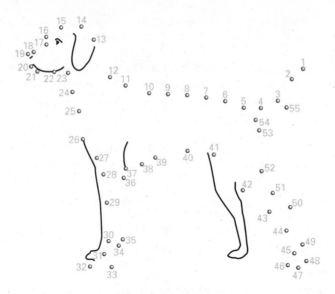

Figure 4-3. Connect the dots.

"Mommy, what are you doing?"

"Learning about a 3D computer graphics rendering engine."

"Boy, that looks easy—*I* could do *that*."

By now you've drawn a flat, 2D dog, but I'm sure you get the idea: By specifying the order in which a set of points are joined, we can define quite complex shapes. In geometry class we called each dot a vertex, and that's how we'll refer to them from now on. A vertex defines the point of intersection of one or more lines, and these are *straight* lines so far as we are concerned. (I'm sure you connected the dots in the dog picture with nice flowing curves. If you connected them with straight lines, you are destined for greatness in the computer graphics world but I doubt many folks would like your dog.) Of course, if the dog picture had an awful lot of dots defining the shape, even Captain Super Nerd, using a ruler to join the dots, would get a pretty good looking dog.

What's the point (no pun intended) of all this business with dogs and dots? The point is that the computer draws only straight lines. If we want shapes that look smooth, we're going to need either a lot of vertices to define the shape or some other way to make it look good. We'll come back to the issues of smoothness later, in the section "Creating Solid Objects" on page 84. For now, let's be satisfied with knowing what a vertex is.

Vectors

To define a vertex in 3D space, we need to specify three coordinate values: X, Y, and Z. The origin of our coordinate system is at 0, 0, 0. A point at the top left of the screen and some way back into the screen might be at –2, 3, 4. We can define the location of a vertex by specifying a vector from the origin to another point in 3D space. Figure 4-4 shows a vector defining the point located at –2, 3, 4.

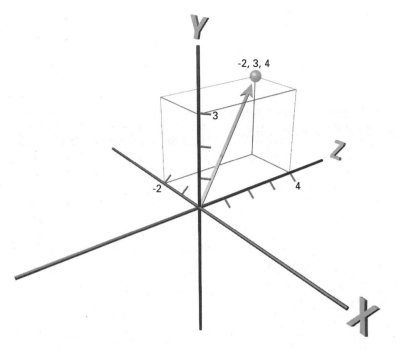

Figure 4-4. *A vector defining the point –2, 3, 4.*

We can also use a vector to define a direction. For example, the vector 0, 1, 0 defines *up* (the positive Y direction) as shown in Figure 4-5.

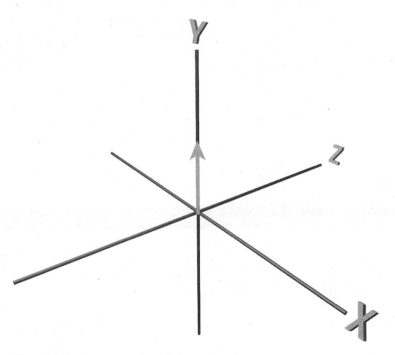

Figure 4-5. *A vector used to define a direction.*

Note that the actual length of the vector is not important when the vector is used to define a direction. As long as at least one of the coordinates is nonzero, the vector can be used to define a direction. It is conventional, however, to use a unit vector to define directions. A unit vector has a length of one, meaning:

$$x^2 + y^2 + z^2 = 1$$

Because it's often not convenient to compute the exact values required to get a unit vector when writing code, there is usually some way to normalize vectors to unit length. The *C3dVector* class includes a *Normalize* function that performs this task. Why do we want direction vectors as unit vectors? When we use direction vectors to modify the orientation of an object, the math that needs to be done on the object's vertices is simpler if the directions are unit vectors. However, you don't need to supply unit vectors for the direction when calling the rendering engine functions because the engine will normalize the vectors before it uses them. The only time you need to be able to normalize a vector is when you are doing your own vector math. (The other common use for a unit vector is to define the normal to a plane, which we'll be looking at in "Normals" on page 78.)

Enough about vectors. Let's summarize: A vector can be used to define the position of a vertex or to define a direction.

Orientation

When we position a 3D object in space, we actually need three vectors to define its position and orientation. One vector is used to define its position (or at least the position of some reference point on the object). Another vector is used to define the way the object is pointing, sometimes referred to as the object's *look* direction. So what's the third vector for? Figure 4-6 on the facing page shows three objects that are the same shape and that look in the same direction. What's different about each one?

The difference is that each object is rotated differently about the look axis. To define the orientation of an object completely, we need to specify the direction it's looking in and also the direction the object considers as *up*. Figure 4-7 shows the up vectors for the three shapes.

We can define an object's position and orientation completely by using these three vectors.

Faces

The dog you drew in Figure 4-3 on page 74 used many vertices to define one irregularly shaped face. A 3D object consists of many faces, and these faces are flat on the computer, of course. To create a smooth looking sphere, we're going to need quite a lot of flat faces. Faces can be any shape, from simple triangles to very complex polygons, so you can design your 3D object from triangles, squares, pentagons, or whatever shape you think will do the job.

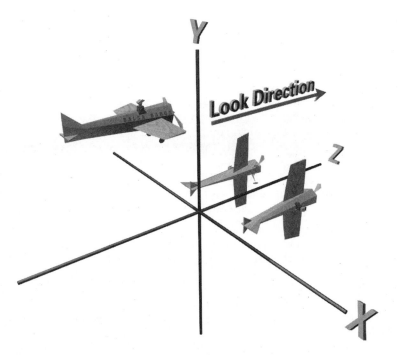

Figure 4-6. *Three objects looking in the same direction.*

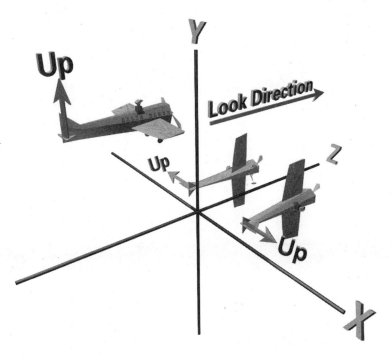

Figure 4-7. *Up vectors used to complete object orientation.*

A point to consider is that no matter how you define your faces, it's very common for the rendering engine to divide polygons into triangles for drawing. If you have some superwonderful video hardware in your computer and some equally wonderful 3D drivers for your hardware, your polygons might be rendered directly by the hardware as polygons instead of triangles. Why do you care? If you design your shapes using some very special polygons to reduce the number of faces so that your shapes draw faster, you might be better off using triangles in the first place, or some other shape that is easier to use, if your machine renders all polygons as triangles. You also might not get quite the effect you expected. If you simply define the vertices of a polygon and let the engine draw it, you might be surprised to see that your "flat" polygon has gained what looks like a lot of triangular lumps. We'll be looking at why this happens a little later, in the section "Creating Simple Shapes" on page 80. For now, we'll make our objects from triangles or squares and see what we get.

One final point you need to be aware of is that when you specify the set of vertices that define a face you must specify them in a clockwise order (see Figure 4-8). This is *very* important because the rendering engine only renders one side of a face. This process is known as *culling.* By culling the back surface of every face, the renderer avoids drawing faces that aren't visible, which obviously saves some time. Be careful when you specify the vertices for a face to make sure it's visible from the side you expect.

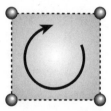

Figure 4-8. *Vector order for a face.*

Of course, you also need to specify them in the correct order around the face to create the shape you want. You can't just randomly supply six or seven vertices and expect to have them connect and become one face. After all, if you don't connect the dots in order you don't get a dog—you get a mess.

Normals

Normals are people who don't do geometry for fun. Just kidding—I love geometry, and I'm terminally normal. (I know this because someone once told me so. I don't make this stuff up.) So what are normals? Normals, as they apply to faces, are vectors that define the direction a face is pointing—the look direction of a face, if you like. Figure 4-9 shows a face and its normal.

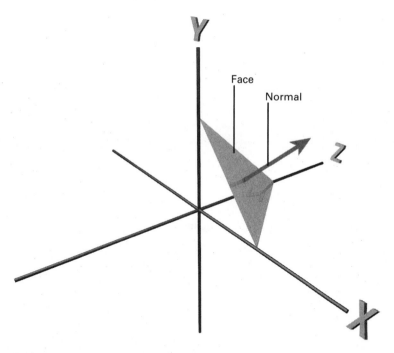

Figure 4-9. A face and its normal.

The face normal is a vector that is perpendicular to the face. And what is the purpose of face normals? Knowing which way a face of an object is oriented is useful when we start applying texture maps to an object. The face normals can be involved in computing how the texture needs to be oriented to get a desired effect. This isn't that important right now, so let's look at another set of normals.

In some rendering techniques the shading of a face is controlled by the direction its normal points and, obviously, where the light sources are in a scene. This kind of shading colors the face evenly and makes it look flat. Since most objects in real life (remember that?) aren't flat, drawing a bunch of flat faces doesn't give much of an illusion of reality. As any artist can show you, shading a flat piece of paper in just the right way can give the illusion of real, solid objects. So if we can find a way to intelligently shade the flat faces of our 3D shapes, we could perhaps end up with objects that appear more realistic. This is where the normals come in handy again.

The rendering engine we're using has several shading models, but the one I have set the sample applications to use is called Gouraud shading (named after Mr. Gouraud). This shading model uses normals at the vertices to control how a face is shaded.

Let's say we have a rectangular face and each vertex has a normal associated with it, as shown in Figure 4-10 on the next page.

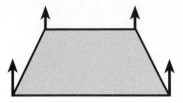

Figure 4-10. *A face showing its vertex normals.*

In Figure 4-10 the normals all point up. When shaded using the Gouraud model, this face will appear flat because all the vertex normals point the same way, so all the points on the face in between the vertices get the same lighting applied to them. I'm sure that's not very obvious or perhaps too clear, but imagine the vertex normals as defining how flat the face looks at the corners. All the vertices in Figure 4-10 point the same way, giving the face the same flatness all over. Consequently, the lighting doesn't vary over the surface.

Let's change the normals and see what effect this has. Figure 4-11 shows the same face with a different set of normals.

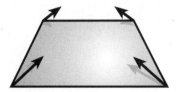

Figure 4-11. *A face with nonperpendicular normals.*

When lit, this face appears "dished" (concave) because the direction of the normals varies from vertex to vertex in a way that suggests the face is curled up at the corners.

If you don't follow any of this, don't worry; we're about to start looking at some code that demonstrates all of this, which I'm sure will make it a lot clearer.

Creating Simple Shapes

Having reviewed a bit of geometry, let's turn our attention to writing some code to create a few simple shapes. The sample application for this chapter can be found in the Shapes directory, and now might be a good time to start the Shapes sample so that you can try out the demonstrations for yourself as you read the text. At first glance the Shapes application looks just like the Stage application from Chapter 2, but if you click on the menu items you'll see a significant difference in menu options. We'll explore what these options do and how to implement them. All the code we're going to look at is in the MainFrm.cpp file in the sample.

We're going to begin with an extremely simple shape—a rectangle—which has four vertices that define one face. If you run the Shapes sample, you'll find the Edit menu has a number of items designating shapes you can insert. We're going to start with the code for the item that says "Flat Face." Here's the code in its entirety:

```
void CMainFrame::OnEditInsface()
{
    // Insert a simple flat face, and
    // define list of vertices
    D3DVECTOR vlist [] = {
        {-2, -2, -2},
        {-2, -2,  2},
        { 2, -2,  2},
        { 2, -2, -2}
    };

    // Get the number of vertices in array
    int nv = sizeof(vlist) / sizeof(D3DVECTOR);

    // Define the vertices used in each face as
    // count, vert1, vert2, and so on
    int flist [] = {4, 0, 1, 2, 3, // 4 Vertices, ...
                    0 // End of the face data list
    };

    // Put this shape into a new scene
    NewScene();

    // Create shape from list of vertices and
    // face data list
    m_pShape = new C3dShape;
    m_pShape->Create(vlist, nv, flist);

    // Add the shape to the scene
    m_pScene->AddChild(m_pShape);
}
```

The vertices of the face are defined using an array of vectors, *vlist*. The vectors define four vertices in a face that lies in the $y = -2$ plane. The rectangle is 4 units by 4 units. The first vector defines the vertex at the front left, the second vector defines the back left corner, the third defines the back right corner, and the fourth defines the front right corner—in other words, clockwise.

The shape is defined using an array of integers representing the face, *flist*. Each face definition in the list consists of a count of the number of vertices followed by the index value of each vertex in the *vlist* array. The face list is terminated by a zero value. A face list can define many faces, but in this sample it is being used to define only one. Note that the face vertex order is 0, 1, 2, 3, which corresponds to front left, back left, back right, and front right in clockwise order as you look down on the face from above. Because the face is at $y = -2$, it is below the camera (which is at 0, 0, −10) and therefore is visible.

The shape is created by calling the *Create* member function on a *C3dShape* object and passing the list of vertices, the number of vertices, and the face list data as arguments. Let's ignore what happens inside the *C3dShape* object for now, as it's pretty much a case of handing the vector and face data to the rendering engine, which actually builds the shape. The *C3dShape* object is then added to the scene to make it visible in the application's window. If you run the Shapes sample and choose Flat Face from the Edit menu, you should see something like Figure 4-12.

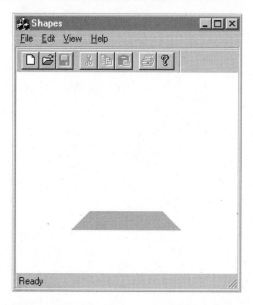

Figure 4-12. *The Shapes sample showing a single flat face.*

Notice that the face appears flat, indicating that the normals for each vertex must all be the same. You can verify this by choosing Normals from the View menu, which adds a pointer to each vertex to show the normal direction. Figure 4-13 shows the face and its normals.

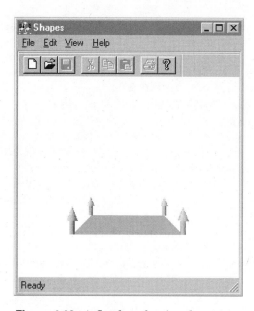

Figure 4-13. *A flat face showing the vertex normals.*

Now let's take the same face data and create a new face, but this time we'll specify a set of normals that look in toward the center of the face. Here's the code to generate the dished face, similar to the one shown in Figure 4-11 on page 80:

```
void CMainFrame::OnEditDishface()
{
    // A dished face
    D3DVECTOR vlist [] = {
        {-2, -2, -2},
        {-2, -2,  2},
        { 2, -2,  2},
        { 2, -2, -2}
    };
    int nv = sizeof(vlist) / sizeof(D3DVECTOR);

    D3DVECTOR nlist [] = {
        { 1,  1,  1},
        { 1,  1, -1},
        {-1,  1, -1},
        {-1,  1,  1}
    };
    int nn = sizeof(nlist) / sizeof(D3DVECTOR);

    int flist [] = {4, 0, 0, 1, 1, 2, 2, 3, 3,
                    0
    };

    NewScene();
    m_pShape = new C3dShape;
    m_pShape->Create(vlist, nv, nlist, nn, flist);
    m_pScene->AddChild(m_pShape);
}
```

As you can see, the vertex vector data is the same except that we've added another vector array, *nlist*. This second array contains several normals. Note that these normals are not unit vectors but instead are values that I found convenient. The rendering engine will normalize the vectors before it uses them.

The face list (*flist*) data has changed and now contains a count of the number of vertices followed by pairs of vertex and normal indices. The *C3dShape* object uses another version of the *Create* member function, which takes both the vertex and normal arrays as well as the face list data.

The result of running this code is shown in Figure 4-14 on the next page. You can view the results on screen by running the Shapes sample and choosing Dished Face from the Edit menu.

Notice how the shading makes the face appear dished in the middle? (This dish effect becomes more apparent if you rotate the shape.) The light source is in the top left corner of the scene in case you'd forgotten. The Shapes sample also includes an example of making the face bulge up by using normals that point out and away from the face. I'll leave it to you to look at that on your own by choosing Bulging Face from the Edit menu.

Figure 4-14. A face with nonperpendicular normals.

Creating Solid Objects

So much for single faces. Let's modify the code a bit and create a cube:

```
void CMainFrame::OnEditDefcube()
{
    D3DVECTOR vlist [] = {
        {-1, -1, -1},
        {-1, -1,  1},
        { 1, -1,  1},
        { 1, -1, -1},
        {-1,  1, -1},
        {-1,  1,  1},
        { 1,  1,  1},
        { 1,  1, -1}
    };
    int nv = sizeof(vlist) / sizeof(D3DVECTOR);

    int flist [] = {4, 0, 3, 2, 1,
                    4, 3, 7, 6, 2,
                    4, 4, 5, 6, 7,
                    4, 0, 1, 5, 4,
                    4, 0, 4, 7, 3,
                    4, 2, 6, 5, 1,
                    0
    };
```

```
    NewScene();
    m_pShape = new C3dShape;
    m_pShape->Create(vlist, nv, flist);
    m_pScene->AddChild(m_pShape);
}
```

The vertex list now has eight entries, one for each corner of the cube, and the face list now has entries to describe each of the six faces of the cube. Figure 4-15 shows you the index values of the cube's vertices, so you can follow the values in the face list in the code above. Remember that each face must be described in a clockwise direction from the side in which it is to be viewed.

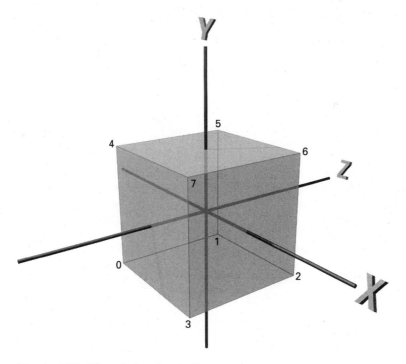

Figure 4-15. *The cube's vertex indices.*

Take the time here to convince yourself that the face descriptions make sense to you. If you take the time to learn this now, you will avoid creating lots of invisible faces that face the wrong way later. The *OnEditDefcube* function creates the shape shown in Figure 4-16 on the next page. You can view this on screen by choosing Default Cube from the Edit menu.

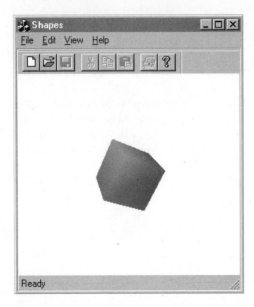

Figure 4-16. *A rotating cube created with default normals.*

Why do you think the shading of the faces looks like that? Choose Normals from the View menu, and you'll see the normals pointing out from the corners, away from the center of the cube. Because we didn't supply any normals, the rendering engine supplied its own set, which it created by averaging the normals of the faces adjacent to each vertex. This might seem like a weird thing to do, particularly for a cube. But it makes a lot of sense when we want to build a sphere or other smooth shape because vertex normals, which are the average of adjacent face normals, help generate a much smoother looking object by using shading to effectively "bend" the edges of adjacent faces to meet each other.

Of course this doesn't really cut it for a cube that we expect to see with flat faces and sharp edges, but we can fix that by supplying our own normals. For the vertices of each face, we supply a normal that is the same as the face normal. Here's the code used to create a cube with flat faces:

```
void CMainFrame::OnEditFlatfacecube()
{
    D3DVECTOR vlist [] = {
        {-1, -1, -1},
        {-1, -1,  1},
        { 1, -1,  1},
        { 1, -1, -1},
        {-1,  1, -1},
        {-1,  1,  1},
        { 1,  1,  1},
        { 1,  1, -1}
    };
    int nv = sizeof(vlist) / sizeof(D3DVECTOR);
```

```
D3DVECTOR nlist [] = {
    { 1,  0,  0},
    { 0,  1,  0},
    { 0,  0,  1},
    {-1,  0,  0},
    { 0, -1,  0},
    { 0,  0, -1}
};
int nn = sizeof(nlist) / sizeof(D3DVECTOR);

int flist [] = {4, 0, 4, 3, 4, 2, 4, 1, 4,
                4, 3, 0, 7, 0, 6, 0, 2, 0,
                4, 4, 1, 5, 1, 6, 1, 7, 1,
                4, 0, 3, 1, 3, 5, 3, 4, 3,
                4, 0, 5, 4, 5, 7, 5, 3, 5,
                4, 2, 2, 6, 2, 5, 2, 1, 2,
                0
};

NewScene();
m_pShape = new C3dShape;
m_pShape->Create(vlist, nv, nlist, nn, flist);
m_pScene->AddChild(m_pShape);
}
```

If you run the sample and display the flat-faced cube in Normal view (choose Edit-Flat Faced Cube then View-Normals), you'll get something like Figure 4-17.

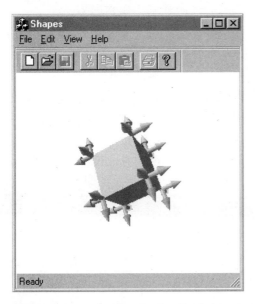

Figure 4-17. *A flat-faced cube showing its vector normals.*

Now you know how to create shapes with smoothed faces simply by letting the engine generate the normals, or you can create sharper edges by specifying values for the normals yourself. Sometimes you might want to create a smooth looking object that has some sharp edges, too. Figure 4-18 shows a cone with rounded sides and a flat bottom (Edit-Cone).

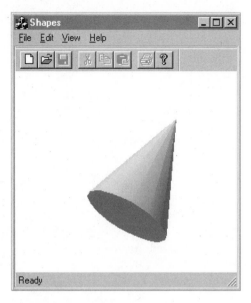

Figure 4-18. *A cone.*

If you look closely at the cone you can see that the sides are made from lots of triangles (16) and that the bottom is a single disk. The shading of the side triangles helps to make the cone look smooth, the shading of the bottom helps to make it look flat, and the transition between the sides and the bottom is a sharp edge. How did we get this effect?

The sides of the cone were generated the same way we created the first cube on page 84, by supplying the vertices of the triangles that form the sides of the cone and letting the rendering engine supply a set of normals created by averaging the face normals. This gives us the nice smooth effect we want for the sides. If we had simply added the bottom face to the face list we used to create the sides, the normals at the bottom of the cone would be generated by averaging the normal for the bottom face with normals from the side faces. This would create a bottom face shaded so that it appears to bulge out, and the edge transition between the sides and the bottom would be smoothed out.

There are two ways to generate a bottom face that looks flat and has a sharp edge transition from the sides. The simplest way is to add the bottom face to the face list using its own set of vertices. The vertices should have the same coordinate values as those that define the bottom edges of the sides to avoid creating any gaps in the final shape. By supplying separate vertices for the bottom face we ensure that the face has no adjacent faces, and, consequently, when the engine generates normals for the vertices of the face it will use the face normal for all of them. This approach gives the result we want—a flat face with a sharp edge transition—but it's a bit wasteful because we need to supply the extra set of vertices (16 in this case).

A better way to create the flat bottom face is to use the same vertices that define the bottom edges of the sides of the cone but also specify normals for the vertices. This is how the code works that generated the cone in Figure 4-18. The advantage of this method is that we don't need a redundant set of vertices. We do need to supply the data for the normals, but this method is economical because we have only one normal that we want to use for all the vertices of the face. We'll look at the code that does this in the next section when we see how solids of revolution such as the cone are generated.

Solids of Revolution

My father introduced me to solids of revolution at an early age. He was in England what we call a turner—a machinist who stands in front of a lathe all day creating pipe flanges, shafts, screw threads, tubes, and so on. (See Figure 4-19.) The lathe rotates a billet of metal which is held in a chuck. A cutting tool is then brought up to the billet to remove unwanted material as the billet rotates. The cutting tool controls the radius of the final shape. By moving the cutting tool in, the radius of the shape is reduced. The cutting tool can be moved along the bed of the lathe as the billet rotates to create a smooth shaft or a thread. Anyway, the point of this is that solid objects can be created by a simple function that determines the radius at any point along the object's length.

Figure 4-19. *A lathe.*

Creating a solid of revolution is no different than creating any other 3D object. We need to create a set of vertices, a description of which vertices belong to which faces, and, if we want to, we can create some normals. Because a solid of revolution can be described by giving its radius as a function of its length, it's a fairly simple matter to write some code that uses such a function to generate the vertex and face data for an object. Figure 4-20 shows a solid of revolution generated in this way. You can see this on screen by choosing Solid Of Revolution from the Edit menu.

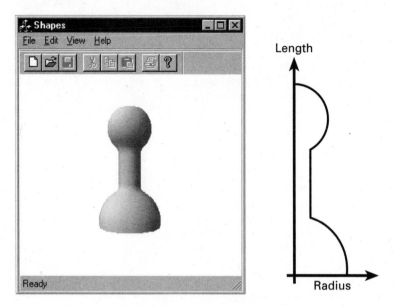

Figure 4-20. *A solid of revolution.*

Here's the code from the Shapes application that generated the object:

```
double RevolveFn(double z, void* pArg)
{
    if (z < -1.1) {
        return sqrt(1 - (z + 2)*(z + 2));
    } else if (z > 0.8) {
        return sqrt(2 - (z - 2)*(z - 2));
    } else {
        return 0.5;
    }
}

// Create a solid of revolution
void CMainFrame::OnEditSolidr()
{
    // Create a shape using a height function
    NewScene();
    m_pShape = new C3dShape;
    m_pShape->CreateRSolid(-3.0, 2.2, 0.2, TRUE, TRUE,
                           RevolveFn, NULL, 16);
    m_pScene->AddChild(m_pShape);

    // Turn it to see its side view
    m_pShape->SetDirection(0, -1, 0);
}
```

As you can see, we have two functions here. *RevolveFn* is used to provide radius values, and *OnEditSolidr* is called when you choose Solid Of Revolution from the Edit menu. *OnEditSolidr* uses the *RevolveFn* and *C3dShape::CreateRSolid* functions to build the object. The arguments to *CreateRSolid* are a bit out of the ordinary, so let me explain them.

When I wrote the *CreateRSolid* function, I wasn't thinking in very general terms. Instead of specifying the coordinates of the ends of the object, I decided to simplify things by always generating the shape along the *z*-axis. So the function you provide, in this case *RevolveFn*, returns the radius as a function of the object's position along the *z*-axis. The arguments to *CreateRSolid* are the start and end *z*-axis values, the *z* increment value, two Booleans that determine whether the ends of the shape should be closed or not, a pointer to the radius function, an optional argument to pass to the radius function, and, finally, the number of facets to use around the shape.

The optional radius function argument isn't used here, but you could use it, for example, to provide a table of data that the radius function generator would use. In this way, you could write a more general function that uses the table data to produce more complex shapes.

Once the object has been created, you will probably want to rotate it and move it to its final position. As you can see in the *OnEditSolidr* function in the preceding code, I rotated the object so that at its initial position it is pointing up along the *y*-axis instead of into the screen along the *z*-axis.

Let's look at how the *C3dShape::CreateRSolid* function works. Here's the code from the 3dPlus library:

```
// Create a solid of revolution
BOOL C3dShape::CreateRSolid(double z1, double z2, double dz,
                            BOOL bClosed1, BOOL bClosed2,
                            SOLIDRFN pfnRad, void* pArg,
                            int nFacets)
{
    New();
    ASSERT(pfnRad);
    ASSERT(dz != 0);
    int iZSteps = (int)((z2 - z1) / dz);
    if (iZSteps < 1) return FALSE;

    int iRSteps = nFacets;
    if (iRSteps < 8) iRSteps = 8;
    double da = _twopi / iRSteps;

    // Create the array for vertices
    int iVertices = (iZSteps + 1) * iRSteps;
    D3DVECTOR* Vertices = new D3DVECTOR [iVertices];
    D3DVECTOR* pv = Vertices;

    // Create the array for face data.
    // Each face has 4 vertices except the ends.
    int iFaces = iZSteps * iRSteps;
```

(continued)

```
int iFaceEntries = iFaces * 5 + 1;
if (bClosed1) iFaceEntries += iRSteps + 1;
if (bClosed2) iFaceEntries += iRSteps + 1;
int* FaceData = new int [iFaceEntries];
int* pfd = FaceData;

// Write out the vertex set
double z = z1;
double r, a;
for (int iZ = 0; iZ <= iZSteps; iZ++) {
    r = pfnRad(z, pArg);
    a = 0;
    for (int iR = 0; iR < iRSteps; iR++) {
        pv->x = D3DVAL(r * sin(a));
        pv->y = D3DVAL(r * cos(a));
        pv->z = D3DVAL(z);
        pv++;
        a += da;
    }
    z += dz;
}

// Write out the face list
int iFirst = iRSteps;
for (iZ = 0; iZ < iZSteps; iZ++) {
    for (int iR = 0; iR < iRSteps; iR++) {
        *pfd++ = 4; // No. of vertices per face
        *pfd++ = iFirst + iR;
        *pfd++ = iFirst + ((iR + 1) % iRSteps);
        *pfd++ = iFirst - iRSteps +
                    ((iR + 1) % iRSteps);
        *pfd++ = iFirst - iRSteps + iR;
    }
    iFirst += iRSteps;
}
*pfd = 0; // End the list

// Create round surface with autogeneration of the
// normals
BOOL b = Create(Vertices, iVertices, NULL, 0, FaceData,
                TRUE);

delete [] FaceData;

FaceData = new int [iRSteps * 2 + 2];
D3DVECTOR nvect [] = {
    {0, 0, 1},
    {0, 0, -1}
};
```

```
if (bClosed1) {
    pfd = FaceData;
    *pfd++ = iRSteps;
    for (int iR = 0; iR < iRSteps; iR++) {
        *pfd++ = iR;
        *pfd++ = 1;
    }
    *pfd = 0;
    m_hr = m_pIMeshBld->AddFaces(iVertices, Vertices,
                                 2, nvect,
                                 (ULONG*)FaceData,
                                 NULL);
    ASSERT(SUCCEEDED(m_hr));
}
if (bClosed2) {
    pfd = FaceData;
    *pfd++ = iRSteps;
    iFirst = iRSteps * iZSteps;
    for (int iR = 0; iR < iRSteps; iR++) {
        *pfd++ = iRSteps - 1 - iR + iFirst;
        *pfd++ = 0;
    }
    *pfd = 0;
    m_hr = m_pIMeshBld->AddFaces(iVertices, Vertices,
                                 2, nvect,
                                 (ULONG*)FaceData,
                                 NULL);
    ASSERT(SUCCEEDED(m_hr));
}

delete [] Vertices;
delete [] FaceData;
m_strName = "Solid of revolution";

return b;
}
```

The first step shown in the code above, after some initialization, uses the radius function to create a list of vertices. Then the face data for the sides is generated, and the initial shape is created. If closed ends have been selected, a new set of face data is created—but this time using normals to control the shading so that the end faces will appear flat. The new faces are then added to the existing shape.

You might also note that the shape is given a name. (The name, in this case, is *Solid of revolution,* and it is stored in *m_strName.*) When we look at selecting objects in a scene, we'll be using that name to show the user what got selected.

We just breezed through quite a big chunk of code, and I'm sure you have a lot of questions about how it works and what some of the functions do. If you want to understand how it works, draw a grid of squares on a piece of paper, roll up the paper into a tube, and then imagine trying to describe every corner and every face in the grid. That's all this piece of code does, and what I just described is how I figured out how to write it. There are also several calls to Direct3D interface functions in here that you can look up in the DirectX 2 SDK documentation. While you're in the SDK, you can look up the *D3DVAL* macro and see what that does, too.

In Chapter 5 we'll look at how to transform a shape using rotation, translation, and scaling. When you've read that chapter you might want to take the code for the *CreateRSolid* function and modify it so that you can provide the coordinates of the end points as arguments to the function, which makes the function a little more useful.

Creating Landscapes

There are times you might want to create varying surfaces for a scene that give an impression of rugged terrain, rolling hills, or whatever your fancy. The Shapes sample includes demonstrations of two techniques for generating randomly varying landscapes. The first technique uses a grid of points and randomly sets the height of each point. The second technique starts with a single face and subdivides it by generating a random height point in the middle of the face. The subdivision is repeated until there are enough new faces to make it look interesting.

Generating a Landscape with a Grid

Let's look at the grid technique first. Figure 4-21 shows an example of a landscape generated using a grid of random height points (Edit-Landscape 1).

Figure 4-21. *A random landscape generated using a grid.*

The code for generating the shape that makes up the landscape is similar to the code used to generate solids of revolution shown on page 91. In this case, you provide a function that generates the height from the X and Z values. Here's the code from the sample:

```
double LandscapeFn(double x, double z, void* pArg)
{
    return -2.0 + (double)(rand() % 100) / 100;
}

// Create a shape to represent landscape
void CMainFrame::OnEditInsland()
{
    // Create a shape using a height function
    NewScene();
    m_pShape = new C3dShape;
    m_pShape->CreateSurface(-5, 5, 1, -10, 10, 1,
                            LandscapeFn, NULL);
    m_pScene->AddChild(m_pShape);
}
```

The height is generated randomly, and the shape is created using *C3dShape-::CreateSurface*. This function is similar to *C3dShape::CreateRSolid*, so I won't bore you with the details.

NOTE

The Landscape you see on your screen may not look exactly like what you see in Figure 4-21. In certain cases there will be a strange spike angling through the scene. This is caused by a bug in this release of the DirectX software. For more information and a possible workaround, see the ReadMe.txt file on the companion CD. In the meantime, try resizing the window to make the spike disappear.

Generating a Landscape by Subdividing Faces

Let's go from the ridiculously simple to something a lot more complicated and look at how to generate a surface by subdividing faces. Figure 4-22 on the next page shows a landscape generated using face subdivision (Edit-Landscape 2).

The faces in Figure 4-22 are all flat and sharp edged because the code that generates them creates a separate set of vertices for each new face. As we saw earlier in the section titled "Creating Simple Shapes" on page 80, the default behavior for a face with no adjacent faces is to create a set of vertex normals that are the same as the face normal, which produces a flat face. You could modify this behavior by generating normals as well as vertices, or you could write some slightly more sophisticated code to create the faces with shared vertices. Let's look at the technique used to create the surface in Figure 4-22 and then the code that was used.

Figure 4-22. *A landscape generated using face subdivision.*

For each face on the surface, a point is chosen within the face. I chose to determine the point by using coordinates that are the average of the coordinates of all the face's vertices. Having picked what will be the new vertex, we then generate a random height for the new vertex and create a new set of faces. Figure 4-23 shows an initial rectangular face that was subdivided using this process.

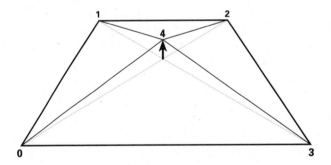

Figure 4-23. *A face subdivided into four faces.*

Once the four new faces have been created, the process is repeated to divide up the four new triangular faces into more triangles, as shown in Figure 4-24.

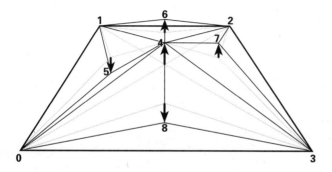

Figure 4-24. *The faces after the second round of divisions.*

It's a little hard to see the faces in the illustration, but I'm sure you get the idea. This technique can generate quite realistic looking mountains if you work at it a bit. Now let's see what the code looks like that generated the landscape in Figure 4-22:

```
void CMainFrame::OnEditInsland2()
{
    // Create the initial shape, which is a simple
    // rectangular face.
    // Insert a simple flat face.
    double x = 10;
    double z1 = -10;
    double z2 = 20;
    D3DVECTOR vlist [] = {
        {-x, -4, z1},
        {-x, -4, z2},
        { x, -4, z2},
        { x, -4, z1}
    };
    int nv = sizeof(vlist) / sizeof(D3DVECTOR);

    int flist [] = {4, 0, 1, 2, 3,
                        0
    };

    NewScene();
    m_pShape = new C3dShape;
    m_pShape->Create(vlist, nv, flist);

    // Progressively subdivide faces
    int iCycles = 5;
    double dHeight = 1.0;
    while (iCycles--) {
```

(continued)

```
// Get current list of faces
int nFaces = m_pShape->GetFaceCount();
IDirect3DRMMeshBuilder* pMB =
                        m_pShape->GetMeshBuilder();
ASSERT(pMB);
IDirect3DRMFaceArray* pIFA = NULL;
HRESULT hr;
hr = pMB->GetFaces(&pIFA);
ASSERT(SUCCEEDED(hr));

// Create new shape to add new faces to
C3dShape* pNewShape = new C3dShape;

// Walk through the face list
for (int iFace = 0; iFace < nFaces; iFace++) {

    IDirect3DRMFace* pIFace = NULL;
    hr = pIFA->GetElement(iFace, &pIFace);
    ASSERT(SUCCEEDED(hr));
    ASSERT(pIFace);

    // Get vertex count
    DWORD nVert = pIFace->GetVertexCount();

    // Allocate buffers
    D3DVECTOR* pVert = new D3DVECTOR [nVert];

    // Get the vertex data
    hr = pIFace->GetVertices(&nVert,
                            pVert,
                            NULL);
    ASSERT(SUCCEEDED(hr));
    ASSERT(pVert);
    ASSERT(nVert > 2);

    // Allocate space for new vertex and face data
    // lists
    D3DVECTOR* NewVert = new D3DVECTOR [nVert + 1];
    int* NewFaceData = new int [4 * nVert + 1];

    // Copy old vertices and generate coordinate
    // sums
    C3dVector vNew(0, 0, 0);
    for (DWORD i = 0; i < nVert; i++) {
        NewVert[i] = pVert[i];
        vNew.x += pVert[i].x;
        vNew.y += pVert[i].y;
        vNew.z += pVert[i].z;
    }

    // Compute new vertex in plane of face
    vNew.x /= nVert;
```

```
            vNew.y /= nVert;
            vNew.z /= nVert;

            // Add a random height factor
            double dh = dHeight * (1.0 - ((double)(rand() %
                        100)) / 50.0);
            vNew.y += dh;

            // Add new vertex
            NewVert[nVert] = vNew;

            // Create face data
            int *pfd = NewFaceData;
            for (i = 0; i < nVert; i++) {
                *pfd++ = 3;
                *pfd++ = i;
                *pfd++ = (i+1) % nVert;
                *pfd++ = nVert; // The new vertex
            }
            *pfd = 0;

            // Add new faces to shape
            pNewShape->AddFaces(NewVert, nVert+1, NULL, 0,
                                NewFaceData);

            // Free the vector and face storage
            delete [] NewVert;
            delete [] NewFaceData;

            // Free the vertex data storage
            delete [] pVert;

            // Release the face
            pIFace->Release();
        }

        // Release the face array
        pIFA->Release();

        pMB->GenerateNormals();

        // Note: Don't release the mesh builder interface.

        // Delete old shape and make new one current.
        delete m_pShape;
        m_pShape = pNewShape;
    }

    // Add final shape to scene
    m_pScene->AddChild(m_pShape);
}
```

As I mentioned earlier, this approach is a bit more long-winded than simply generating a grid of height values. I'm not going to explain all the code here but leave it to you to read through it for yourself. It uses some functions from the *C3dShape* class and some direct calls to interfaces in the rendering engine for the few cases where I haven't exposed that functionality through a *C3dShape* class member function.

Building a Whole Forest

Let's say that we'd like to create a pretty forest scene: The birds are singing happily in the trees, the brook burbles merrily down the mountain, and the spotted owl hoots as it dodges another bullet. Nice idea—but for now let's settle for a few things that look vaguely like fir trees. Figure 4-25 shows the kind of fir tree I have in mind (Edit-A Tree).

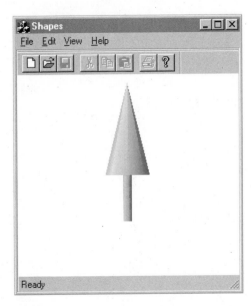

Figure 4-25. *A fir tree.*

OK, so it's not quite all that it might be, but it will do for now. This tree consists of about 25 vertices and 19 faces. If we want to create an entire forest of, say, 100 trees (most of the rest were chopped down to make the book you're reading), we could add 99 more trees just like the one in Figure 4-25. Or we could find some way to tell the rendering engine to draw the 99 other trees exactly like the first one but at different positions in the scene.

Do you remember when we talked about frames and visuals in Chapter 3? A *C3dShape* object contains a frame that determines its position, size, orientation, and so on, and it also contains a visual that is essentially the set of vertices, faces, and so on for the object we want to see. We can actually add the same visual to many different frames by using the *C3dShape::Clone* method. This method creates a new *C3dShape* object from an existing one, but instead of creating a new visual for the new shape, it attaches the visual from the original shape. So to create a forest, we can create one tree and clone it 99 times. Figure 4-26 shows the result (Edit-A Forest).

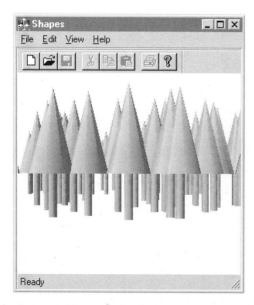

Figure 4-26. *An entire forest.*

Let's look at the code that built the forest, because a few details of how the clone trees were created aren't particularly obvious.

```
void CMainFrame::OnEditForest()
{
    NewScene();

    // Create the first tree and its trunk
    m_pShape = new C3dShape;
    m_pShape->CreateCone(0, 0, 0, 1, TRUE, 0, 4, 0, 0,
                         FALSE);
    C3dShape trunk;
    trunk.CreateRod(0, -2, 0, 0, 0, 0, 0.2);
    m_pShape->AddChild(&trunk);

    // Add tree to scene
    m_pScene->AddChild(m_pShape);

    // Get position and orientation of tree trunk
    // relative to its parent, the tree
    C3dVector p, d, u;
    trunk.GetPosition(p);
    trunk.GetDirection(d, u);

    // Clone tree 99 times
    for (int i = 0; i < 99; i++) {
```

(continued)

```
// Clone tree and trunk
C3dShape* pTree = m_pShape->Clone();
C3dShape* pTrunk = trunk.Clone();
pTree->AddChild(pTrunk);

// Set relative position of the trunk
// to the tree
pTrunk->SetPosition(p);
pTrunk->SetDirection(d, u);

// Add clones as children of first tree
// so we can rotate entire forest
m_pShape->AddChild(pTree);

// Place new tree in scene
pTree->SetPosition((((double)(rand() % 100) / 5)
                   - 10.0,
                   0,
                   (double)(rand() % 100) / 5,
                   m_pScene);

// Delete containers
delete pTrunk;
delete pTree;
    }
}
```

One important point to note is that the trunk is attached as a child of the cone that forms the body of the tree. So when you clone the tree and its trunk, it's important that the cloned trunk is added to the cloned tree using the same relative positioning. If you don't do this, the trunk will point in some interesting direction and most likely won't be connected to the tree. Try commenting out the trunk positioning (*pTrunk->SetPosition*) and directioning (*pTrunk->SetDirection*) code and rebuilding the sample to see what effect it has.

The other point to note is that the clone trees were added as children of the first tree just so that I could rotate the entire forest using the *m_pShape* variable (the first tree). Because the clones are added as children of the first tree, you need to set the position of the clones relative to the scene. If you leave out the optional relative frame argument (*m_pScene*) from the *PTree->SetPosition* call, the positions will be set relative to the parent, which puts them in the wrong place. Try it and see what happens.

So Much for Shapes

Well, that does it for shapes. We've seen how to create simple faces and more complex solid shapes. We looked at how the vertex normals affect the shading of a shape and how to efficiently replicate a shape by reusing its visual component. In the next chapter we're going to look at how to move shapes around and change their size and orientation using transforms.

CHAPTER 5

Transforms

n this chapter you'll learn how to move an object in a scene by applying various transforms (also called "transformations") to it. We'll also look at how to change an object's position, the direction it's facing, and even its size by using appropriate transforms. As you'll see, these transforms can be combined to create a single transform that moves, orients, and sizes an object all at once. Neat, eh? The nasty part is that all of this magic is done using matrices. But fear not: As usual we will take this serious mathematical stuff and render it harmless by hiding it inside some C++ classes. If you want to know more about the math involved in 3D transforms, I suggest you dig out a copy of Foley et al., *Computer Graphics Principles and Practice* (see page 314 for a complete reference), and read Chapter 5, "Geometrical Transformations."

The sample for this chapter can be found in the TransFrm directory. You might want to run it while you read the chapter to try out the demonstrations for yourself.

Using Matrices for Transformations

Most of the transformations we'll use can be represented using a 3-by-3 matrix of floating-point values. If we use a 3-by-3 matrix, though, the math gets a bit complicated because we need to treat some transformations differently from others. For example, you would perform a translation by adding the matrix values and perform a rotation by multiplying the matrix values. However, if we insert our 3-by-3 matrix values into a 4-by-4 matrix and fill in the spare values appropriately, all transformations can be achieved by multiplying by the matrix values. For this reason, we'll use a 4-by-4 matrix to represent our transformations. If you're not familiar with using a *homogenous coordinate system* to represent transformations in 3D coordinate space (and who is?), I'm sure you're already feeling lost. Let's fix that problem right away by looking quickly at an example of how to use a matrix to transform a point in space. Because the math for the 3D case is a bit long, we'll look at a 2D example instead, and you can trust me that it works just as well for 3D.

A 2D coordinate x, y in a homogenous coordinate system is represented by a vector like this:

$$\begin{bmatrix} x \\ y \\ 1 \end{bmatrix}$$

A matrix that can translate 2D points looks like this:

$$\begin{bmatrix} 1 & 0 & dx \\ 0 & 1 & dy \\ 0 & 0 & 1 \end{bmatrix}$$

where dx is the amount of displacement in the x-axis and dy is the displacement in the y-axis. Now let's multiply the original vector by the matrix and see what we get. Remember: To multiply a matrix by a column vector, the rows in the result-ant vector are computed by multiplying the elements from the same row of the matrix by the values in the source vector, like this:

$$\begin{bmatrix} 1 & 0 & dx \\ 0 & 1 & dy \\ 0 & 0 & 1 \end{bmatrix} \times \begin{bmatrix} x \\ y \\ 1 \end{bmatrix} = \begin{bmatrix} 1*x + 0*y + 1*dx \\ 0*x + 1*y + 1*dy \\ 0*x + 0*y + 1*1 \end{bmatrix} = \begin{bmatrix} x + dx \\ y + dy \\ 1 \end{bmatrix}$$

As you can see, by multiplying the vector for the point by the translation matrix, we end up with a vector displaced by just the right amount. Amazing. When I first learned how to use a homogenous coordinate system to reduce all transformations to multiplications, I thought it was totally awesome. Even if you're not so impressed, at least you can see how it works.

Having seen how a matrix can represent a transformation, let's look at a prac-tical example of using a *C3dMatrix* object that contains a 4-by-4 array of floating-point values to apply a translation to a vector. As an introduction to the *C3dMatrix* class, here's the code for its constructor:

```
C3dMatrix::C3dMatrix()
{
    m_00=1.0; m_01=0.0;  m_02=0.0; m_03=0.0;
    m_10=0.0; m_11=1.0;  m_12=0.0; m_13=0.0;
    m_20=0.0; m_21=0.0;  m_22=1.0; m_23=0.0;
    m_30=0.0; m_31=0.0;  m_32=0.0; m_33=1.0;
}
```

The constructor sets the initial state of the matrix to be an *identity matrix*. If a vector were multiplied by this matrix, the result would be the same as the origi-nal vector. Using a *C3dMatrix* object, the code below translates the vector x, y, z by an amount dx, dy, dz.

```
C3dVector v (x, y, z);
C3dMatrix m;
m.Translate(dx, dy, dz);
v = m * v;
```

A *C3dVector* object is initialized with the original vector values. A *C3dMatrix* object is constructed (as an identity matrix), and then its *Translate* member is used to add a translation transform to the matrix. Finally, the vector is multiplied by the matrix, and the result is assigned back to the vector.

The *C3dMatrix::Translate* function doesn't simply initialize the matrix, it actually combines a translation transform with any existing transform the matrix might hold, as you can see on the next page.

```
void C3dMatrix::Translate(double dx, double dy, double dz)
{
    C3dMatrix tx( 1, 0,  0, 0,
                  0, 1,  0, 0,
                  0, 0,  1, 0,
                 dx, dy, dz,1);

    *this *= tx;
}
```

A temporary matrix is initialized with the translation values. The current matrix is then multiplied by the temporary translation matrix and assigned back to itself.

By using the various member functions of the *C3dMatrix* class, you can combine many different transformations into a single matrix that can then be used to map as many vectors as you want. You can also create separate *C3dMatrix* objects, each with a single transformation, and then simply multiply all the matrices together to get the final transformation:

```
mFinal = m1 * m2 * m3;
```

Transforming 3D Objects

Now let's look at some practical applications of using matrix transformations on 3D objects. To apply a transformation matrix to a *C3dShape* object, we won't perform any vector multiplications ourselves. Instead we'll attach our transformation to the existing transformation that is contained in the object's frame. If you recall, the frame that determines an object's position and orientation in a scene is really just a transformation that is applied to all of the points in the shape. Remember, too, that an object's frame is a child of another frame above it in the hierarchy and that all the transformations in the frame hierarchy need to be combined to compute the object's final position. What we are going to do is modify the transformation contained in the object's own frame, which is somewhere at the bottom of the frame hierarchy. Figure 5-1 shows an example of a frame hierarchy.

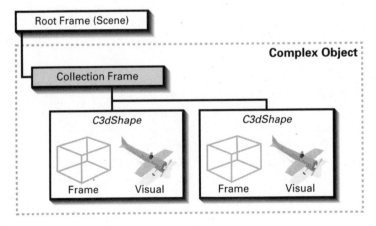

Figure 5-1. An object's frame hierarchy.

In Figure 5-1, the complex object consists of two component shapes, each of which has its own frame and visual. The collection frame, which is the common parent frame of the component parts, is the frame we need to modify to transform the whole object.

There are three ways to modify the transform for a frame. We can add the new transform before the existing transform, after the existing transform, or we can replace the existing transform with the new one. How do we know which technique we should use? I hope that will be clear to you when we are finished with the examples.

All of the transforms we are going to look at are implemented in the TransFrm sample, which uses an airplane as the object to transform. The airplane is very convenient because you can easily see both its position in the scene and its orientation. Figure 5-2 shows the initial condition of the sample with the plane sitting at the origin.

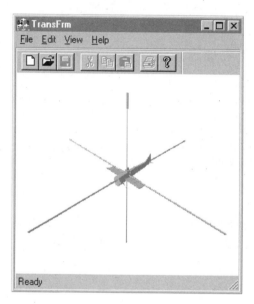

Figure 5-2. The initial condition before any transforms have been applied.

Translating

The first type of transform we'll explore is a *translation*. A translation is a simple linear movement in one direction. To translate an object, we add some delta value to each of its *x*-, *y*-, and *z*-coordinates. Figure 5-3 on the next page shows the result of a translation along the *x*-axis.

The code that implemented the translation looks like this:

```
void CMainFrame::OnEditTranslatex()
{
    if (!m_pCurShape) return;
    C3dMatrix m;
    m.Translate(2, 0, 0);
    m_pCurShape->AddTransform(m, D3DRMCOMBINE_AFTER);
}
```

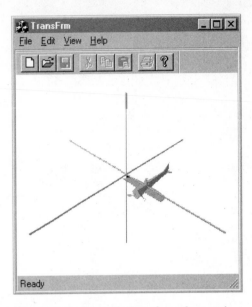

Figure 5-3. A translation along the x-axis.

A *C3dMatrix* is created with the translation we require—in this case, 2 units along the x-axis. The transform is then added to the current shape. Note that we specified D3DRMCOMBINE_AFTER to add this transformation after any existing transform. In other words, after all other transformations are complete, an additional translation along the x-axis is required.

Rotation

Now let's apply a rotation to the airplane. Starting from the origin, we'll rotate the airplane 45 degrees about the y-axis. The result is shown in Figure 5-4.

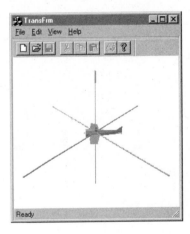

Figure 5-4. A rotation about the y-axis.

Here's how the rotation was implemented:

```
void CMainFrame::OnEditRotatey()
{
    if (!m_pCurShape) return;
    C3dMatrix m;
    m.Rotate(0, 45, 0);
    m_pCurShape->AddTransform(m, D3DRMCOMBINE_AFTER);
}
```

I'm sure you're getting the hang of transformation by now, but bear with me.

Scaling

Another type of transformation we can apply is to scale the object, making it bigger or smaller. What's most interesting, however, is that we can scale it differently in each axis. Figure 5-5 shows the result of increasing the size in the *x*- and *y*-axes only.

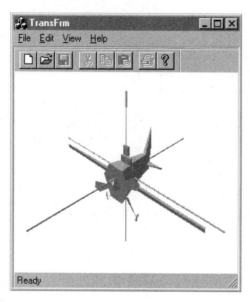

Figure 5-5. *A scale increase in* x-*axis and* y-*axis only.*

We end up with a rather stubby looking airplane! Adding similar scaling to the *z*-axis results in the object shown in Figure 5-6 on the next page.

The code for scaling is similar to the other transformations we've applied so far. Here's an example of adding a scale factor to just the *x*-axis:

```
void CMainFrame::OnEditscalex()
{
    if (!m_pCurShape) return;
    C3dMatrix m;
    m.Scale(2.0, 1.0, 1.0);
    m_pCurShape->AddTransform(m, D3DRMCOMBINE_AFTER);
}
```

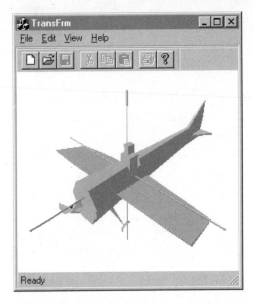

Figure 5-6. The object after equal scaling in the x-, y-, *and* z-*axes.*

Note that the *y* and *z* values are set to unity, not zero. If you set them to zero, you're going to find it hard to see the object!

Applying Multiple Transforms

We've looked at single transforms for translation, rotation, and scaling. Now we'll look at what happens when we apply a sequence of transforms. Let's start by applying a translation along the *x*-axis followed by a rotation about the *y*-axis. Figure 5-7 on the facing page shows the result.

Is that what you expected? Here's the code:

```
void CMainFrame::OnEditTranrot()
{
    if (!m_pCurShape) return;
    C3dMatrix m;
    m.Translate(3, 0, 0);
    m.Rotate(0, 45, 0);
    m_pCurShape->AddTransform(m, D3DRMCOMBINE_AFTER);
}
```

As you can see, we translated 3 units in the *x*-axis and then rotated the object 45 degrees about the *y*-axis. So the rotation was applied with the airplane out at a radius of 3 units from the origin. Therefore, the plane has traveled 45 degrees around a circle of 3 units' radius.

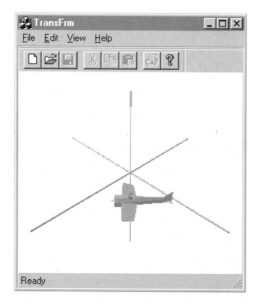

Figure 5-7. *A translation along the x-axis followed by a rotation about the y-axis.*

Let's apply the same two transforms again, but this time in the opposite order. Figure 5-8 shows the result.

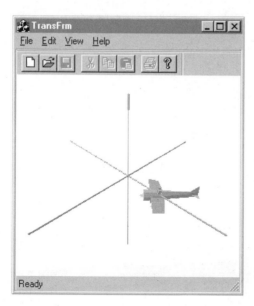

Figure 5-8. *A rotation about the y-axis followed by a translation along the x-axis.*

As you can see, this is very different from what happened last time. The effect this time is as if the plane were translated and then rotated about its own *y*-axis instead of about the *y*-axis of the scene.

We have made an important discovery: The order in which we apply transformations is critical. We have also learned that to rotate about the scene's axes, we must apply the rotation *after* we apply any translation; and to rotate about the object's axes, we must apply the rotation *before* we apply the translation. This knowledge is vital if you want to be able to control the motion of objects. In Chapter 6 we'll be using these techniques to fly objects through a scene, just like real aircraft.

The sample includes menu items to rotate the object about the scene's axes, which we saw implemented in the code on page 110. The sample also includes code to rotate the object about its own axes. Here's an example of rotation about the object's *y*-axis.

```
void CMainFrame::OnEditRobjy()
{
    if (!m_pCurShape) return;
    C3dMatrix m;
    m.Rotate(0, 45, 0);
    m_pCurShape->AddTransform(m, D3DRMCOMBINE_BEFORE);
}
```

At first glance, this code looks the same as the code we saw on page 109, but close inspection shows that the transform here is applied *before* the existing transform, not after, as we did earlier.

Getting Back to Base

So we've been out flying for a while and now we'd like to get home. The sample includes a Reset menu option on the Edit menu that returns the object to the origin, orienting and sizing the object the same as it was originally. Here's the code:

```
void CMainFrame::OnEditReset()
{
    if (!m_pCurShape) return;
    C3dMatrix m;
    m_pCurShape->AddTransform(m, D3DRMCOMBINE_REPLACE);
}
```

This looks more like a mistake than anything else because there seems to be no transform set in the matrix at all. But actually that's what we want. Notice that the D3DRMCOMBINE_REPLACE option is used to replace any existing transform with the new matrix. The matrix constructor established an identity transform, and by replacing whatever has been set in the frame with this identity value, we return to the original state. Replacing the existing transform rather than adding to it is just another way of determining the result.

Playtime

The sample includes a modeless dialog box you can access by selecting Transform Shape from the Edit menu. You can use it to apply translations, rotations, and scales, as you see fit. In each case, you can choose to apply the transform before or after the existing transform, or you can replace the existing transform with the new one. A few minutes spent playing with the Transforms dialog box, shown in Figure 5-9, should fill in any holes in your understanding of how these transformations work in combination.

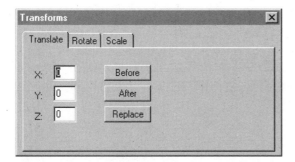

Figure 5-9. *The Transforms modeless dialog box.*

The Silly Department

We haven't actually covered all the possible transformations you can apply to a shape. The ones we've looked at are the common useful ones. I'd like to finish up this chapter with something a little on the random side and show you one last transform—the shear. A *shear* is a transform that slides an object sideways. For example, place a neatly stacked deck of playing cards on a table. Now push the stack sideways so that the edges of the stack are still straight but no longer perpendicular to the table, as shown in Figure 5-10.

Figure 5-10. *A "sheared" deck of cards.*

You just sheared the stack of cards. Figure 5-11 shows the result of applying a shear to the airplane.

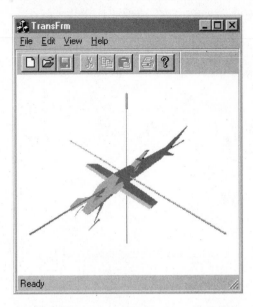

Figure 5-11. *The result of a shear transformation.*

To make it easier to see the transformation, I made the airplane a bit bigger by applying equal scaling to the three axes before applying the shear. I can't see many uses for shear transformations in 3D applications but I bet you can, so here's the code I used to create the shear shown in Figure 5-11:

```
void CMainFrame::OnEditShear()
{
    if (!m_pCurShape) return;
    C3dMatrix m;
    m.m_12 = 2;
    m_pCurShape->AddTransform(m, D3DRMCOMBINE_BEFORE);
}
```

As you can see, the *C3dMatrix* class doesn't have a *Shear* member function, so I've simply set up the matrix manually by entering a value into one of the matrix cells. In this case I applied the shear in the *z*-axis. You can shear in the other axes as well, of course. I'll leave it up to you to research what values you need for those shears. (Perhaps when you've done that you can add the missing *Shear* function to the *C3dMatrix* class.)

Summary

Objects can be moved, oriented, sized, and sheared using simple matrices. By combining transformations together, complex transformations can be created and held in a single matrix. In the next chapter we'll apply some of these transforms in ways that make objects move about in a scene.

3D GRAPHICS PROGRAMMING FOR WINDOWS 95

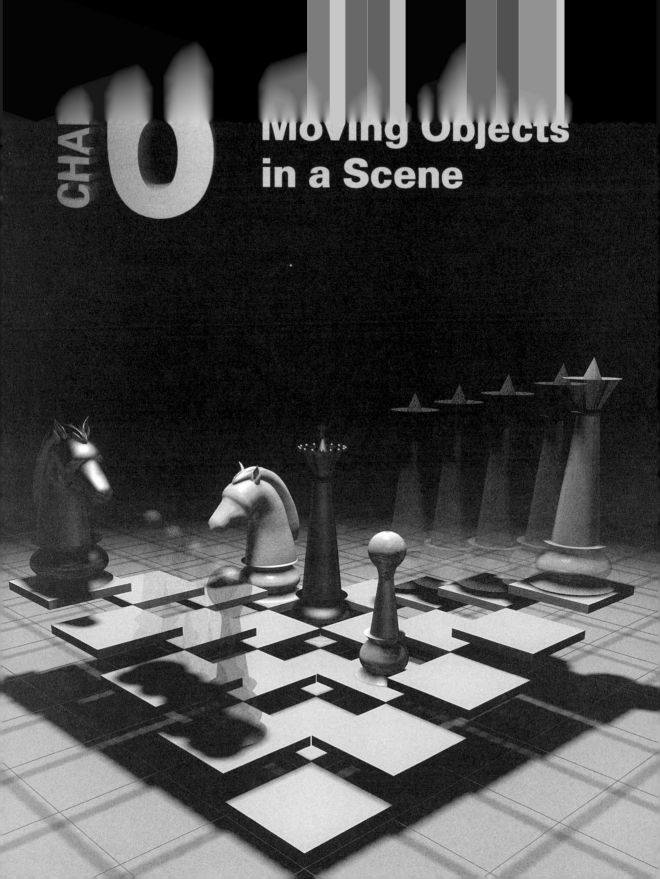

CHAPTER 10

Moving Objects in a Scene

Welcome to Chapter 6! In this chapter we're going to look at ways to let a user move objects around or fly them through a scene. We'll also discuss how to have objects move by themselves in various ways and learn how to set the camera flying off on a perilous aerial mission. The main sample for this chapter can be found in the Moving directory. I'll introduce the other samples as we need them.

Input Devices

It's my experience that when I write an application for Microsoft Windows, I often spend more time working on the user interface than I do on the core components. In fact, I'd say that for any reasonably usable product maybe 75 percent of the work goes into the user interface. To be fair, I don't put that amount of effort into my own applications (as those of you who have struggled to use them will know).

I think I've done my best user interface work creating applications for my children. These applications accomplish their tasks in the simplest way possible. For example, I wrote a paint application with almost no user interface for my son Mark when he was 18 months old. There is no menu, no buttons, no keyboard interface, and you don't even need to use the mouse buttons. Despite this, you can paint quite a nice picture with the tools available.

Mark had his third birthday last week (as I write), and he's developed quite an interest in rockets, so some of my tinkering time has been devoted to making rockets on the computer. When I started to work on the samples for this book, I had all sorts of ideas for games that Mark would like. But it was soon obvious that the keyboard and the mouse were not going to provide the sort of usability in a 3D application I'd like for a three-year-old. To be honest, my first attempts at any sort of interface designed to move 3D objects weren't even suitable for me. The problem was that I was trying to create an interface using just the mouse and a few keyboard keys. Now I'm sure that many of you, like myself, have played with 3D applications that have quite usable keyboard and mouse interfaces. But there's no way my son could deal with holding down both the left mouse button and the Shift key while dragging an object and tapping his right foot at the same time.

Enter the joystick. Many moons ago when computers were still powered by steam and the 80286 was a mean processor, I had the dubious privilege of writing the original joystick driver for the Multimedia Extensions to Microsoft Windows.

That was a long time ago, however, and I had pretty much forgotten about joysticks until a few weeks ago when I found a huge pile of them in the Microsoft company store. That's when I thought I'd use a joystick to control my 3D applications and bought myself a Microsoft SideWinder 3D Pro. I quickly found that the joystick was a much better input device than a mouse for my 3D applications. The SideWinder has four axes that generate data: X, Y, rotation, and velocity. By using some of the buttons on the side of the joystick, I could control all three rotational axes of an object as well as its position.

A little later, I was given a SpaceBall Avenger, which is a very cool device by Spacetec IMC Corp. It has 6 degrees of freedom, which means that you get outputs for the x-, y-, and z-axes and also for r, u, and v rotational movements. The device itself uses pressure sensors to detect how you're trying to push and twist it, which makes for very sensitive control.

So now I had two joysticks that work differently from each other, and my code was dedicated to only one of them. What I wanted was a nice, general input model that I could attach any input device to and configure the model just how I wanted. It didn't sound like a lot of work to me—until I got started. What I ended up with isn't exactly wonderful, but it's quite configurable, and if you have 10 or 15 minutes to spare, you can set up your joystick in all sorts of fascinating ways. Having done all this work, I thought the least I could do was pass it on to you as an example of how you *might* build a general input model. I don't suggest shipping this to any of your customers unless you like being unpopular.

When you do take the time to set up the joystick device, the results are great: My son loves to whiz the objects around the screen by making great stirring motions with the joystick or by shoving the SpaceBall wildly in all directions.

To get the most from the sample applications for this chapter and those that follow, I recommend acquiring a joystick—it's so much more fun than a mouse.

The Input Device Model

Figure 6-1 on the next page shows the input model from the application's point of view. When the application needs to perform an update cycle, it calls the input controller's *Update* function. The input controller asks the input device for an update on the hardware status. When the input controller receives the new hardware state from the input device, it modifies the position and orientation of the frame to which it's attached in the application and then notifies the application of what has changed state. All this activity typically happens when the application is idle. In addition to what's shown in Figure 6-1, there are some other events that occur. In particular, any mouse or keyboard messages received by the window showing the 3D scene are passed down to the controller and the input device. This is done so that an input device can be mouse or keyboard driven without having to poll for this data.

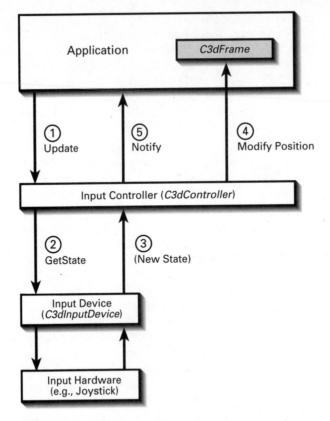

Figure 6-1. *The input model's update cycle.*

The Input Device

The role of the input device is to take data from the hardware and generate six axis data values: x, y, z, r, u, and v. Values x, y, and z are linear displacements, and r, u, and v are rotational components. These axis values do not necessarily relate to the axes in the scene or the axes of a particular object; they are just the raw input data the controller uses to position an object. Figure 6-2 on the facing page shows the general relationship between the rotational components and the axes.

Obviously, if you use a device like the SpaceBall, generating x, y, z, r, u, and v data is simply a matter of sampling the hardware, applying some scale factor, and returning the results. For physical devices that don't generate six axes of data, the input device must take the available hardware data and process it in such a way as to create data for all six axes. For example, the input device in the 3dPlus library that works with the mouse takes the x and y mouse-position data and uses the Shift and Control keys to determine which output values should be updated. So if you hold down the left mouse button while you move the mouse, without pressing any keys, the x and y output values change. Holding the Shift key down maps the x input to the v output and the y input to the z output.

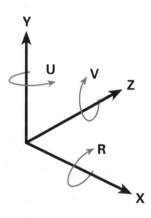

Figure 6-2. *The relationship between* r, u, v *and* x, y, z.

The 3dPlus library includes support for three different input devices: keyboard, mouse, and joystick. Each device is implemented in a C++ class derived from *C3dInputDevice*.

KEYBOARD INPUT DEVICES

The keyboard input device class processes *WM_KEYDOWN* messages sent to it from the controller. The keyboard messages are used to increment or decrement the current value for the *x*-, *y*-, *z*-, *r*-, *u*-, and *v*-axes. Table 6-1 shows how the various key combinations control the axis outputs.

TABLE 6-1
Keyboard Axis Mappings

Key	Normal	Shift	Control
Left arrow	X--	V--	U--
Right arrow	X++	V++	U++
Up arrow	Y++	Z++	R++
Down arrow	Y--	Z--	R--
Keypad Plus sign	Z--		
Keypad Minus sign	Z++		
Page Up	V++		
Page Down	V--		
Home	U++		
End	U--		
Insert	R++		
Delete	R--		

Remember that the axis outputs still need to be processed by the controller before they affect an object, so the axes shown here as x, y, z, r, u, and v aren't necessarily related to axes in the object or scene.

The code that drives the keyboard input device is just a switch statement that processes the various key messages. Here's the first part of the code taken from 3dInpDev.cpp in the 3dPlus library Source directory, which handles the Left and Right arrow keys:

```
void C3dKeyInDev::OnKeyDown(UINT nChar, UINT nRepCnt,
                            UINT nFlags)
{
    double dInc = 0.02;
    switch (nChar) {
    case VK_SHIFT:
        m_bShift = TRUE;
        break;
    case VK_CONTROL:
        m_bControl = TRUE;
        break;
    case VK_RIGHT:
        if (m_bShift) {
            Inc(m_st.dV);
        } else if (m_bControl) {
            Inc(m_st.dU);
        } else {
            Inc(m_st.dX);
        }
        break;
    case VK_LEFT:
        if (m_bShift) {
            Dec(m_st.dV);
        } else if (m_bControl) {
            Dec(m_st.dU);
        } else {
            Dec(m_st.dX);
        }
        break;
        ⋮
```

MOUSE INPUT DEVICES

The mouse input device is a little simpler. Because the mouse has two degrees of freedom, we just need to determine how those two input axes will be mapped to the six output axes. Table 6-2 shows the mouse axis mappings.

TABLE 6-2
Mouse Axis Mappings

Input Axis	Normal	Shift	Control
X	X	-V	-U
Y	-Y	-Z	-R

Note that some axes are shown as negative. I reversed some axes to give the most reasonable control effect. The code for the mouse device consists of two separate functions: *C3dMouseInDev::OnUserEvent* and *C3dMouseInDev::GetState*. The first function, shown below, can also be found in 3dInpDev.cpp. This function handles mouse movements and captures the mouse position when the left button is pressed:

```
void C3dMouseInDev::OnUserEvent(HWND hWnd, UINT uiMsg,
                                WPARAM wParam,
                                LPARAM lParam)
{
    switch (uiMsg) {
    case WM_LBUTTONDOWN:
        ::SetCapture(hWnd);
        m_bCaptured = TRUE;
        break;

    case WM_LBUTTONUP:
        if (m_bCaptured) {
            ::ReleaseCapture();
            m_bCaptured = FALSE;
        }
        break;

    case WM_MOUSEMOVE:
        if (m_bCaptured) {
            // Note: screen coords. (See C3dWnd.)
            m_ptCur.x = LOWORD(lParam);
            m_ptCur.y = HIWORD(lParam);
            m_dwFlags = wParam;
        }
        break;

    default:
        break;
    }
}
```

The mouse position is kept in a local *CPoint* structure, *m_ptCur*. The second function, which follows, is called when a controller requests the current input state:

```
BOOL C3dMouseInDev::GetState(_3DINPUTSTATE& st)
{
    if (m_ptPrev.x < 0) {
        m_ptPrev = m_ptCur;
    }

    // Set initial state
    m_st.dX = 0;
    m_st.dY = 0;
    m_st.dZ = 0;
    m_st.dR = 0;
    m_st.dU = 0;
    m_st.dV = 0;

    // See how far mouse has moved
    int dx = m_ptCur.x - m_ptPrev.x;
    int dy = m_ptCur.y - m_ptPrev.y;

    // If it's a big move, ignore it to stay on screen
    if ((abs(dx) > 100) || (abs(dy) > 100)) {
        dx = 0;
        dy = 0;
    }

    // Provide a deadband so the object doesn't wander
    int idb = 3;
    if (dx > idb) {
        dx -= idb;
    } else if (dx < -idb) {
        dx += idb;
    } else {
        dx = 0;
    }
    if (dy > idb) {
        dy -= idb;
    } else if (dy < -idb) {
        dy += idb;
    } else {
        dy = 0;
    }

    double dScale = 0.1;
    if (dx != 0) {
        double d = dx * dScale;
        if (m_dwFlags & MK_SHIFT) {
            m_st.dV = -d;
        } else if (m_dwFlags & MK_CONTROL) {
```

```
                m_st.dU = -d;
            } else {
                m_st.dX = d;
            }
        }
        if (dy != 0) {
            double d = dy * dScale;
            if (m_dwFlags & MK_SHIFT) {
                m_st.dZ = -d;
            } else if (m_dwFlags & MK_CONTROL) {
                m_st.dR = -d;
            } else {
                m_st.dY = -d;
            }
        }

        m_ptPrev = m_ptCur;

        st = m_st;
        return TRUE;
    }
```

The mouse's *x*- and *y*-axis values are processed to provide a small deadband zone that helps prevent shapes from wandering. A scale factor is applied so that the object will always appear in the display in the proper proportions. Then the current state of the Shift and Control keys is used to determine which output axis value to modify.

JOYSTICK INPUT DEVICES

The joystick input device is just a little more complicated than both the keyboard and the mouse input devices. Figure 6-3 shows the Joystick Settings dialog box.

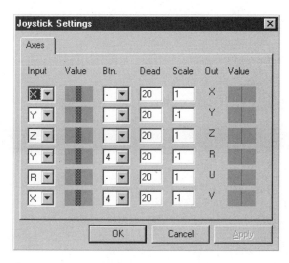

Figure 6-3. *The Joystick Settings dialog box.*

Each output axis can be generated from any of the available input axes, and you can select a button to act as a qualifier. For example, looking at Figure 6-3, we see that the *v* output actually comes from the *x* input but is active only when button 4 is pressed. The boxes in the Value columns show the current axis values. The left column shows the current input value as read from the joystick. The dark gray band is a deadband zone. If the input value lies inside the deadband, the output doesn't change. This helps prevent objects from wandering around the screen when the joystick is released but doesn't quite return to the exact center. The value boxes in the right column show the output values.

You can alter the scale values, making a value greater for more sensitivity or using a negative value to reverse the axis direction. The settings shown here are how I configured my Microsoft SideWinder. When I'm using the SpaceBall I don't need to do much more than map *x* to *x*, *y* to *y*, and so on. Figure 6-4 shows a typical axis output value plotted against the input value. The flat area in the middle is the deadband.

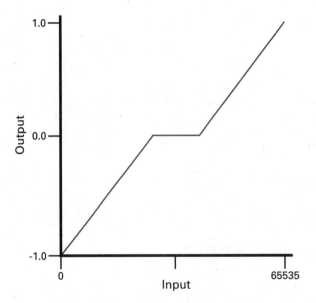

Figure 6-4. *A typical joystick input/output mapping function.*

The configuration data for the joystick is kept in the system registry, and I chose to keep separate configurations for each type of joystick and also for each application. If you have more than one joystick, it's convenient not to have to reconfigure the settings when you change the active joystick. Having different configurations for each application might sound bizarre, but I found that for some applications I wanted different mappings. The configuration data is under the key:

```
HKEY_CURRENT_USER\Software\3dPlus\<AppName>\Settings
\Joystick\<JoystickName>
```

<AppName> is the name of the application, and *<JoystickName>* is the name of the joystick.

The joystick code is a bit long-winded to include here, so I'll leave you to browse through 3dJoyDev.cpp in the 3dPlus library Source directory later.

The Input Controller

The function of the input controller is to take the raw *x*-, *y*-, *z*-, *r*-, *u*-, and *v*-axis data from the input device and apply it to a *C3dFrame* in some way. I created two different types of controllers, which I refer to as the *position controller* and the *flying controller*. Either one can be used to manipulate an object in the scene or to manipulate the camera. The controller just needs to know which frame is to be manipulated and the rest is automatic. In addition to moving an object, the application can request notification events from the controller, when, for example, the *x*-axis value changes or a button is pushed, so the application can take some other action. Figure 6-5 shows the dialog box, accessed from the Edit menu in the Moving sample, that you can use to select the object to be controlled, the type of controller, and the input device.

Figure 6-5. *The Control Device dialog box.*

You use the position controller to move objects in a scene. The *x*-, *y*-, and *z*-axes change the object's position, using the scene's frame as the reference; so if you move the joystick to the left, the object moves along the *x*-axis of the scene. Rotation is relative to the object's origin, which provides the effect that feels most reasonable. For example, if you twist the joystick the object rotates in place. Almost anyone can quickly learn to use this controller to place objects in a scene.

The position controller can also be used to move the camera, which, in effect, moves the entire scene in front of you. This tends to feel strange, however, because the motion is relative to the scene and not relative to the camera; if you turn the camera about its *y*-axis 90 degrees to look left, any forward motion is now perceived as movement to the right.

You can use the flying controller to fly either an object or the camera through a scene. This controller uses the *x* and *y* data to control roll and pitch, the *z* data to control velocity, and the *u* data to control yaw. The idea is to set the object in forward motion by giving it some velocity and then to use the roll, pitch, and yaw controls to affect its path. My original code multiplied the roll and pitch by the velocity to give a more realistic effect. I found that I'm not much of a flyer and that the controls were much too difficult for me to use, so I opted for a simpler approach that lets you alter the object's roll, pitch, and yaw even if it's stationary. If this doesn't make much sense to you, I suggest you try the code the way it is and then modify it to use the velocity effect. What code? This code, located in 3dInCtlr.cpp:

```
void C3dFlyCtlr::OnUpdate(_3DINPUTSTATE& st,
                          C3dFrame* pFrame)
{
    // Get velocity (use z-axis for this)
    double v = st.dZ / 10;

    // Get roll, pitch, and yaw from x-, y-, and u-axes
    double pitch = st.dY / 3;
    double roll = -st.dX / 3;
    double yaw = st.dU / 5;

    // Multiply pitch and roll by velocity for
    // extra realism
    // pitch *= v;
    // roll *= v;

    pFrame->AddRotation(1, 0, 0, pitch,
                        D3DRMCOMBINE_BEFORE);
    pFrame->AddRotation(0, 0, 1, roll, D3DRMCOMBINE_BEFORE);
    pFrame->AddRotation(0, 1, 0, yaw, D3DRMCOMBINE_BEFORE);

    // Get current direction vector
    double x1, y1, z1;
    pFrame->GetDirection(x1, y1, z1);

    // Multiply direction vector by velocity
    x1 *= v;
    y1 *= v;
    z1 *= v;

    // Get current position
    double x, y, z;
    pFrame->GetPosition(x, y, z);

    // Update position
    x += x1;
    y += y1;
    z += z1;
    pFrame->SetPosition(x, y, z);

}
```

The preceding function, *C3dFlyCtlr::OnUpdate*, is the function in the flying controller that uses the raw axis data to modify the controlled object's frame position and orientation. This function is called each time an update of the object's position is required. The input arguments include a description of the current state of the input device being used (the raw axis data) and a pointer to the frame to be manipulated. Out of all the input device and controller code, this function is by far the most interesting, so we'll look at it step by step.

Let's begin with the input data structure:

```
typedef struct __3DINPUTSTATE {
    double dX;       // -1 <= value <= 1
    double dY;       // -1 <= value <= 1
    double dZ;       // -1 <= value <= 1
    double dR;       // -1 <= value <= 1
    double dU;       // -1 <= value <= 1
    double dV;       // -1 <= value <= 1
    double dPov;     //  0 <= value <= 359
                     // (< 0 indicates not valid)
    DWORD dwButtons;// 1 = active (pressed)
} _3DINPUTSTATE;
```

As you can see, six of the axis data values range from −1.0 through 1.0. There is also a value that represents a "point-of-view," which is the direction you're looking—forward, left, right, and so on. (Some joysticks include a button control to select a point of view in a game.) The *dPov* value here is an angle in degrees from the front position.

The controller sets the velocity, roll, pitch, and yaw from the input values for the *z*-, *x*-, *y*-, and *u*-axes, respectively. I applied some scaling to provide better sensitivity. I found the scale values empirically.

If you want more of a challenge, you can uncomment the lines that alter the pitch and roll by the velocity factor.

Having established the current velocity and the amount the object's position needs to be altered, the next step is to apply the rotational changes to the frame. This is done using the *AddRotation* member function and specifying that the rotation transform should be applied *before* any existing transform. This is required to rotate the object about its own axes rather than those of the scene.

The final step is to move the object to the new position. This is done by first calling *GetDirection* to obtain the forward vector for the object, which represents the direction that it is flying. The forward vector is then multiplied by the velocity to produce the incremental change in position. Finally, the object's current position is retrieved, the incremental changes are added, and the object is set in its new position.

You might note that I used versions of the *GetDirection*, *GetPosition*, and *SetPosition* functions that have separate *x*, *y*, and *z* arguments, rather than using the versions that use *C3dVector* arguments. There's no particular reason for this choice, and perhaps you'd like to rewrite it using vector arguments as an exercise.

One final note: The rate of movement is not constant. The update functions are called when the application is idle, and redrawing the scene takes a variable amount of time depending on the location of the objects in the scene. If you need a constant rate of motion, your update functions will need to sample the current time by calling *timeGetTime* (declared in Mmsystem.h), for example, and using the elapsed time to modify how far each object moves.

Creating Objects That Move by Themselves

The flying controller does actually give you a way to set an object in motion by itself, but the client still needs you to control where it flies. I find this quite limiting when I'm in the driver's seat, so I've created some examples of how objects can be set in motion on fixed paths and fly by themselves.

The first example, which can be found in the Cruise directory, involves setting the camera in motion to give the effect of flying in a circle, following an airplane around a mountain. Figure 6-6 shows a screen shot of the application. (Also see the color version in the color insert.)

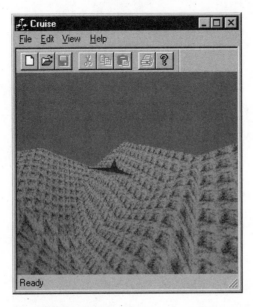

Figure 6-6. *Cruising through the valley.*

To create this application I drew the plan for the scenery on a sheet of graph paper, showing the edges of all the mountains. I then hand-coded all the vertices and face data to construct the landscape. I won't include the code here, because it consists simply of a long array of vertex values followed by a long list of face data values. You can find the code in the MainFrm.cpp file in the Cruise directory.

I also created the little airplane manually and then added a texture map to the terrain to make it more interesting. (We'll look at how to create and apply texture maps in Chapter 8.) The last part of creating the scene was to set the camera in its initial position and increase the camera's field of view to give a more expansive effect:

```
BOOL CMainFrame::SetScene()
{
    ⋮
    // Set up the camera flight path
    m_vCamera = C3dVector(5, 5, 0);
    m_dRadius = 5.0;
```

```
    // Set field of view
    m_pScene->SetCameraField(1.5);
    ⋮
}
```

The camera is set to rotate about a fixed point on a circular path. Figure 6-7 shows the path of the camera around the scene.

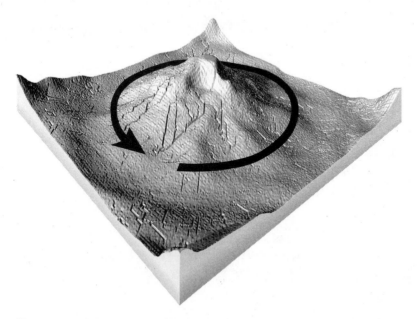

Figure 6-7. *The flight path of the camera.*

Now all that's needed is to move the camera and the small airplane together with each iteration of the scene:

```
BOOL CMainFrame::Update(double d)
{
    // Update camera position
    C3dMatrix r;
    r.Rotate(0, 2.0, 0);
    m_vCamera = r * m_vCamera;

    m_pScene->SetCameraPosition(m_vCamera);

    // Set the up vector
    C3dVector vu(0, 1, 0);

    // Generate forward vector
    C3dVector vf = m_vCamera * vu;
    m_pScene->SetCameraDirection(vf, vu);

    // Set airplane position in front of camera
    r.Rotate(0, 20, 0);
```

(continued)

```
C3dVector vp = r * m_vCamera;
m_pPlane->SetPosition(vp);

// Set direction
C3dMatrix rp;
rp.Rotate(0, 0, 10); // A bit wobbly!
vu = rp * vu;
vf = vp * vu;
m_pPlane->SetDirection(vf, vu);

return m_wnd3d.Update(TRUE);
}
```

I chose to use a *C3dVector* object to hold the camera's current position. To compute the new position, the vector is multiplied by a rotation matrix. The camera is then set in its new position—but that's not all we need to do. We need to change the camera's direction so that it stays tangential to the circle. To compute the new camera direction, we multiply an up vector (*vu*) by the camera's position vector (*m_vCamera*). The resultant vector (*vf*) gives the look direction for the camera. Figure 6-8 shows these vectors.

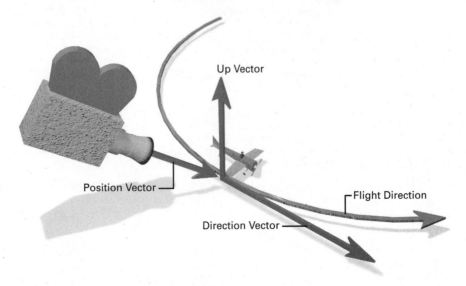

Up Vector

Position Vector

Flight Direction

Direction Vector

Figure 6-8. *Computing the camera's forward direction vector.*

The vector product is very useful when we need a vector perpendicular to the plane defined by two other vectors, as in the case here.

The last step is to compute the position and direction of the small airplane in front of the camera. The plane is following the same path as the camera but moving a few degrees ahead of the camera. To compute the plane's position we take the camera position vector and rotate it a bit further using another matrix (*r*). To set the direction, I originally computed a cross product for the plane exactly as we did above for the camera, but it looked a bit boring to watch the plane flying straight and level (well, sort of) ahead of the camera. Instead, I rotated the up vector slightly, which makes the plane appear to wobble. Not a great effect, but certainly easy to create.

Using Relative Motion

The object in the next example is a clock mechanism comprised of several sets of parts that are in constant motion relative to one another. Figure 6-9 shows a screen shot of the application, which can be found in the Clock directory. (Look in the color insert for a better view of this screen shot.)

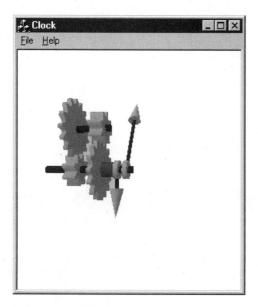

Figure 6-9. *The clock mechanism.*

The mechanism is made up of three rotating shafts. The center shaft is connected to the minute hand and a small gear. The hour hand and a large gear are connected to the second shaft, which is wrapped around part of the center shaft. The third shaft has a big gear and a small gear that mesh with the gears on the minute hand (center) and hour hand (outer) shafts.

In my original attempt at building this application, I used disks to represent the gears, and it took only one hour to create. The gears took me three more hours to get right! The code to construct the entire mechanism is simple and consists of creating each shaft and adding the gears and hands as child frames to the shafts. The shafts are then set in motion about their own center lines. I chose rates of rotation that give the effect that the gears are actually driving the mechanism. If you watch it closely, you'll see that the illusion is not quite perfect.

To make the entire clock rotate, I used one frame as the parent for all the shafts. The frame can then be set in motion about the *y*-axis to rotate the entire mechanism as it works. (Astute readers might notice that the gear reduction is 4:1 instead of the more conventional 12:1 found in most other clocks.) Let's finish up by taking a look at the code in MainFrm.cpp that makes the minute hand shaft work. The other two shafts are created in much the same way:

```
BOOL CMainFrame::SetScene()
{
    ⋮
    // Build clock
    C3dFrame clock;
    clock.Create(m_pScene);
    double dSpin = -0.1;

    // Create the minute hand shaft
    C3dFrame s1;
    s1.Create(&clock);
    C3dShape r1;
    r1.CreateRod(0, 0, -0.5, 0, 0, 10, 0.4, 16);
    r1.SetColor(0, 0, 1);
    s1.AddChild(&r1);

    // Add big hand
    CHand bighand(10);
    s1.AddChild(&bighand);
    bighand.SetPosition(0, 0, 0);

    // Add gear
    CGear g1(1.5, 1.5, 8);
    s1.AddChild(&g1);
    g1.SetPosition(0, 0, 5.5);

    // Make shaft rotate
    s1.SetRotation(0, 0, 1, dSpin);
    ⋮
}
```

The shaft frame is created using the clock frame as its parent. A rod is then added to the shaft frame to represent the visual part of this shaft. The big hand is created from *CHand*, a class derived from *C3dShape*, which we'll look at in a minute. The gear is also created from a class derived from *C3dShape*, *CGear*, and added to the shaft frame. The last task is to set the frame rotating by calling *C3dFrame::SetRotation*.

The hands are created from two rods and a cone:

```
CHand::CHand(double l)
{
    CreateRod(0, 0, 0, 0, 0, 0.5, 1, 16);
    SetColor(1, 1, 0);
    C3dShape r;
    r.CreateRod(0, 0, 0.25, 0, l-3, 0.25, 0.20, 16);
    r.SetColor(0, 0, 1);
    AddChild(&r);
    C3dShape c;
    c.CreateCone(0, l-3, 0.25, 0.75, TRUE, 0, l, 0.25, 0,
                 FALSE, 16);
    c.SetColor(1, 1, 0);
    AddChild(&c);
}
```

The gears are rather more complicated to create. Two circles define the inside and outside radii of the teeth, and the number of teeth requested determines how these circles are subdivided to get the vertex positions for the teeth. (See Figure 6-10.) A face list is constructed for the outside faces of the teeth, and the first part of the shape is created.

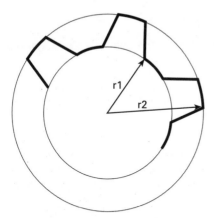

Figure 6-10. *Constructing the gear teeth.*

The side faces of the gears are created using normals to make sure they're rendered as flat surfaces. If you fail to supply the normals, the renderer rounds off the sides of the gears and produces weird triangular facets on the faces of the gears. Of course, five minutes spent in Autodesk 3D Studio would probably have created some perfectly serviceable gears without all this code:

```
CGear::CGear(double r, double t, int teeth)
{
    double twopi =  6.28318530718;
    double r1 = r - 0.3;
    double r2 = r + 0.3;
    int nFaceVert = teeth * 4;
    int nVert = nFaceVert * 2;
    D3DVECTOR* Vertices = new D3DVECTOR[nVert];
    D3DVECTOR* pv = Vertices;
    double da = twopi / (teeth * 4);
    double a = 0;
    for (int i = 0; i < teeth; i++) {
        pv->x = r1 * cos(a);
        pv->y = r1 * sin(a);
        pv->z = 0;
        pv++;
        a += da;
        pv->x = r2 * cos(a);
        pv->y = r2 * sin(a);
        pv->z = 0;
        pv++;
        a += da;
```

(continued)

```
            pv->x = r2 * cos(a);
            pv->y = r2 * sin(a);
            pv->z = 0;
            pv++;
            a += da;
            pv->x = r1 * cos(a);
            pv->y = r1 * sin(a);
            pv->z = 0;
            pv++;
            a += da;
        }

        pv = Vertices;
        D3DVECTOR* pv2 = &Vertices[nFaceVert];
        for (i = 0; i < nFaceVert; i++) {
            *pv2 = *pv;
            pv2->z = t;
            pv++;
            pv2++;
        }

        // Generate face data for teeth.
        // Cross your fingers.
        int nf = (teeth * 5 * 4) + (teeth * 26) + 10;
        int* FaceData = new int[nf];
        int* pfd = FaceData;

        for (i = 0; i < teeth*4; i++) {
            *pfd++ = 4;
            *pfd++ = i;
            *pfd++ = (i + 1) % (teeth*4);
            *pfd++ = nFaceVert + ((i + 1) % (teeth*4));
            *pfd++ = nFaceVert + (i % (teeth*4));
        }

        // End the list
        *pfd++ = 0;

        Create(Vertices, nVert, NULL, 0, FaceData, TRUE);

        // Add end faces using normals
        D3DVECTOR nvect [] = {
            {0, 0, 1},
            {0, 0, -1}
        };

        delete [] FaceData;
        FaceData = new int [teeth * 9  + teeth * 4  + 10];

        pfd = FaceData;
```

```
    for (i = 0; i < teeth; i++) {
        *pfd++ = 4;
        *pfd++ = i*4;
        *pfd++ = 1;
        *pfd++ = i*4+3;
        *pfd++ = 1;
        *pfd++ = i*4+2;
        *pfd++ = 1;
        *pfd++ = i*4+1;
        *pfd++ = 1;
    }
    *pfd++ = teeth*2;
    for (i = teeth-1; i >= 0; i--) {
        *pfd++ = i*4+3;
        *pfd++ = 1;
        *pfd++ = i*4;
        *pfd++ = 1;
    }
    *pfd++ = 0;
    AddFaces(Vertices, nVert, nvect, 2, FaceData);

    pfd = FaceData;
    for (i = 0; i < teeth; i++) {
        *pfd++ = 4;
        *pfd++ = nFaceVert + i*4;
        *pfd++ = 0;
        *pfd++ = nFaceVert + i*4+1;
        *pfd++ = 0;
        *pfd++ = nFaceVert + i*4+2;
        *pfd++ = 0;
        *pfd++ = nFaceVert + i*4+3;
        *pfd++ = 0;
    }
    *pfd++ = teeth*2;
    for (i = 0; i < teeth; i++) {
        *pfd++ = nFaceVert + i*4;
        *pfd++ = 0;
        *pfd++ = nFaceVert + i*4+3;
        *pfd++ = 0;
    }
    *pfd = 0;
    AddFaces(Vertices, nVert, nvect, 2, FaceData);
    delete [] Vertices;
    delete [] FaceData;

    SetColor(1, 1, 0);
}
```

This code should look pretty familiar to you by now. When I have some free time I plan to use the code in this sample to create a real clock with second, minute, and hour hands, a real face, and a pendulum.

Moving Objects Along Other Paths

Of course, you can move your objects along any path you like. All you need is either a set of coordinates in space or a function such as a spline generator, which can generate smooth curves along a path you describe with a few control points. At each iteration of the scene, you compute the object's new position and place it there. Don't forget that unless you're moving a sphere you are going to have to compute the object's look direction and maybe its up direction as well.

Implementing Your Own Controller

The ability to position an object or make it fly is all very nice, but what if that's not the behavior you have in mind? Let's look now at building a controller for a slightly more interesting object: the Mark VII Interplanetary Battle Tank with X-Band Doppler Radar. The tank can move across the surface of a planet at varying velocities and turn as it moves. Its turret rotates with lightning speed and its gun can be elevated to fire its shells. Oh, and did I mention the radar that spins happily on top of the tank? Figure 6-11 shows the tank in action.

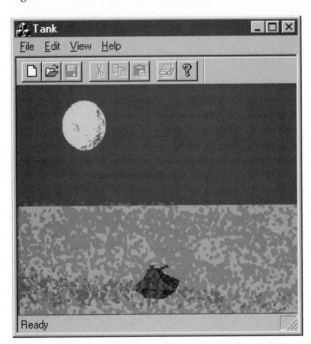

Figure 6-11. *The Mark VII Interplanetary Battle Tank with X-Band Doppler Radar in action.*

Hmmm, notice the lack of wheels? There could be two reasons for this:

◆ It's a flying tank.

◆ Making the wheels was too hard.

You decide.

Figure 6-12 shows a diagram of the tank parts, with wheels added, that can be moved relative to one another. (This figure is also included in the color insert.)

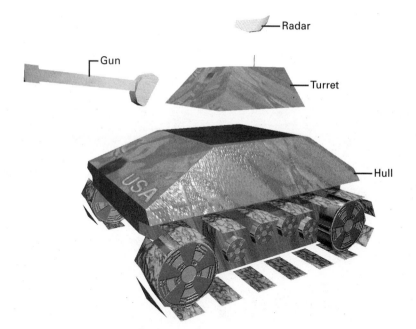

Radar

Gun

Turret

Hull

Figure 6-12. *The tank parts.*

In the Tank sample, the *C3dTank* object is derived from *C3dFrame*. The tank is built by attaching the hull shape to a containing frame, attaching the turret to the hull, and then attaching the gun and radar to the turret. The radar is made to rotate constantly. The gun can be raised and lowered by rotating it about a horizontal axis. The turret can be rotated about a vertical axis through the hull.

Before learning how to create a controller for the tank, let's look at the code that implements the tank so that we can see how it's controlled.

```
C3dTank::C3dTank()
{
    // Create the frame
    C3dFrame::Create(NULL);

    // Load tank parts and build tank
    m_hull.Load(IDX_HULL);
    AddChild(&m_hull);
    m_turret.Load(IDX_TURRET);
    m_hull.AddChild(&m_turret);
    m_gun.Load(IDX_GUN);
    m_turret.AddChild(&m_gun);

    // The radar has its own frame for better control
    // of the rotation axis
    C3dFrame rframe;
    rframe.Create(&m_turret);
    C3dShape radar;
```

(continued)

```
radar.Load(IDX_RADAR);
rframe.AddChild(&radar);
radar.SetPosition(0, 0, -0.3);
rframe.SetPosition(0, 0, 0.3);
rframe.SetRotation(0, 1, 0, 0.1);

SetGun(25);
}
```

The only odd thing in the code is that I used a separate frame for the radar because the original art for the tank had the *y*-axis of the radar displaced from where I wanted it to rotate. So I set the frame's origin on the turret where I wanted the axis of rotation and displaced the radar object inside the frame to position it over the point of rotation. (See Figure 6-13.)

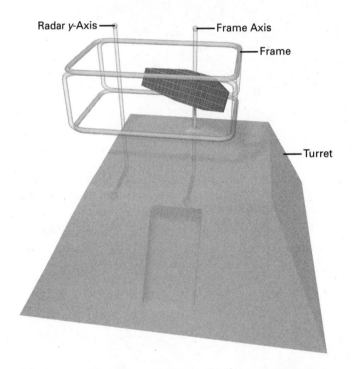

Figure 6-13. *The placement of the radar image inside its frame.*

All the objects that make up the tank were created using 3D Studio and converted to .X file format using the conv3ds utility in the DirectX 2 SDK. They were added to the application's RC2 file as resources:

```
//
// STAGE.RC2 - resources Microsoft Visual C++ does not edit
// directly
//

#ifdef APSTUDIO_INVOKED
    #error this file is not editable by Microsoft Visual C++
#endif //APSTUDIO_INVOKED
```

```
//////////////////////////////////////////////////////
// Add manually edited resources here

#include "3dPlus.rc"

// Tank parts
IDX_HULL      XOF          res\T_hull.x
IDX_TURRET    XOF          res\turret.x
IDX_GUN       XOF          res\gun.x
IDX_RADAR     XOF          res\radar.x
camo.bmp      BITMAP       res\camo.bmp
camousa.bmp   BITMAP       res\camousa.bmp
// Sounds
IDS_BANG      WAVE         res\bang.wav


//////////////////////////////////////////////////////
```

The XOF tag used in the resource file could actually have been any string. I chose XOF because it was originally the file extension used in the shape files. The only place the XOF string is referenced is in the *C3dShape::Load* function, where it is used to distinguish XOF file resources from other types of resources.

The tank has three methods, found in 3dTank.cpp, that provide controls for the turret angle, the gun angle, and the firing of the gun:

```
#define D2R  0.01745329251994

void C3dTank::SetTurret(double angle)
{
    if ((angle < 0) || (angle >= 360)) {
        angle = 0;
    }
    double x = sin(angle * D2R);
    double z = cos(angle * D2R);
    m_turret.SetDirection(x, 0, z, &m_hull);
}

void C3dTank::SetGun(double angle)
{
    if (angle < 0) {
        angle = 0;
    } else if (angle >= 60) {
        angle = 60;
    }
    double y = -sin(angle * D2R);
    double z = cos(angle * D2R);
```

(continued)

```
        m_gun.SetDirection(0, y, z, &m_turret);
    }

    void C3dTank::FireGun()
    {
        PlaySound(MAKEINTRESOURCE(IDS_BANG),
                  AfxGetResourceHandle(),
                  SND_RESOURCE);

    }
```

As you can see, the positions of the turret and gun are set by computing a direction vector. Then we set the object's direction *relative to its parent,* which is actually the default action for *SetDirection*. But I wanted to be obvious here, so I included the reference frame as an argument each time.

We have a functional tank. Now we need a way to control it.

The Tank Controller

Most of the code for implementing the controller is inside the *C3dWnd* and *C3dController* classes. All you need to do to build your own controller is derive a new class from *C3dController*, override the *OnUpdate* function, and install the new controller in your application. Before you can implement the controller's *OnUpdate* function, you must decide which input axes will be used for what function. The configuration I chose is shown in Table 6-3.

TABLE 6-3
Tank Control Channel Mappings

Input Channel	Tank Parameter
y	Forward velocity
x	Turning
r	Turning
POV	Turret direction
Buttons 3 & 4	Gun elevation
Button 1	Fire gun

I chose to use both x and r to control turning so that if you had a simple two-axis joystick you could still drive the tank. I used my SideWinder Pro joystick for this application because it has more of a tank-driving kind of feel than the SpaceBall. The point-of-view button on top of a SideWinder Pro is also great for setting the turret direction.

Having decided on how the controls will work, we can write the controller code. The entire code consists of just two functions:

```
CTankCtrl::CTankCtrl()
{
    m_dGunAngle = 25;
    m_bWasFire = FALSE;
}


void CTankCtrl::OnUpdate(_3DINPUTSTATE& st,
                         C3dFrame* pFrame)
{
    // Set velocity (use y-axis for this)
    double v = st.dY / 2;

    // Get current position
    C3dVector pos;
    pFrame->GetPosition(pos);

    // Get current direction vector
    C3dVector dir, up;
    pFrame->GetDirection(dir, up);

    // Set new direction.
    // Both x and r affect direction.
    double dr = -st.dX + -st.dR;
    C3dMatrix r;
    r.Rotate(0, dr * 3, 0);
    dir = r * dir;

    // Multiply direction vector by velocity to get
    // position delta
    C3dVector ds = dir * v;

    // Set new position and direction
    pos += ds;
    pFrame->SetPosition(pos);
    pFrame->SetDirection(dir);

    // Use POV info to set turret direction.
    // To do this we must be controlling a C3dTank,
    // not just a C3dFrame.
    C3dTank* pTank = (C3dTank*) pFrame;
    ASSERT(pTank->IsKindOf(RUNTIME_CLASS(C3dTank)));

    if (st.dPov >= 0) {
        pTank->SetTurret(st.dPov);
    }
```

(continued)

```
                // Use buttons 3 and 4 to raise or lower the gun
                if (st.dwButtons & 0x04) {
                    m_dGunAngle += 0.1;
                }
                if (st.dwButtons & 0x08) {
                    m_dGunAngle -= 0.1;
                }
                if (m_dGunAngle < 0) {
                    m_dGunAngle = 0;
                } else if (m_dGunAngle > 45) {
                    m_dGunAngle = 45;
                }
                pTank->SetGun(m_dGunAngle);

                // Check whether it's time to fire
                if (st.dwButtons & 0x01) {
                    if (!m_bWasFire) {
                        pTank->FireGun();
                        m_bWasFire = TRUE;
                    }
                } else {
                    m_bWasFire = FALSE;
                }
            }
```

The constructor is used to initialize some local data; the real work is done in the *OnUpdate* function. The *y*-axis value is used to set the current velocity. The current position and direction of the tank is saved in some *C3dVector* objects. The *x*- and *r*-axis data is used to set up a rotation matrix that is then used to rotate the direction vector to the new heading. The direction vector is multiplied by the velocity to give a position delta vector that is added to the tank's old position. The tank is then moved to its new position and set in the new direction.

The point-of-view data is used to set the turret direction. The number 3 and number 4 buttons are tested and, if pressed, are used to alter the gun's elevation by a small amount. Holding one of these buttons down slowly changes the gun's elevation.

The final task is to test the fire button. A local variable *m_bWasFire* is used to prevent multiple firing when the button is held down—fully automatic weapons are illegal in the U.S.A.

Putting the Application Together

I used the code for the Moving sample as the basis for the Tank application. I removed some inappropriate menu items and replaced the concept of the current shape with a *C3dTank* object. I also added a background image, which provides the entire scene. Here's part of the code that sets up the main window of the tank application:

```
int CMainFrame::OnCreate(LPCREATESTRUCT lpCreateStruct)
{

    ⋮
    // Load images
    m_imgBkgnd.Load(IDB_BKGND);

    NewScene();
    ASSERT(m_pScene);

    // Create controller object
    m_pController = new CTankCtrl;
    m_pController->Create(&m_wnd3d,
                          OnGetCtrlFrame,
                          this);

    // Restore controller settings
    m_pController->SelectDevice(m_iObjCtrlDev);

    return 0;
}
```

The *NewScene* function creates the scene and sets the initial conditions:

```
BOOL CMainFrame::NewScene()
{
    // Delete any scene we might have
    if (m_pScene) {
        m_wnd3d.SetScene(NULL);
        delete m_pScene;
        m_pScene = NULL;
    }

    // Create an initial scene
    m_pScene = new C3dScene;
    if (!m_pScene->Create()) return FALSE;

    // Set lighting
    C3dDirLight dl;
    dl.Create(0.8, 0.8, 0.8);
    m_pScene->AddChild(&dl);
    dl.SetPosition(-2, 2, -5);
    dl.SetDirection(1, -1, 1);
    m_pScene->SetAmbientLight(0.4, 0.4, 0.4);

    // Reset camera position and direction
    m_pScene->SetCameraPosition(C3dVector(0, 5, -25));
    m_pScene->SetCameraDirection(C3dVector(0, 0, 1));
```

(continued)

```
    m_wnd3d.SetScene(m_pScene);

    // Set up scenery
    m_pScene->SetBackground(&m_imgBkgnd);

    // Place tank in scene
    m_pScene->AddChild(&m_Tank);
    m_Tank.SetPosition(0, 0, 0);
    m_Tank.SetDirection(0, 0, 1);

    return TRUE;
}
```

You can choose New from the File menu to call *NewScene* and start the game again if your tank wanders off and gets lost. The only other change I made was to return a pointer to the tank when the controller requests the frame to control:

```
C3dFrame* CMainFrame::OnGetCtrlFrame(void* pArg)
{
    CMainFrame* pThis = (CMainFrame*) pArg;
    ASSERT(pThis);
    ASSERT(pThis->IsKindOf(RUNTIME_CLASS(CMainFrame)));
    return pThis->m_Tank;
}
```

It's important to note here that we're returning a pointer to a *C3dFrame*, but it is actually a pointer to a *C3dTank* object. We used this knowledge in the controller's *OnUpdate* function shown on page 141. If you thought that casting a *C3dFrame* pointer to be a *C3dTank* pointer was a bit cheesy, you can see now the reason it was OK to do that.

Moving On

So much for moving planes, clocks, and tanks. Now we can move on and look at how we can enable object selection in a scene.

CHAPTER 7

Hit Testing

When I was much younger—even before my punched card programming days—we had a TV program on the BBC in the UK called *Top of the Pops*, which played the hit records of the day. If you made it on to *Top of the Pops*, your record was a hit. I guess that was a kind of hit test, but it has nothing to do with what we're going to talk about next.

Our kind of hit testing is used to determine if a mouse click in a 3D scene occurs on any of the visible objects. This process is also sometimes called *selection* or *picking*. The rendering engine documents refer to it as picking, but I'm going to call it hit testing because that's the terminology I grew up with in Microsoft Windows programming.

There are several uses for hit testing. The first use we'll look at is when we want to select an object in a scene so that we can control it with the mouse or joystick. Once we have a way to select individual objects, we can move them independently and build a scene by placing each object exactly where we want it.

The second example we'll look at is determining which face of an object has been hit. This can be useful if you want to set the colors of an object's faces, for example. The third case we'll look at involves computing the actual point on the object that was hit. Having figured out the exact point on the object, you could modify the object in some way, such as adding a dimple to a flat surface.

The sample code for this chapter can be found in the Select directory. Once again I invite you to open the laptop and sing along as we progress through the story.

The Selection Process

Selecting an object in a scene with the mouse is very intuitive. The user just puts the cursor on the object and clicks a mouse button. For the application to know which object was selected, however, isn't quite so simple. Just for starters, the user might also be using the mouse to manipulate objects, so the messages that Windows sends to your main window—about where the mouse is and which buttons have been clicked—need to go to more than one place. This means that usually some central piece of code traps the mouse messages and makes that data available for any other piece of the application's code that needs it. You could simply store the current mouse state in some globally available variables and let any code peek at those values directly, or you can do what I chose to do, which was write some simple routines to handle the mouse events and then make calls to other areas of the application's code to notify it of some of those mouse events.

Given that you know where the mouse is on the screen and that the user has clicked a button in an attempt to select an object in the scene, how do you know which object was hit? Your first step is to convert the mouse coordinates to values which are relative to the client area of your window. Then you need to effectively reverse the transform that the rendering engine uses to convert your 2D screen coordinates into 3D coordinates. That's not quite as simple as it might at first seem. As we'll see shortly, the Direct3D engine does this for us—to a limited degree. Instead of converting the screen position of the mouse to a 3D value, it gives you a list of objects that lie underneath the point you choose. It also sorts the list by depth so that you can find the object which is at the front of the scene and which is (we're hopeful) the object the user is trying to select. All of this involves quite a bit of transform matrix juggling.

In my sample applications, I chose to be able to select only one object at a time. This makes the selection code a little simpler since I can have a variable (*m_pCurShape*) that points to the currently selected shape or is NULL if no shape is selected. As we'll see later, I also include the concept of the *currently selected face of an object*, which is the face of the currently selected object that the mouse was positioned over when the object was selected.

Implementing the code in the sample applications in order to support hit testing involved adding bits of code to quite a lot of different places. In the following sections, I'll try to explain which bits go where and how it all works. If you don't follow the explanation and want to see for yourself how the code works, then I strongly suggest that you run the sample under the debugger, set a breakpoint on the routine *C3dWnd::OnWndMsg* (in 3dWnd.cpp in the 3dPlus library), and follow the execution path from there. Once again I want to point out that there are lots of ways I could have implemented this code, and the one here is probably no better than any other. So if you have a design of your own that you think is better, then it probably is, and that's the one you should use.

Selecting an Entire Object

Most of the tasks for object selection are handled by the rendering engine's viewport code. Before we look at how that works, however, I want to review the sequence of events that start at the point where you click the mouse over an object in a scene. We'll walk through the various bits of code involved, beginning with the 3D window in which the scene is displayed.

Before your application can use the hit-testing support in the *C3dWnd* class, it must call a function that installs a notification function that is called each time an object is hit. After all, there wouldn't be much point in implementing hit detection if you weren't going to do anything with it. The story starts in the code that creates the application's main frame window:

```
int CMainFrame::OnCreate(LPCREATESTRUCT lpCreateStruct)
{
    ⋮
    // Enable mouse selection of objects
    m_wnd3d.EnableMouseSelection(OnSelChange, this);
    ⋮

}
```

The preceding line of code installs the notification function *OnSelChange*. The *OnSelChange* function is a static member of the *CMainFrame* window class, so it has no *this* pointer. As we'll see in a minute, the second argument passed to *Enable-MouseSelection* is returned in the *pArg* argument of the notification function. You can see that we are passing a pointer to the C++ object here. (See the code for the *EnableMouseSelection* function in C3dWnd.cpp for reference if this seems a bit confusing.) Let's look now at how a mouse click gets handled in the *C3dWnd* class, which will lead our discussion back to the actual notification function. Here's the part of the window's message handler that deals with hit testing:

```
BOOL C3dWnd::OnWndMsg(UINT message, WPARAM wParam,
                      LPARAM lParam, LRESULT* pResult )
{
    ⋮


    // See if we are looking for mouse selections
    if (m_bEnableMouseSelection
        && (message == WM_LBUTTONDOWN)) {
        CPoint pt(LOWORD(lParam), HIWORD(lParam));
        C3dShape* pShape = HitTest(pt);
        if (m_pSelChangeFn) {
            // Call notification function
            m_pSelChangeFn(pShape, pt, m_pSelChangeArg);
        }
    }

    return CWnd::OnWndMsg(message, wParam, lParam, pResult);
}
```

If mouse detection has been enabled (as we just saw), a *CPoint* object is created from the mouse coordinates passed in the WM_LBUTTONDOWN message and a call is made to the *HitTest* function to see if a shape has been hit. The results of the test (which could be NULL if no object was under the mouse) are returned to the application via the notification function it installed when it enabled mouse hit selection. Let's see now how that notification function is used in the application:

```
void CMainFrame::OnSelChange(C3dShape* pShape, CPoint pt,
                             void* pArg)
{
    // Get a pointer to class
    CMainFrame* pThis = (CMainFrame*) pArg;
    ASSERT(pThis);
    ASSERT(pThis->IsKindOf(RUNTIME_CLASS(CMainFrame)));

    if (pShape) {

        // Make sure it's not a hit on selection box or hit-
        // pointer shapes
        if (!pShape->IsPartOf(pThis->m_pSelBox)
            && !pShape->IsPartOf(pThis->m_pHitPtr)) {
```

```
        // Identify which face was hit
        C3dViewport* pViewport =
            pThis->m_wnd3d.GetStage()->GetViewport();
        pShape->HitTest(pt, pViewport,
                        &pThis->m_iHitFace,
                        &pThis->m_vHitPoint);

    } else {

        pShape = NULL;

    }
}

    // Make selected shape current
    pThis->MakeCurrent(pShape);
}
```

The newly selected object gets passed down to the *MakeCurrent* function, which puts a selection box around the object so we can see it's been selected. (We'll look further at *MakeCurrent* on page 159). The most important point about this piece of code is that it's a *static* member of the class, so, as we stated earlier, it has no *this* pointer. We get around this problem by passing the address of the C++ object as an argument to the routine that enabled mouse hit detection (*EnableMouseSelection*). The notification function passes back the value that we cast as a pointer to our class. Cunning stuff, eh? Making a callback to a class member function is quite a bit more involved, so I chose to make the notification function static to keep the code simple.

Let's look now in a bit more detail at how the hit detection was actually achieved. The *C3dWnd::HitTest* function simply passes the request down to the viewport:

```
// Test for hit on visible object
C3dShape* C3dWnd::HitTest(CPoint pt)
{
    ASSERT(m_pStage);
    return m_pStage->GetViewport()->HitTest(pt);
}
```

The viewport code, which can be found in 3dStage.cpp, makes the actual test in this way:

```
C3dShape* C3dViewport::HitTest(CPoint pt)
{
    IDirect3DRMPickedArray* pIPickArray = NULL;
    ASSERT(m_pIViewport);
    m_hr = m_pIViewport->Pick(pt.x, pt.y, &pIPickArray);
    if (FAILED(m_hr)) return NULL;
```

(continued)

```
// See if there are any items in the array
   if (pIPickArray->GetSize() == 0) {
       pIPickArray->Release();
       return NULL;
   }

   // Get the first (topmost) element
   IDirect3DRMVisual* pIVisual = NULL;
   IDirect3DRMFrameArray* pIFrameList = NULL;
   m_hr = pIPickArray->GetPick(0, &pIVisual, &pIFrameList,
                               NULL);
   ASSERT(SUCCEEDED(m_hr));
   ASSERT(pIVisual);
   ASSERT(pIFrameList);

   // Get last frame in list
   IDirect3DRMFrame* pIFrame = NULL;
   pIFrameList->GetElement(pIFrameList->GetSize() - 1,
                           &pIFrame);
   ASSERT(pIFrame);

   // Get 'AppData' value of the frame which should be a
   // C++ class pointer

   C3dShape* pShape = (C3dShape*) pIFrame->GetAppData();

   if (pShape) {
       if(!pShape->IsKindOf(RUNTIME_CLASS(C3dShape))) {
           pShape = NULL;
       }
   }

   pIFrame ->Release();
   pIFrameList->Release();
   pIVisual->Release();
   pIPickArray->Release();

   return pShape;
}
```

The first step is to ask the viewport to create what the rendering engine refers to as a *pick list,* which is a list of all the visual elements under a particular point in the window. The visual list (*pIPickArray*) is sorted so that the frontmost element is at the top of the list. The second step is to get a pointer (*pIVisual*) to this first visual element and use this pointer to get the list of frames (*pIFrameList*) to which the visual element is attached. Figure 7-1 shows the relationship between the various objects.

The frame list has the root frame (the scene) at the top and then lists successive child frames down to the last frame, which contains the visual object that was hit.

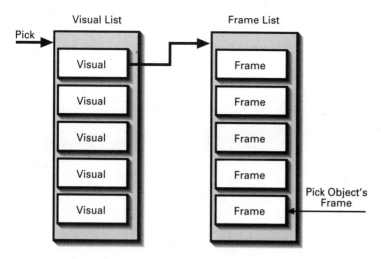

Figure 7-1. *The pick list data structures.*

The last step is to extract the *AppData* value from the frame interface. The *C3dFrame* and *C3dShape* classes store their *this* pointers in this variable in the interface. The AppData value is cast as a pointer to a *C3dShape* object, and the pointer is tested to see if it's NULL. If not, a check is made to see if the pointer is a pointer to a *C3dShape* object using the MFC run-time class information functions.

There are three possible values that could be in the *AppData* value: NULL, a pointer to a *C3dFrame* object, or a pointer to a *C3dShape* object. The hit detection code works only if the pointer references a *C3dShape* object and if the C++ class that created the visual and frame has not been destroyed. The destructor for the *C3dFrame* class (from which *C3dShape* is derived) sets the value of *AppData* back to NULL so you won't get a pointer to a deleted C++ object by accident. The relevance of all of this is that the *HitTest* function is useful only with 3D shapes that have a current *C3dShape* class object associated with them.

Showing the Selection

If you run the Select sample and click on an object in the scene, you'll see the object inside a selection box like the one shown in Figure 7-2 on the next page.

The selection box is displayed as a tubular frame that is positioned to show the object's bounding box, which is the smallest cuboid that encloses all of the object's vertices. A rod and cone are used to show the object's look direction, and another rod and cone (the stubbier looking cone) are used to show the object's up direction. These two direction pointers intersect at the object's 0, 0, 0 coordinate point. In the case of the sphere shown in Figure 7-2, the origin is actually inside the object.

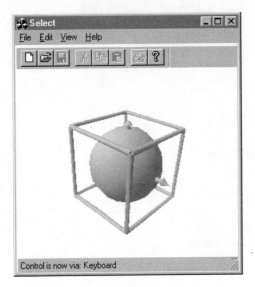

Figure 7-2. *A selected object.*

The code that shows the selection box is quite simple, if a little long:

```
void CMainFrame::ShowSelection()
{
    ⋮

        // Get bounding box of shape
        double x1, x2, y1, y2, z1, z2;
        BOOL b = m_pCurShape->GetBox(x1, y1, z1, x2, y2,
                                        z2);

        ASSERT(b);

        // Create new selection box around shape
        m_pSelBox = new C3dShape;

        double r = 0.03;
        double rc = r * 2;
        C3dShape r1, r2, r3, r4, r5, r6, r7, r8, r9,
                 r10, r11, r12, rd, ru, cd, cu;
        // Create rods for tubular frame
        r1.CreateRod(x1, y1, z1, x2, y1, z1, r);
        m_pSelBox->AddChild(&r1);
        r2.CreateRod(x1, y1, z1, x1, y2, z1, r);
        m_pSelBox->AddChild(&r2);
        r3.CreateRod(x1, y1, z1, x1, y1, z2, r);
        m_pSelBox->AddChild(&r3);
        r4.CreateRod(x1, y2, z1, x2, y2, z1, r);
        m_pSelBox->AddChild(&r4);
        r5.CreateRod(x2, y1, z1, x2, y2, z1, r);
        m_pSelBox->AddChild(&r5);
        r6.CreateRod(x1, y2, z1, x1, y2, z2, r);
        m_pSelBox->AddChild(&r6);
```

```
r7.CreateRod(x2, y2, z1, x2, y2, z2, r);
m_pSelBox->AddChild(&r7);
r8.CreateRod(x2, y1, z1, x2, y1, z2, r);
m_pSelBox->AddChild(&r8);
r9.CreateRod(x1, y1, z2, x1, y2, z2, r);
m_pSelBox->AddChild(&r9);
r10.CreateRod(x1, y1, z2, x2, y1, z2, r);
m_pSelBox->AddChild(&r10);
r11.CreateRod(x2, y1, z2, x2, y2, z2, r);
m_pSelBox->AddChild(&r11);
r12.CreateRod(x1, y2, z2, x2, y2, z2, r);
m_pSelBox->AddChild(&r12);
// Create rods and cones for look and up
rd.CreateRod(0, 0, 0, 0, 0, z2 * 1.2, r);
m_pSelBox->AddChild(&rd);
cd.CreateCone(0, 0, z2 * 1.2, rc, TRUE, 0, 0,
              z2 * 1.4, 0, FALSE);
m_pSelBox->AddChild(&cd);

ru.CreateRod(0, 0, 0, 0, y2 * 1.1, 0, r);
m_pSelBox->AddChild(&ru);
cu.CreateCone(0, y2 * 1.1, 0, rc, TRUE, 0,
              y2 * 1.2, 0, 0, FALSE);
m_pSelBox->AddChild(&cu);

// Set position and orientation of box to
// match shape
double x, y, z, xd, yd, zd, xu, yu, zu;
m_pCurShape->GetPosition(x, y, z);
m_pCurShape->GetDirection(xd, yd, zd, xu, yu, zu);
m_pSelBox->SetPosition(x, y, z);
m_pSelBox->SetDirection(xd, yd, zd, xu, yu, zu);

// Attach selection box to current shape
// to move with shape
m_pCurShape->AddChild(m_pSelBox);
⋮
```

The bounding box for the shape is used to position the set of rods that form the enclosing tubular frame and the rod and cone pairs that show the look and up vectors. All the rods and cones are attached to a single selection box object, which is set in position and oriented in the same direction as the selected object. The selection box is then attached to the selected object so that it will move with it.

Because the selection box consists of a set of visual objects, you might wonder why they won't be "selected" with the mouse. If you look at the code that handles the selection notification on page 148, you'll see this statement:

```
pShape->IsPartOf(pThis->m_pSelBox)
```

This test forms part of the logic to reject selection of the visible parts of the selection box. The *IsPartOf* function tests to see whether a frame is the same as the frame passed as the argument or whether the frame is the same as one of the argument's parent frames. In other words, it tests to see whether the frame is a part of some other frame set.

You might also recall that I mentioned that visible objects having no attached C++ object can't be selected. If you look at the code that built the selection box frame, you'll see that the C++ objects used to create the rods and cones were destroyed once the box was created. So why do we need the *IsPartOf* test? Because one C++ object remains—the one referenced by the *m_pSelBox* variable. To ensure that we stay out of trouble, the code makes the test even though it might not be absolutely necessary. After all, at some point in the future I could alter the code that creates the selection box in a way that leaves all the C++ objects intact. If I made that change, I wouldn't want all the selection logic to break.

Now that we have a mechanism for selecting an object in a scene, you can run the Select application, insert a few objects, and click on them. You'll find that you can move the currently selected object and see its selection box if you have the Selection Box menu option enabled. The View menu includes the Selection Box option to turn the selection box on or off.

Selecting a Single Face

The version of the rendering engine that I used to create the code for this book doesn't have any support for selecting individual faces, so I added this support. I want to show you how I did it because it demonstrates another good use of coordinate transforms.

The problem is that, given a point in the 3D scene window, we need to determine the face of the object below the point. We'll assume that there is an object below the point, which was found using the shape hit detection logic we looked at in the previous section. Figure 7-3 shows a diagram of the problem.

Given the mouse position in the window, we need to find a face on the object that contains the mouse position when projected onto the window. What's more, if there is more than one face under the mouse position, we need to select the frontmost face (with the lowest *z* value).

Here's how we do it. First we get a list of all the faces in the object, and then for each face we project its vertices onto the viewing plane, testing to see if the hit point lies inside the polygon formed by the projected vertices on the viewing plane. If we find a projected face that encloses the hit point, we see if it's closer to the front than any previous match. When all the faces have been tested, the result is the face we want.

One slight complication is in actually projecting the face vertices onto the viewing plane, which is a three-step process. Each vertex coordinate must first be transformed from its local coordinate value in the object's frame to a world coordinate value. The world coordinate value is then transformed to a homogeneous coordinate in the viewing plane. Finally, the homogeneous vector is converted to a point in the window.

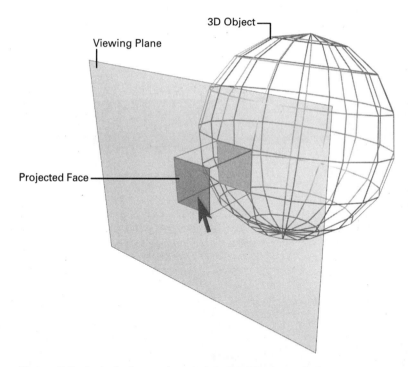

Figure 7-3. *A single face projected onto the 3D scene window.*

The other issue is actually figuring out if the hit point lies inside the polygon of points projected onto the viewing plane. We'll see how this is done in a moment. Let's look now at the code that implements the face hit detection logic:

```
BOOL C3dShape::HitTest(CPoint pt,
                       C3dViewport* pViewport,
                       int* piFace,
                       D3DVECTOR* pvHit)
{
    ⋮

    int iHitFace = -1;
    double dHitZ = 0;
    ⋮

    // Read through the face list
    D3DVECTOR lv;
    D3DVECTOR wv;
    D3DRMVECTOR4D sv;
    for (int i = 0; i < nFaces; i++) {
```

(continued)

```
// Get the face
IDirect3DRMFace* pIFace = NULL;
m_hr = pIFaceList->GetElement(i, &pIFace);
ASSERT(SUCCEEDED(m_hr));

// Get vertex count and allocate screen
// coordinate data array
int nVert = pIFace->GetVertexCount();
ASSERT(nVert > 2);
POINT* pScrnVert = new POINT [nVert];

// Convert each vertex to screen coordinates
double dZ = 0;
for (int v = 0; v < nVert; v++) {

    // Get vector in local (frame) coordinates
    m_hr = pIFace->GetVertex(v, &lv, NULL);
    ASSERT(SUCCEEDED(m_hr));

    // Convert it to world coordinates
    m_hr = m_pIFrame->Transform(&wv, &lv);
    ASSERT(SUCCEEDED(m_hr));

    // Convert world coordinates to screen
    // coordinates
    m_hr = pIViewport->Transform(&sv,
                                 &wv);
    ASSERT(SUCCEEDED(m_hr));

    // Convert homogeneous values to absolute pixel
    // values
    double w = sv.w;
    if (w != 0) {
        pScrnVert[v].x = (int) sv.x / w;
        pScrnVert[v].y = (int) sv.y / w;
        dZ += sv.z / w;
    } else {
        pScrnVert[v].x = 0;
        pScrnVert[v].y = 0;
    }
}
dZ /= nVert;

// See if hit point lies inside screen polygon
if (::_3dPointInPolygon(pScrnVert, nVert, pt)) {
    if (iHitFace < 0) {
        iHitFace = i;
        dHitZ = dZ;
```

```
        } else {
            if (dZ < dHitZ) {
                iHitFace = i;
                dHitZ = dZ;
            }
        }
    }

    // Release face when finished
    delete [] pScrnVert;
    pIFace->Release();
}

  ⋮

    // Set return value
    *piFace = iHitFace;

    return TRUE;
}
```

I've omitted some of the code for brevity and also because there's a part of the code I want to leave until later. You can follow the parts of the code that take the vertex values and convert them to the homogeneous vector. Let's pick up the story from there.

A homogeneous vector has values for x, y, z, and w. Why do we need all this information to represent a point in the window when just x and y will do? Because if a vertex gets very close to the camera position, the transform that maps world coordinates onto the viewing plane starts to approach a divide-by-zero condition, which, of course, is something we need to avoid. By using a homogeneous vector to represent the result, we can actually avoid the divide-by-zero condition. (Trust me—or dig out the reference texts if you want.) Given that we do have this homogeneous vector, we need to figure out the actual window coordinates by dividing the x, y, and z values in the homogeneous vector by the w value. If w is zero, we force the result to be the 0, 0 point. So why do we care about the z value? How can a point in the screen plane have a z value anyway? Well, it doesn't, but the z value is an indicator of the z-axis position of the face we projected onto the viewing plane. We need this information to resolve which one of the many possible faces contains the hit point that is frontmost.

As you can see, the code above goes on to test whether the hit point lies inside the polygon defined by the projected vertices and then tests to see if the current face is more forward than any other face we might have already found.

The test to determine whether the point lies inside the polygon took me a long time to get right. One way to test whether a point lies inside a polygon is to draw a line from the point to some other point inside the polygon and count how many times that line crosses the edge of the polygon. An odd number of crossings means the point is outside the polygon, as shown in Figure 7-4 on the next page.

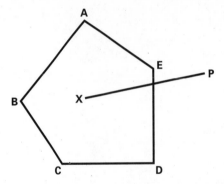

Figure 7-4. *Testing for a point inside a polygon.*

My initial approach was a little silly because I decided to implement the test code myself. I spent quite a few hours trying to make sure that every possible condition was covered, and I got quite close before sanity took over. I reasoned that this problem had been solved before, and therefore the code might be easily available. Indeed it is. I found the code I needed in the *Graphics Gems* series (Academic Press) and was just about to include it when I had yet another idea. Maybe this function already exists in Windows? After a quick search in the Microsoft Developer Library for "point in polygon," I found what I was looking for, and the final function to make the test, which is in 3dMath.cpp, came out like this:

```
BOOL _3dPointInPolygon(POINT* Points, int nPoints,
                       CPoint pt)
{
    HRGN hrgn = ::CreatePolygonRgn(Points, nPoints,
                                   WINDING);
    ASSERT(hrgn);
    BOOL b = ::PtInRegion(hrgn, pt.x, pt.y);
    ::DeleteObject(hrgn);
    return b;
}
```

I used the Windows GDI system to create a polygonal region and then used the *PtInRegion* function to complete the test. I learned a lesson from this exercise: just because I'm not using GDI functions for most of my current project doesn't mean I can't use them for some of it.

I ended up with a nice, compact solution. I didn't bother to evaluate the performance of the test because it's used only in response to a user event, and even a slow test isn't going to give you much response delay. If you wanted to do thousands of these tests, this technique might not be as good as many of the other published methods.

One final note: the face hit detection code I've implemented doesn't take into account which way the face is facing. What this means is that you could potentially get a hit on a face that is facing away from the user and consequently not visible. This will happen only if there is a visible face behind the invisible one—assuming that you got a valid object hit in the first place—because the viewport pick code doesn't return objects that have hits only on back faces.

The Select sample application uses the face hit value to color the faces red as they are hit. Also, the status bar shows the name of the selected object, the face number that was hit, and the coordinates of the hit point on the object. (We'll discuss how to retrieve the hit point coordinates in the next section.) This is done in the *MakeCurrent* function, shown here:

```
void CMainFrame::MakeCurrent(C3dShape* pShape)
{
    HideSelection();
    m_pCurShape = pShape;
    ShowSelection();
    if (m_pCurShape != NULL) {
        if (m_iHitFace >= 0) {
            Status("Selected: %s (%d @ %3.1f,%3.1f,%3.1f)",
                    m_pCurShape->GetName(),
                    m_iHitFace,
                    m_vHitPoint.x,
                    m_vHitPoint.y,
                    m_vHitPoint.z);
            m_pCurShape->SetFaceColor(m_iHitFace, 1, 0, 0);
        } else {
            Status("Selected: %s", m_pCurShape->GetName());
        }
    } else {
        Status("No selection");
    }
}
```

Finding the Point of Contact

Having successfully detected a hit on an object and which face of the object was hit, we can now add just a little more code to determine the actual coordinates of the point on the object that was hit, as shown in Figure 7-5 on the next page.

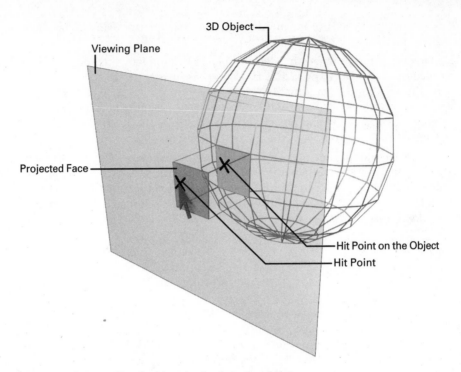

3D Object

Viewing Plane

Projected Face

Hit Point on the Object

Hit Point

Figure 7-5. *Projecting the hit point back to the object.*

What we need to do is to take the coordinates of the hit point on the screen and change them back to a homogeneous vector, then to world coordinates, then back to local coordinates on the object. Here's the final piece of the hit detection code in *C3dShape::HitTest*:

```
 ⋮
// Compute the point on face where hit occurred.
// Set up a vector to describe screen point.
// We'll use the average z value.
sv.x = pt.x;
sv.y = pt.y;
sv.z = dHitZ;
sv.w = 1.0;

// Convert to world coordinates
m_hr = pIViewport->InverseTransform(&wv, &sv);
ASSERT(SUCCEEDED(m_hr));

// Convert to local coordinates in frame
m_hr = m_pIFrame->InverseTransform(&lv, &wv);
ASSERT(SUCCEEDED(m_hr));

// Return result
*pvHit = lv;
 ⋮
```

This works fairly well, but in order to keep it simple I've used a bad approximation for the z value of the screen point. The value here is actually the average z value of all the vertices that define the projected face. This is wrong, as it doesn't account for where the exact hit occurred in the polygon. A better approach would be to do something like what's shown in Figure 7-6.

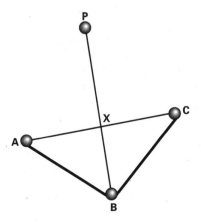

Figure 7-6. *Computing the z value at point P.*

In Figure 7-6 the points A, B, and C are three vertices of the face. Draw a line from A to C and another line from B to the hit point P. Use the ratio of the lengths of the AX and XC lines to compute the z value at X from the z values at A and C. Use the ratio of the lines PB and XB to compute the z value at P from the z values at B and X. I'll leave this as an exercise for you to do.

The Select sample includes a menu option to display the hit point on the object (View-Hit Point). The code for this, found at the end of the *CMainFrame-::ShowSelection* function, creates a cone and attaches the point of the cone to the hit point using the normal of the selected face to determine the orientation of the cone:

```
⋮
// Get hit point on shape and
// convert from local to world coordinates
C3dVector vh = m_pCurShape->Transform(m_vHitPoint);

// Get face normal
ASSERT(m_pCurShape);
C3dVector vn = m_pCurShape->GetFaceNormal(m_iHitFace);

// Alter length as needed, add it to hit
// point, and convert to world coordinates
C3dVector vx = vn * 0.5 + m_vHitPoint;
vx = m_pCurShape->Transform(vx);
```

(continued)

```
                    // Point to the hit point with cone
                    m_pHitPtr = new C3dShape;
                    m_pHitPtr->CreateCone(vh.x, vh.y, vh.z, 0, FALSE,
                                          vx.x, vx.y, vx.z, 0.1, TRUE);

                    // Attach cone to the shape
                    m_pCurShape->AddChild(m_pHitPtr);
                    }
            }
```

To place the cone correctly, the local object coordinates need to be converted to world coordinates. Figure 7-7 shows a screen shot of the cone in use. (You can see the cone pointing to a selected sphere in the color insert.)

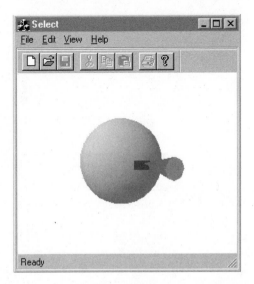

Figure 7-7. *Showing the hit point on an object.*

To illustrate the inaccuracy of the hit point position created by using the average *z* value, try selecting a face on the side of a cone-shaped object. You'll see that the tip of the cone that indicates the hit point is either just off the selected face or just inside it, instead of coinciding exactly with it.

Putting Hit Testing to Work

As an illustration of what you might do with the hit detection code, I created the Blobs sample, which allows you to create some stunningly exciting space creatures, as you can see in Figure 7-8. (Turn to the color insert to get a better look at the Blobs sample.)

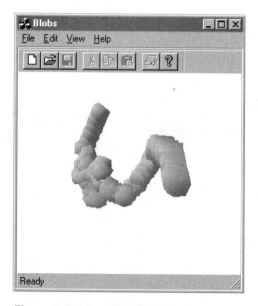

Figure 7-8. *The Blobs application.*

This application adds a new blob to the object at the point you click. The blobs are actually spheres created using four bands, which gives a sphere with only a few faces that is still kind of spherical. The application was created by taking the Select sample, removing all the superfluous menu items, and modifying the hit notification code to add the new blobs. Here's the modified notification function:

```
void CMainFrame::OnSelChange(C3dShape* pShape, CPoint pt,
                             void* pArg)
{
    // Get pointer to the class
    CMainFrame* pThis = (CMainFrame*) pArg;
    ASSERT(pThis);
    ASSERT(pThis->IsKindOf(RUNTIME_CLASS(CMainFrame)));

    if (pShape) {

        // Find which face was hit
        C3dViewport* pViewport =
            pThis->m_wnd3d.GetStage()->GetViewport();
        int iFace;
        C3dVector vHit;
        if (pShape->HitTest(pt, pViewport, &iFace, &vHit)) {
            pThis->AddBlob(pShape, vHit);
        }
    }
}
```

As you can see, the point of contact is found and the *AddBlob* function is called to modify the shape that was hit:

```
void CMainFrame::AddBlob(C3dShape* pShape, C3dVector& vHit)
{
    // Get hit point on shape and
    // convert from local to world coordinates
    ASSERT(pShape);
    C3dVector vh = pShape->Transform(vHit);

    // Create a blob to add
    C3dShape* pBlob = new C3dShape;
    pBlob->CreateSphere(0.5, 4);

    // Center it on hit point
    pBlob->SetPosition(vh);

    // Attach it to shape
    pShape->AddChild(pBlob);

    // Keep track of new blob so we can hit test it
    m_pScene->m_ShapeList.Append(pBlob);
}
```

The point of contact on the shape that was hit is converted to world coordinates. A new blob is created, set in position, and added to the shape. The new object (the blob) is added to the shape list so that it will be destroyed when the scene is destroyed. Remember that we need to keep the C++ object around for the hit test logic to work.

Here's an exercise for you. Look at the *AddBlob* function above. Do we need to convert the hit point on the object to world coordinates? Is there a way to achieve the same functionality without doing this conversion? Try modifying the code to see if your solution works.

Summary

We've learned how to select an object with a mouse click in the window, how to determine the face of the object that was hit, and also how to find the point on the object that was hit. Now we have all the tools required to select and modify 3D objects.

Let me again suggest that if you didn't follow how this code works, fire up the debugger and trace the mouse event processing.

ow that we have created a variety of shapes and added the ability to select them and move them around, we can add some color and texture for a bit more realism. In this chapter we're going to look at using color with our shapes, loading images for use as backgrounds, and applying texture maps to objects. The main sample for this chapter can be found in the Color directory. Because this chapter is about color but the diagrams are in beautiful shades of gray, you really need to run the Color sample to see the true results.

Color

Having an entire section dedicated to color is perhaps a bit extravagant, but we need to start this discussion somewhere, and setting an object's color is about as basic as it gets. As you recall from Chapter 1, a color consists of red, green, and blue components and the values of each component can vary from zero to unity (one). Each time we set a color value we're going to use a set of RGB values specified as floating-point fractional values. For example, red is specified as 1.0, 0.0, 0.0. Blue is 0.0, 0.0, 1.0, and so on. Because the compiler will blithely cast an integer constant to a double, you'll occasionally see some colors specified like this: 1, 0, 0 (red). Just remember that they are always fractional values.

NOTE

Windows programmers might well groan at having yet another way to specify colors, and I did consider using a C++ class with several constructors to make using colors a bit easier. In the end, though, I thought this just added complexity and didn't really help all that much. So I'm afraid that if you're accustomed to red being 255, 0, 0, then you're going to have to get used to dividing your color component values by 255 to use them here.

The simplest thing we can do with color is to apply one color to an entire object. Let's leap right in and see how we do that. The Color sample includes a Color option in its Edit menu, which displays the standard Microsoft Windows Color dialog box from which you can choose the color you want applied to the currently selected object:

```
void CMainFrame::OnEditColor()
{
    ASSERT(m_pCurShape);
    CColorDialog dlg;
```

```
if (dlg.DoModal() != IDOK) return;
m_pCurShape->SetColor(GetRValue(dlg.m_cc.rgbResult) /
                      255.0,
                      GetGValue(dlg.m_cc.rgbResult) /
                      255.0,
                      GetBValue(dlg.m_cc.rgbResult) /
                      255.0);
}
```

The Color dialog box returns the chosen color in a *COLORREF* structure (*rgbResult*). The Windows macros *GetRValue*, *GetGValue*, and *GetBValue* extract the individual red, green, and blue components, which are then converted to floating-point values in the range 0.0 through 1.0. The *C3dShape::SetColor* function completes the job:

```
BOOL C3dShape::SetColor(double r, double g, double b)
{
    ASSERT(m_pIMeshBld);
    m_hr = m_pIMeshBld->SetColorRGB(r, g, b);
    return SUCCEEDED(m_hr);
}
```

As you can see, this is all no big deal. The mesh builder interface supports a *SetColorRGB* function that really does the work. If you look through the DirectX 2 SDK documentation, you'll see that the mesh builder interface also supports a *SetColor* function that takes a *D3DCOLOR* structure argument. I didn't provide any way to use this structure in the *C3dShape* class, but it would be trivial to add one should you feel the need for it. If you're into color in a big way, you might also want to derive a C++ class from *D3DCOLOR* in much the same way I created the *C3dVector* class from the *D3DVECTOR* structure. Your class could then support conversion from *COLORREF* values, addition, and so on.

Let's do something a bit more interesting with color and randomly color the faces of an object. (See Figure 8-1 on the next page, and the Randomly Colored Airplane in the color insert.) Why? I found it interesting to load an object generated originally in 3D Studio and see how the faces were constructed. Random coloring shows up the face patterns nicely. The *C3dShape* class supports the *SetFaceColor* function that applies a color to a given face, which makes it simple to randomly color the entire object:

```
void CMainFrame::OnEditRandcolor()
{
    ASSERT(m_pCurShape);
    int iFaces = m_pCurShape->GetFaceCount();
    for (int i = 0; i < iFaces; i++) {
        m_pCurShape->SetFaceColor(i,
                                  (rand() % 100) / 100.0,
                                  (rand() % 100) / 100.0,
                                  (rand() % 100) / 100.0);
    }
}
```

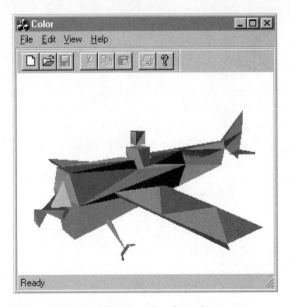

Figure 8-1. *A randomly colored airplane.*

Using Frame Colors

You might think that we've exhausted all the possibilities for using color, but there's one technique left to show you, which although simple is actually quite important. When we were looking at creating our own shapes in Chapter 4, I told you that the visual element of a shape could be attached to several frames, which in effect clones the shape of the object with minimal overhead. This technique is useful if we want 97 objects that all have the same color, but what if we want many objects of the same shape but different colors?

Our method so far has applied color to the mesh of an object. We can also apply a color to the frame that contains the visual of an object. We then tell the frame that when that visual is rendered, its color should be taken from the frame rather than from the mesh. As we'll see later in this chapter, this technique can also be used to apply different textures to clones of a common shape by applying the texture to the frame rather than to the visual element of the object.

The *C3dShape::SetFrameColor* function is used to apply a color to the shape's frame. You also need to enable the frame color by calling *C3dFrame::SetMaterial-Mode(D3DRMMATERIAL_FROMFRAME)*. The Color sample includes a demonstration of this function that creates a red sphere and then clones it to create several other spheres of different colors (Edit-Color from Frame). Here's a part of that code that creates the red sphere and the first clone:

```
void CMainFrame::OnEditClrframe()
{
    // Create a sphere for first shape
    C3dShape* pShape = new C3dShape;
```

```
pShape->CreateSphere(1);
pShape->SetColor(1, 0, 0); // Red
m_pScene->AddChild(pShape);
m_pScene->m_ShapeList.Append(pShape);
MakeCurrent(pShape);
pShape->SetName("Red master");

// Create clone
C3dShape* pClone1 = m_pCurShape->Clone();
m_pScene->m_ShapeList.Append(pClone1);
m_pScene->AddChild(pClone1);
pClone1->SetPosition(-2, 0, 0);

// Set color of clone's frame
pClone1->SetMaterialMode(D3DRMMATERIAL_FROMFRAME);
pClone1->SetFrameColor(0, 1, 0); // Green
pClone1->SetName("Green clone");
    ⋮
}
```

Setting the color of the cloned object is simply a matter of applying the color to the cloned object's frame instead of its visual and calling the *SetMaterialMode* function with the *D3DRMMATERIAL_FROMFRAME* option.

Material Properties

Different materials reflect light in different ways. Plastic surfaces tend to reflect light dully, whereas shiny metallic surfaces reflect light more sharply. The rendering engine we're using doesn't actually generate reflections, but it does render objects in a way that takes into account an object's reflective properties.

For example, let's say that we want to show a billiard ball, which has a hard, polished surface that is highly reflective. The reflected light rays don't get scattered very much because the surface of the ball is smooth. If we place the billiard ball on a table with a light above it, we see a distinct highlight on the ball from the light. A closer examination reveals that the reflection of highest intensity is actually the color of the light, not the color of the ball.

This phenomenon occurs because there are two kinds of reflected light: *diffuse* and *specular*. Diffuse reflections are what we see from an object that give the object its own natural color. Specular reflections come from shiny surfaces and show the color of the illumination. So a red billiard ball illuminated by a white light gives off red diffuse reflections and a white specular reflection.

Specular reflections vary according to how shiny the surface is. For a very shiny surface, the specular reflection occurs over a small angle, resulting in a small, sharp highlight on the object. For a less shiny object like a balloon, for example, the specular reflection occurs over a larger area and gives a duller reflection.

To make an object look shinier, we can narrow the angle of specular reflection; to make it look more plastic, we can widen the angle. In practice, we don't actually specify an angle. Instead we specify a power to which the cosine of the angle is to be raised in computing the intensity of the reflected ray as the angle increases. In short, a low number (like 5) gives a plastic-looking surface and a high number (like 300) gives a metallic-looking surface.

A small number of surfaces (colored metals, for example) have specular reflections that are not the color of the light source but the color of the material instead. If you look at a polished gold ring under a bright light, you'll see that the highlights are gold in color rather than the white of the light source.

Some surfaces also give off, or emit, light. An example of such a surface would be the frosted glass of a light bulb or the phosphor of a cathode-ray tube. Because these surfaces also reflect light, their behavior is quite complex.

We can specify how a material will be rendered and affect to some degree how shiny it looks and whether it appears to emit light. The *IDirect3DRMMaterial* interface defines three methods that determine the properties of a material: the color it emits (if any), its specular reflection color, and the power factor for the specular reflection equation.

I'm sure that you either understand this fully or are feeling just a bit confused. In case it's the latter, let's look at an example. Figure 8-2 shows some spheres created using different specular power and emissive light material properties, but it's quite hard to see the differences on paper so I suggest you look at these more closely on your computer. (Also check out the color version of this figure in the color insert.) Run the Color sample, and choose Materials from the Edit menu.

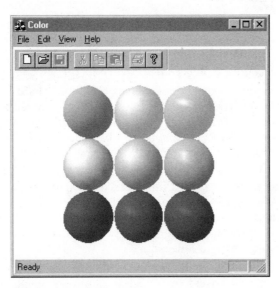

Figure 8-2. *Different material properties.*

In the top row, the ball at the left is created using the default material properties. The ball in the center has been configured to emit red light so it appears to glow. The ball on the right is also emitting red light but has a higher specular power

3D GRAPHICS PROGRAMMING FOR WINDOWS 95

value (400), which gives the surface a more metallic look. The balls in the middle row are all white but with specular powers of 3, 10, and 50. The bottom row of balls are all red and have specular power values of 100, 500, and 2000.

To make manipulating the material properties a little easier, I created the *C3dMaterial* class:

```
class C3dMaterial : public C3dObject
{
public:
    DECLARE_DYNAMIC(C3dMaterial);
    C3dMaterial();
    virtual ~C3dMaterial();
    void SetEmissiveColor(double r, double g, double b);
    void SetSpecularPower(double p);
    void SetSpecularColor(double r, double g, double b);
    IDirect3DRMMaterial* GetInterface() {return m_pIMat;}

protected:
    IDirect3DRMMaterial* m_pIMat;
};
```

Below is a part of the code that created the red ball in the middle of the bottom row in Figure 8-2. You can see how the *C3dMaterial* class is typically used:

```
void CMainFrame::OnEditMaterials()
{
    ⋮
    pShape = new C3dShape;
    pShape->CreateSphere(1);
    pShape->SetName("Specular power 500");
    m_pScene->AddChild(pShape);
    m_pScene->m_ShapeList.Append(pShape);
    pShape->SetPosition(0, -2, 0);
    pShape->SetColor(1, 0, 0);
    C3dMaterial m7;
    m7.SetSpecularPower(500);
    pShape->SetMaterial(&m7);
    ⋮
```

Images

Let's leap forward a bit from simple colors and look at images that can be used in several ways. We're going to use them now for backgrounds to a scene and, later, as the basis for texture maps. At the time of writing, the Direct3D functions handled images only in the Public Pixel Map (PPM) format, so I created a *C3dImage* class that loads Windows bitmaps from either a disk file or a bitmap resource in your application. This makes experimenting with images easier because every Windows system has at least one tool for creating bitmaps.

Windows bitmaps can be created in a wide variety of formats. All of the sample images included with this book on the companion CD are 8 bits per pixel, which means that they have a maximum of 256 colors. In practice, the number of colors on a 256-color display is limited to fewer than that. Let's look at why by considering what happens when an image is used to texture map a surface.

Let's say one pixel of the image in the texture map is green. When the surface is rendered, that green pixel may need to be drawn in one of many different shades of green according to how the surface is lit. In other words, for every color that you include in your image, the rendering engine needs to create several shades of that color. If your video hardware has no practical color limit (you have a 24-bit-per-pixel display, for example), you have no worries. If, however, you want to run your application on a 256-color screen, you must give some consideration to how the colors in the palette will be split up. If your images have many colors, a lot of palette entries get taken trying to render them. To ensure the best overall effect, you should experiment with color usage before you tell the art department to create thousands of bitmaps.

The default number of colors used to render a texture map is eight and the default number of shades used for each color is 16. The short story is that you should try to create a decent looking background image using only eight colors.

The simplest use of an image is to provide the background for a scene. The Color sample includes a menu item (Edit-Background Image) that allows you to load any bitmap image for use as a background to the current scene. The code is very simple:

```
void CMainFrame::OnEditBkgndImg()
{
    C3dImage* pImg = new C3dImage;
    if (!pImg->Load()) {
        delete pImg;
        return;
    }

    ASSERT(m_pScene);
    m_pScene->m_ImgList.Append(pImg);
    m_pScene->SetBackground(pImg);
}
```

A new *C3dImage* object is created and its *Load* member function called with no arguments. The *Load* function displays a File Open dialog box with the filter set to show only BMP files. Once the user has selected a file and clicked the OK button, the image file is opened and loaded into memory. The image data is stored in the *C3dImage* C++ object using the *D3DRMIMAGE* structure that the rendering engine uses for image manipulation.

Once the image has been loaded, it is added to the scene's image list and then added to the scene as the current background image.

NOTE

It's very important that you don't delete an image while it's still in use. The *D3DRMIMAGE* structure is not a COM object and has no reference count associated with it, so it's up to you to keep track of the images you have loaded. If you use the *C3dImage* class, then you can keep track of your *C3dImage* objects by adding them to the image list in the scene. This way, your images are kept alive until the scene is deleted. This warning also applies to texture maps, which are just another variant of an image.

If you run the Color sample and set a background image, you will notice that the background image is stretched to fit the scene so its aspect ratio varies according to the shape of the application's window.

In implementing the *C3dScene::SetBackground* function, I have cheated a little bit perhaps. The rendering engine actually requires a texture map for the background image, but I felt that it was more logical to supply just an image. I arranged the implementation so that you can supply an image object and the texture map gets created for you. Figure 8-3 shows an example of a simple scene that contains only one object, a tank, and a background image—the front lawn of my house. A background image makes a lot of difference to a scene.

Figure 8-3. *A tank drawn against a background image.*

Texture Maps

I think that texture maps are one of the most interesting elements to play with in the 3D world. A good texture map can transform a boring shape into a more lively object. For example, a texture map can transform a cone into a fir tree or a sphere into a planet. Of course, it's a bit more complicated than perhaps that makes it sound—but a bit of enthusiasm never hurt anyone.

A texture map is really just a bitmap image that is stretched to fit over a surface to color it in a specific way. The texture map doesn't actually alter the coordinates of the surface to make it rougher, but paints the surface—much in the same way that flats are painted in the theater to give an illusion of paneling, windows, doors, and so on in a set for a room. It is possible to alter a surface by physically adding lumps or depressions, which can be done on some systems with a bump map. Because we don't have bump map capabilities, we'll rely on the artwork for our texture maps to give the effects we want.

The image used to create a texture map needs to have some specific attributes. The most important of these attributes are the image's dimensions. The length of the sides of the image must be integral powers of two. So images that are 32 by 32, 128 by 256, or 4 by 4, for example, are all valid sizes for a texture map image. An image of, say, 320 by 240 pixels can't be used as a texture map. This restriction is imposed to help with rendering performance. Of course, the rendering engine *could* take any size image and stretch its sides to conform to the power of two rule, but the designers of the rendering engine thought that you'd rather do that yourself to retain as much control over the final image quality as possible.

While I'm on the subject of quality, I want to remind you that if your application is to run on machines with 256-color displays (which are still the most popular), you need to limit the number of colors used in your texture maps to as few as possible. As I explained in the "Images" section on page 171, I try to create mine with as few as eight colors, which is the default maximum number of colors for a texture map. This gives the rendering engine more flexibility in how it uses the system palette to represent all the shades it needs to render an entire scene. Of course, many objects have similar colors, and this helps to reduce the overall requirements. Since there are no hard and fast rules for how you decide how many colors you need for a given texture map or image, I suggest you invest some time in experimenting with different amounts of color before committing to the creation of any final artwork.

The rendering engine includes functions to limit the number of shades that the rendering device will use (default 32) and also to limit the number of shades a texture will use (default 16). Of course, if all your users have 24-bit-per-pixel displays, you don't need to worry about any of these issues because the renderer can generate all the shades it needs. If you want, you can change the default number of colors used per texture and the number of shades per color that the rendering engine will create, by calling *C3dTexture::SetColors* and *C3dTexture::SetShades*.

Applying Texture Maps

Nothing in the computing world is simple. (Take OLE, for example. Now there's a job preservation system if ever I saw one.) Fortunately, texture maps are not quite as nasty to use as adding OLE support to an application, but they do require a bit of work.

Texture maps can be applied to the surfaces of an object in four different ways. Each way involves a different math routine that determines how the image will be wrapped around the object's surfaces. In the simplest case, the flat wrap, the texture map is more or less stretched to fit. The more complex techniques, cylindrical, spherical, and chrome wraps, involve effectively bending the texture image around the object. We're going to look now at each of these four ways of wrapping a texture map around an object.

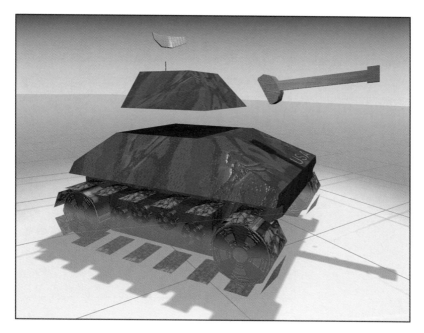

The Tank

You can use frame hierarchies to attach the separate objects to the scene and to each other. See Chapter 1 for more details on frame hierarchies and Chapter 6 for details on the tank.

A Sprite

The monster in this scene is a sprite rendered from a single bitmap that contains all the possible states the sprite can be viewed in. Refer to Chapter 9 to find out more about sprites and how this scene was created.

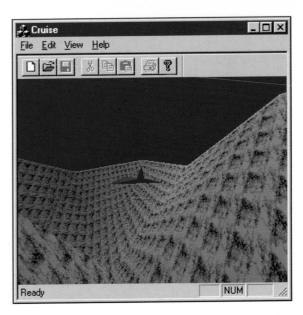

Cruise

An example of moving an object, this airplane flies through the scene on a fixed path without any user interaction. See Chapter 6 for details on how to move an object along a fixed path.

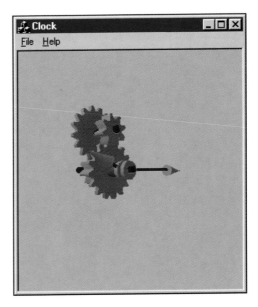

A Clock

A good example of relative motion, the gears of a clock must work together for the hands to move correctly. All the objects in this scene are in constant motion relative to one another. How to move objects is discussed in Chapter 6.

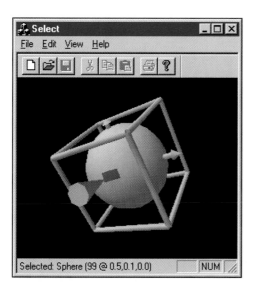

Hit Testing

Chapter 7 covers how to select an object in a scene and to figure out exactly what point on a 3D object has been selected. This figure shows a sphere that has been selected; the red rectangle indicates exactly which area on the sphere was hit.

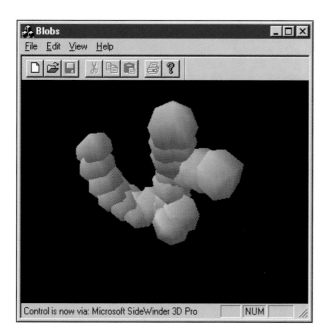

Blobs

You can create fascinating creatures using hit testing. Click on an existing blob and a new blob will be attached at the hit position. See Chapter 7 for details.

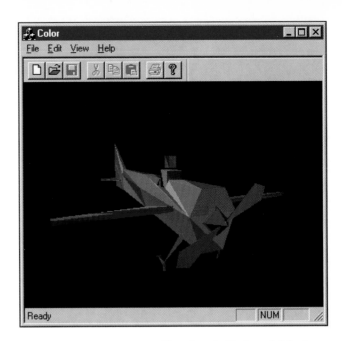

Randomly Colored Airplane

Chapter 8 explores the many uses of color. Here an airplane object has been inserted into the scene. Random colors were then applied to show the airplane's many faces.

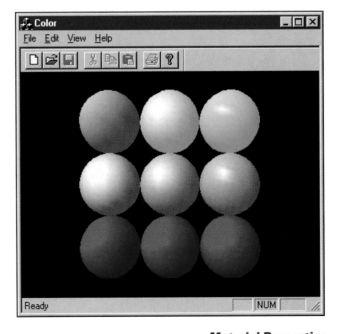

Material Properties

Different materials have different reflective qualities, which affects the color of an object. These spheres were created using different specular power and emissive light material properties. For a description of the properties of each sphere, read about material properties in Chapter 8.

Texture Mapping

Cylindrical texture wraps have been applied to the tree and to the trunk to make the tree appear more realistic. Texture mapping is discussed in Chapter 8.

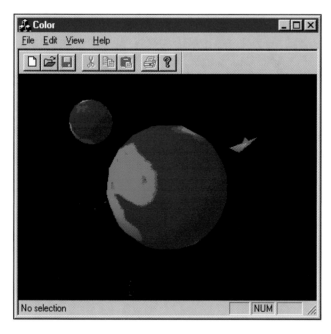

Worlds

You can also apply texture mapping as a spherical wrap. Here a flat map of the world has been wrapped around spheres to create globes. See Chapter 8 to find out what the map looks like flat.

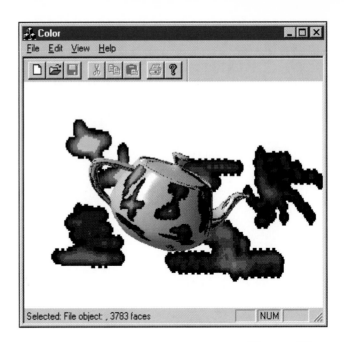

Chrome Wrap

When a shape, such as this teapot, needs to appear to have a very reflective surface, you can wrap a texture map around the object to give the illusion of a reflection. This map must change as the shape moves. This type of wrap is called a chrome wrap and is discussed in Chapter 8.

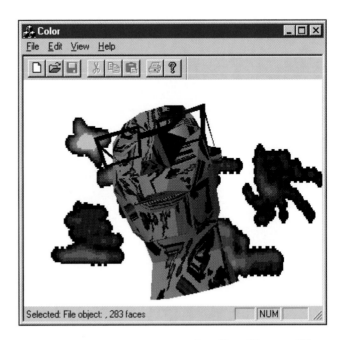

Another Chrome Wrap

You can apply a chrome wrap to any object, so even a face can be reflective! See Chapter 8 for more details.

A Spot Light

You can choose from numerous types of lighting and use them together or individually to produce different effects. The effect here was produced by a spot light. Chapter 10 discusses lighting.

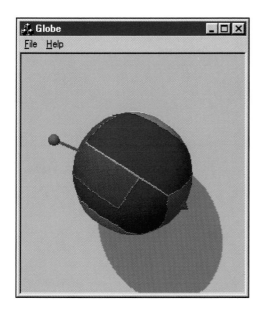

A Globe

In reality, shining light on an object produces a shadow. To learn how to make shadows like the one shown here, see Chapter 10.

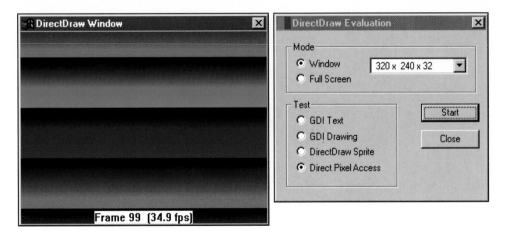

DirectDraw Interface

Chapter 12 discusses the DDEval sample application, shown running here. This application demonstrates how DirectDraw works and how to use it.

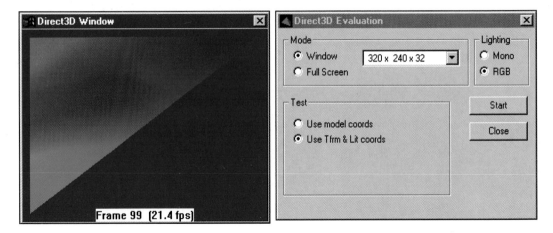

Direct3D Interface

Chapter 13 discusses the D3DEval application, shown running here, which is designed to test the functions and capabilities of Direct3D Immediate Mode.

Flat Wraps

The simplest way to apply a texture map to a surface is with a *flat wrap*. It probably shouldn't be called a *wrap* at all because it doesn't really wrap anything—it's more like draping a colored cloth over the surface. We'll begin with the most trivial example, which is to apply a texture map to a single-faced object, using a flat wrap. The Color sample includes a menu option (Edit-Insert Tex Map Face) to insert a texture-mapped face as shown in Figure 8-4.

Figure 8-4. *A texture map applied to a single face that has been rotated.*

The face in Figure 8-4 has been rotated about the *y*-axis, and you can see that the texture map looks just like an angled view of a photograph. The texture map actually has a perspective correction applied to it to get this result. What you see in Figure 8-4 is not the default behavior for the rendering engine but the behavior I think most useful so the 3dPlus library configures the engine to apply the perspective correction. However, I'm getting a bit ahead of myself here, so let's look first at the code used to generate the object in Figure 8-4 and then we can see what all the fuss is about with perspective correction. Here's the code that created the single-faced object:

```
void CMainFrame::OnEditInstxface()
{
    // Create a shape with only one face, and apply
    // a texture map to face
    C3dShape* pShape = new C3dShape();

    D3DVECTOR vlist[] = {
        {-1.0, -1.0,  0.0},
        { 1.0, -1.0,  0.0},
```

(continued)

```
                { 1.0,  1.0,  0.0},
                {-1.0,  1.0,  0.0}
        };
        int iVectors = sizeof(vlist) / sizeof(D3DVECTOR);
        int iFaces[] = {4, 0, 3, 2, 1,  // Front face
                        4, 0, 1, 2, 3,  // Back face
                        0};

        pShape->Create(vlist, iVectors, iFaces);

        // Color the back face so we can identify it
        pShape->SetFaceColor(1, 0, 0, 1); // Blue

        // Load texture
        C3dTexture* pTex = new C3dTexture;
        if (!pTex->Load(IDB_G1)) {
            return;
        }
        m_pScene->m_ImgList.Append(pTex);

        // Attach texture to front face
        pShape->SetFaceTexture(0, pTex);

        // Create a wrap.
        // The face is 2x2 units, so we scale the texture
        // to fit exactly once. We also invert the texture so
        // the texture map image appears the right way up.
        C3dWrap wrap;
        wrap.Create(D3DRMWRAP_FLAT,
                NULL,
                -1, -1, 0,  // Origin
                0, 0, 1,    // Direction
                0, 1, 0,    // Up
                0, pTex->GetHeight()-1,    // Texture origin
                0.5, -0.5);    // Texture scale (invert)

        // Apply wrap to front face
        wrap.Apply(pShape, 0);

        pShape->SetName("Face");
        m_pScene->AddChild(pShape);
        m_pScene->m_ShapeList.Append(pShape);
        MakeCurrent(pShape);

    }
```

This code might look like a lot of work for just one face, but it's really not so bad if you take it one step at a time. The first task is to create the object itself. I created a vertex list and a face list and then used *C3dShape::Create* to construct the object. I deliberately created the object with two faces so that if you turn the object around you can still see it. The back face is colored blue.

The texture map for the front face is loaded into a new *C3dTexture* object from a bitmap resource in the application. I added the texture map bitmap to the application just like I would any other bitmap resource using AppStudio in Microsoft Visual C++. Because all texture maps must be kept in memory while they are in use, the C++ object that encapsulates the texture map is added to the scene's image list so it won't be destroyed until the scene is destroyed. The texture map is then attached to the required face of the object by calling *C3dShape::SetFaceTexture*.

Simply adding the texture to the object's face isn't enough, however. We also need to create a wrap object that will control how the texture is rendered to the face. A *C3dWrap* object is created using the option to create a flat wrap, D3DRM-WRAP_FLAT. This wrap is then applied to the front face of the object by calling *C3dWrap::Apply* and providing both the wrap and the face number to apply it to. The object is rendered with the texture map stretched to fit the specified face.

Perhaps you've noticed that I sneakily avoided mentioning most of the 15 parameters needed to create the wrap. Let's look at what those parameters do now.

WRAP PARAMETERS

Figure 8-5 shows a texture map being applied to a face using a flat wrap.

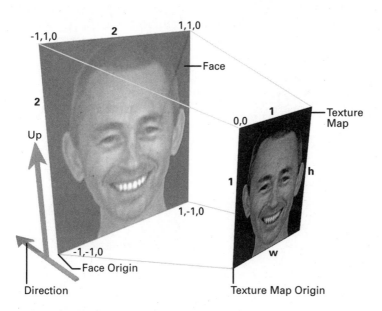

Figure 8-5. *Mapping a texture map to a face.*

Looking at Figure 8-5, let's examine the parameters required to create a wrap. The first item to define, in the third through fifth parameters, is the origin of the wrap on the face. In Figure 8-5, it's the point –1,–1,0. The next two sets of parameters contain a direction vector and an up vector to determine the orientation of the wrap with respect to the face. The direction vector controls the direction in which the texture is moved to cover the object, and the up vector rotates the texture map into a particular direction. Next we need to set the origin of the texture map. You can see that, in Figure 8-5, the texture map origin has been set to the lower left corner of the image. (The image origin is at the upper left.) The last two parameters are the scale factors for the x- and y-axes. To determine these, the texture map is considered to be one unit by one unit. Because the face is actually two units by two units, we need to scale the texture map to fit, and a factor of 0.5 provides the correct scale factor in this case. Note that because we set the origin of the texture map to be the bottom of the image, we need to set the y-axis scale factor as negative. I used the origin and scale this way to make the image come out the right way up on the face.

It might seem to you that there are a lot of parameters to set up, and while this is true, none of them are redundant. Imagine trying to wrap a picture of the front of a house over an object the same shape as the house. You'd want to be pretty sure that the front door image mapped exactly onto the front door of the shape and that the chimney was on the roof, not on the side of the house. To be able to control the map to this degree, you need a lot of parameters.

The direction vector is probably the hardest parameter to understand. Consider this parameter as the direction the texture map needs to be moved to drape it over the face. I found that setting up these wrap parameters was quite hard initially. I experimented a lot to convince myself that I understood what was going on, which paid off when I started using the more complex wraps we'll see shortly.

PERSPECTIVE CORRECTION

Let's return to the issue of perspective correction, which I mentioned earlier on page 175. Consider a texture map that consists of a black cross centered on a white square. Let's see how this texture map gets applied to a square face that is at some angle to the camera. Figure 8-6 shows the problem.

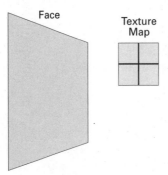

Figure 8-6. *A square texture map being applied to a square face that is at an angle to the camera.*

In order to render the texture map to the face, the face and the map are divided into triangles, as shown in Figure 8-7.

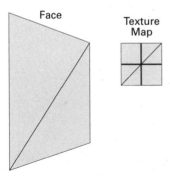

Face   Texture Map

Figure 8-7. *The face and texture map divided into triangles for rendering.*

Now we copy the triangles from the map to the face, interpolating linearly as we go. When the mapping is complete, the ends of the cross that lie at the center of the edges of the texture map will lie at the center of the edges of the face, as shown in Figure 8-8.

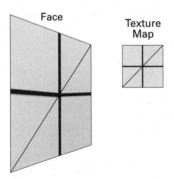

Face   Texture Map

Figure 8-8. *The face mapped without perspective correction.*

As you can see, the face looks as if it has been bent along the dividing line formed by the common edge of the two triangles. To avoid this problem, the algorithm that maps the texture to the surface needs to perform a division to compute the correct position instead of using a simple linear interpolation technique. Obviously, the extra division slows things down, but that's the price you pay for realism.

The perspective correction is applied by calling the *SetPerspective* function in the mesh builder interface. This is done every time you use the *C3dShape::Create* function or one of the other shape creation functions that call *C3dShape::Create*. So if you're using the *C3dShape* class, the perspective correction is already turned on for you.

APPLYING DIFFERENT TEXTURES TO ADJACENT FACES

Having worked out how to apply a texture to a single face, my next project was to build a picture cube—a cube with a different picture on each side. I used *C3d-Shape::CreateCuboid* to create the shape, loaded six different texture maps, and applied them all with a single flat wrap. This technique created two sides with reasonable pictures, but the other four were just streaky lines.

"Me, me, please sir, I know, pick me."

"Yes, Molesworth?"

"Sir, you need to use different wraps for the different directions, sir."

"Good try, Molesworth. See me after class."

Well, that's what I thought too, so I dutifully created some more wraps with different direction vectors and tried again. It still didn't work. This really confused me. I thought I had this stuff down and had to resort to sending e-mail to the rendering engine folks to find out what was going wrong. I learned that texture map wrap information is stored on a per-vertex basis, not per-face. This means that each time I thought I was applying a texture wrap to a face, the rendering engine was actually applying it to the *vertices* of the face. Therefore each vertex received the information for the texture wrap, and when I inadvertently applied a different texture wrap to that same vertex by trying to apply it to an adjacent face, it overwrote the existing wrap and "disfigured" the previous face. The result is that the last face to get wrapped has the right information but the other faces adjacent to that face get messed up.

The solution is to create a cube that consists of six faces with no common vertices. The texture maps can then be applied to the faces, and I get the result I want, which you can see in the Color sample by selecting Insert Picture Cube from the Edit menu. Here's the code I used to create the picture cube:

```
void CMainFrame::OnEditPiccube()
{
    // Create a 2-unit cube with separate faces
    double s = 2;

    C3dShape* pShape = new C3dShape;

    D3DVECTOR vlist[] = {
        {-1.0, -1.0,  -1.0},
        { 1.0, -1.0,  -1.0},
        { 1.0, -1.0,   1.0},
        {-1.0, -1.0,   1.0}, // Bottom

        {-1.0,  1.0,  -1.0},
        { 1.0,  1.0,  -1.0},
        { 1.0,  1.0,   1.0},
        {-1.0,  1.0,   1.0}, // Top

        {-1.0, -1.0,  -1.0},
        {-1.0,  1.0,  -1.0},
```

```
           {-1.0,  1.0,   1.0},
           {-1.0, -1.0,   1.0}, // Left

           { 1.0, -1.0,  -1.0},
           { 1.0,  1.0,  -1.0},
           { 1.0,  1.0,   1.0},
           { 1.0, -1.0,   1.0}, // Right

           {-1.0, -1.0,  -1.0},
           {-1.0,  1.0,  -1.0},
           { 1.0,  1.0,  -1.0},
           { 1.0, -1.0,  -1.0}, // Front

           {-1.0, -1.0,   1.0},
           {-1.0,  1.0,   1.0},
           { 1.0,  1.0,   1.0},
           { 1.0, -1.0,   1.0}  // Back

};
int iVectors = sizeof(vlist) / sizeof(D3DVECTOR);
int iFaces[] = {4, 0, 1, 2, 3,
                4, 4, 7, 6, 5,
                4, 8, 11, 10, 9,
                4, 12, 13, 14, 15,
                4, 16, 17, 18, 19,
                4, 20, 23, 22, 21,
                0};

pShape->Create(vlist, iVectors, iFaces);

for (int i = 0; i < 6; i++) {

    // Load texture map
    char buf[64];
    sprintf(buf, "g%d.bmp", i+1);
    C3dTexture* pTex = new C3dTexture;
    m_pScene->m_ImgList.Append(pTex);
    if (pTex->Load(IDB_G1+i)) {

        // Attach texture to face
        pShape->SetFaceTexture(i, pTex);

        // Get face normal
        C3dVector vn = pShape->GetFaceNormal(i);

        // Reverse face normal so it represents the wrap
        // direction
        vn = -vn;
```

(continued)

```
            // Compute an arbitrary up vector
            C3dVector vu = vn.GenerateUp();

            // Create a wrap oriented to this face
            C3dWrap wrap;
            wrap.Create(D3DRMWRAP_FLAT,
                        NULL,
                        -s/2, -s/2, -s/2, // Origin
                        vn.x, vn.y, vn.z, // Direction
                        vu.x, vu.y, vu.z, // Up
                        // Texture origin
                        0, pTex->GetHeight()-1,
                        // Texture scale (invert)
                        1.0/s, -1.0/s);

            // Apply wrap to face
            wrap.Apply(pShape, i);
        }
    }

    pShape->SetName("Picture cube");
    m_pScene->AddChild(pShape);
    m_pScene->m_ShapeList.Append(pShape);
    MakeCurrent(pShape);
}
```

Cylindrical Wraps

Let's look now at a different kind of wrap, used to wrap a texture map around an object cylindrically. Figure 8-9 shows an example of applying a cylindrical wrap to an object.

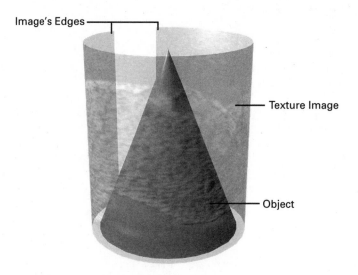

Figure 8-9. *A cylindrical wrap.*

The texture map image is bent around to form a cylinder, which is then projected onto the object. I found this technique a very good way to make the leaves and trunks of my trees look more realistic. Figure 8-10 shows the results of applying textures using cylindrical wraps. You can view this on screen by running the Color sample and selecting Insert A Tree from the Edit menu. (Also see the color insert for another view.)

The code for the tree isn't much different from the code that we used to map a single face, except that the tree consists of two objects instead of one and the wrap is cylindrical instead of flat.

Figure 8-10. *Cylindrical wrapping of textures.*

```
void CMainFrame::OnEditTree()
{
    // Load texture maps
    C3dTexture* pTex1 = new C3dTexture;
    pTex1->Load(IDB_LEAVES);
    m_pScene->m_ImgList.Append(pTex1);
    C3dTexture* pTex2 = new C3dTexture;
    pTex2->Load(IDB_BARK);
    m_pScene->m_ImgList.Append(pTex2);

    // Create cylindrical wrap
    C3dWrap wrap;
    wrap.Create(D3DRMWRAP_CYLINDER,
            NULL,
            0, 0, 0, // Origin
            0, 0, 1, // Direction
            0, 1, 0, // Up
            0, 0,    // Texture origin
            1, 1);   // Texture scale
```

(continued)

```
// Create tree and its trunk
double h = (rand() % 100) / 50.0 + 1.0;
double x = ((rand() % 100) - 50) / 10.0;
double z = ((rand() % 100) - 50) / 10.0;
double y = -2;

C3dShape* pTree = new C3dShape;
pTree->CreateCone(x, y+h/4, z, h/4, TRUE,
                  x, y+h, z, 0, FALSE);
m_pScene->m_ShapeList.Append(pTree);
C3dShape* pTrunk = new C3dShape;
pTrunk->CreateRod(x, y, z,
                  x, y+h/4, z,
                  h/20);
m_pScene->m_ShapeList.Append(pTrunk);
pTree->AddChild(pTrunk);

// Apply textures
pTree->SetTexture(pTex1);
wrap.Apply(pTree);

pTrunk->SetTexture(pTex2);
wrap.Apply(pTrunk);

pTree->SetName("Tree");
m_pScene->AddChild(pTree);

MakeCurrent(pTree);
}
```

Note that only one wrap object was required to wrap both the tree and the trunk. The scale factor was 1:1 in both cases and the orientation was the same, so I didn't need to use different wrap objects. As an exercise, try running the Color sample and inserting a tree. Now rotate the tree away from you so that you can see the bottom of the cone. Can you explain why the texture map looks the way it does? How would you fix that?

Spherical Wraps

No guesses for what we will use a spherical wrap for: it's time for the Genesis effect. Trekkies, stand by, we're going to build a planet. Before the excitement gets too intense, let's take a look at the result. Figure 8-11 shows the result of applying a texture map to a sphere using a spherical wrap. You can view this on screen by choosing Insert A World from the Edit menu. (You can also see a more elaborate version of this scene in the color insert.)

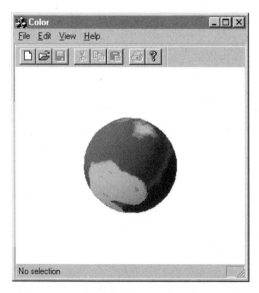

Figure 8-11. *A world created using a spherical wrap.*

Figure 8-12 shows the bitmap I used for the texture map.

Figure 8-12. *The world texture map.*

As you can see, to get much of a polar ice cap you need a lot of ice on the texture map. I messed about with the texture map image for quite a while before I got acceptable results. The code is very similar to what we've already seen, except that the wrap is now spherical:

```
void CMainFrame::OnEditInsworld()
{
    // Create sphere for planet
    C3dShape* pPlanet = new C3dShape;
    pPlanet->CreateSphere(2);
```

(continued)

```
// Load texture map of world
C3dTexture* pTex1 = new C3dTexture;
pTex1->Load(IDB_WORLD);
m_pScene->m_ImgList.Append(pTex1);

// Attach texture to shape
pPlanet->SetTexture(pTex1);

// Create spherical wrap
C3dWrap wrap;
wrap.Create(D3DRMWRAP_SPHERE,
            NULL,
            0, 0, 0, // Origin
            0, 0, 1, // Direction
            0, 1, 0, // Up
            0, 0,    // Texture origin
            1, 1);   // Texture scale

// Apply wrap to shapes
wrap.Apply(pPlanet);

pPlanet->SetDirection(0.5, 0.8, 0);

pPlanet->SetName("World");
m_pScene->AddChild(pPlanet);
m_pScene->m_ShapeList.Append(pPlanet);
MakeCurrent(pPlanet);
}
```

Chrome Wraps

The wraps we've seen so far involve simply applying the texture map to the object in a fixed orientation. After all, the appearance of an object's surfaces doesn't vary as you move the object (ignoring lighting effects). But what if the object was very shiny? If we had a chrome-plated object, it would reflect whatever was around it. As the object moved, the image in the reflection would change a bit but wouldn't rotate with the object.

A chrome wrap is a special kind of wrap that is applied to an object in a way that keeps the texture map oriented to the scene rather than to the axis of the object. The net result is to give the effect of a reflective surface on the object as it moves. To get the best effect, the texture map and the scene's background image need to be related. Figure 8-13 shows an example of a chrome wrap using the same image for the texture map and the scene's background.

It's a little difficult to see the effect on paper because the object isn't rotating and, consequently, it looks more like it's been covered in bad wallpaper rather than reflecting its surroundings. (The color version of this figure, which appears in the color insert, may give you a slightly better idea of what this will look like on your screen.)

Figure 8-13. *A chrome wrap.*

Implementing a chrome wrap requires a little bit more effort than the other wraps do because you can't simply apply the wrap to the shape and forget about it. Each time the object moves, the wrap has to be reapplied so that the texture map used to simulate the reflections can be oriented correctly before being applied to the object. You can think of the chrome wrap as a stationary spherical wrap sitting around a rotating object. So whatever the position of the object, the wrap is shrunk to fit onto the object's surface with the texture map of the wrap oriented to the scene the same way it was before the object rotated. It might sound a bit slow to have to reapply the wrap each time, but in practice it isn't—and in any case, you don't have a choice!

To apply the wrap correctly each time the object moves, we need to do one of two things: either we can add some code to the rendering loop that reapplies any chrome wraps to their objects just before the scene is updated; or we can ask each object to notify the application when it moves so the object's chrome wrap can be reapplied. The second technique is more efficient because it avoids applying the wrap when the object hasn't moved and it avoids having to keep a table of all the objects in a scene that have chrome wraps.

The *IDirect3DRMFrame* interface includes an *AddMoveCallback* method that allows us to install a function that will be called when the frame is moved. I thought it would be tidier if the application didn't have to deal with this notification business and we could instead just use chrome wraps pretty much the way we used the other types of wraps. To accomplish this, I created a class called *C3d-ChromeWrap* that is derived from *C3dWrap* and that implements the callback function required to handle frame movements. The application code required to use a chrome wrap then becomes similar to the code we used for the other wrap demonstrations:

```
void CMainFrame::OnEditChrome()
{
    // Load shape
    C3dShape* pShape = new C3dShape;
```

(continued)

```
    if (!pShape->Load()) {
        delete pShape;
        return;
    }

    NewScene();
    ASSERT(m_pScene);

    // Create chrome wrap
    m_pChromeWrap = new C3dChromeWrap;
    m_pChromeWrap->Create(pShape,
                          m_wnd3d.GetStage()->GetCamera());

    // Load scene background
    C3dImage* pImg = new C3dImage;
    pImg->Load(IDB_CHROME);
    m_pScene->m_ImgList.Append(pImg);
    m_pScene->SetBackground(pImg);

    // Load texture map
    C3dTexture* pTex = new C3dTexture;
    pTex->Load(IDB_CHROME);
    m_pScene->m_ImgList.Append(pTex);

    // Apply texture
    pShape->SetTexture(pTex);

    // Make it very shiny
    C3dMaterial mat;
    mat.SetSpecularPower(2000);
    pShape->SetMaterial(&mat);

    // Add new shape
    m_pScene->AddChild(pShape);
    m_pScene->m_ShapeList.Append(pShape);
    MakeCurrent(pShape);

    // Rotate shape a bit
    pShape->SetRotation(1, 1, 1, 0.03);

}
```

I thought it would be interesting to apply chrome wraps to different objects, so I display the object loading dialog box first thing. Having loaded the object the user selected, I created a chrome wrap, which needs two parameters: the shape to be wrapped and a reference frame. I chose to use the camera in the scene as the reference point. This ensures that the wrap will always be applied in the same way relative to the camera, which gives a consistent effect as objects move.

I used the same image, IDB_CHROME, for the scene background and the texture map. The texture is attached to the shape by calling *C3dShape::SetTexture*. Note that we're not calling *C3dWrap::Apply* here as we did for the other types of wraps because it is called later when the frame moves. I used a *C3dMaterial* object to alter the reflective appearance of the shape, adding to the overall chrome effect. The final steps were to add the shape to the scene and set it rotating to show off the chrome effect.

The code that implements the *C3dChromeWrap* class can be found in 3dImage.cpp and has two main parts: creating the wrap and applying it as the object moves. Here's how it's created:

```
BOOL C3dChromeWrap::Create(C3dShape* pShape,
                           C3dCamera* pCamera)
{
    if (!C3dWrap::Create(D3DRMWRAP_CHROME,
                    pCamera,
                    0, 0, 0,
                    0, 1, 0,
                    0, 0, -1,
                    0, 0,
                    1, -1)) {
        return FALSE;
    }

    // Install movement callback
    ASSERT(pShape);
    m_pShape = pShape;
    IDirect3DRMFrame* pIFrame = pShape->GetInterface();
    ASSERT(pIFrame);
    m_hr = pIFrame->AddMoveCallback(C3dChromeWrapCallback,
                                    this);
    return SUCCEEDED(m_hr);
}
```

The first part of this code is similar to creating the other wraps, but there are a couple of subtle differences. The up vector is set to 0, 0, –1, which actually causes the join in the texture map to occur at the back of the object where you can't see it. If you set the up vector to 0, 0, 1, you'll see some irritating effects in the middle of the object (depending somewhat on exactly what your texture map has at its edges). The second trick is to set the Y scale to –1 so that the "reflections" on the object are oriented the same way as the background image (assuming you used the same image for both).

Having created the wrap, the next step is to add a callback function to the frame by calling *AddMoveCallback*. Let's see how the callback function works:

```
static void C3dChromeWrapCallback(IDirect3DRMFrame* pIFrame,
                                  void* pArg,
                                  D3DVALUE delta)
{
    C3dChromeWrap* pThis = (C3dChromeWrap*) pArg;
    ASSERT(pThis);
    ASSERT(pThis->IsKindOf(RUNTIME_CLASS(C3dChromeWrap)));
    pThis->ApplyRelative(pThis->m_pShape,
                         pThis->m_pShape);
}
```

Note that this function is a static function and not a member of the *C3dChromeWrap* class. Consequently it has no *this* pointer. The second argument to *AddMoveCallback* was used to pass the class's *this* pointer to the callback function so the function could access the class data.

The callback's only task is to apply the wrap, using the *ApplyRelative* function. The first argument for *ApplyRelative* is the frame the wrap is to be applied to, and the second argument is the shape whose visuals will be affected by the chrome texture map. Since the *C3dShape* object contains both of these, the arguments to *ApplyRelative* are identical.

Loading Objects with Textures

If you use 3D Studio to create some nicely texture-mapped objects, then save the objects as 3DS files and the texture maps as Windows bitmaps (BMP files), you can load the object with its texture maps in one go. You need only to convert the 3DS file to a .X file, using the converter in the DirectX 2 SDK. In fact, the *C3dShape::Load* function handles loading the texture maps for you. I'd like to look at how this works, because the process is a bit unreliable and I'm sure you're going to have problems with it at some point. Once we've looked at loading shapes with textures from disk files, I want to look at how you can also build the same object and texture map files into your application as resources and load the objects more reliably from there.

Loading from Files

The names of the texture map image files are stored in the object file. When the object loader code encounters the name of one of these texture map files, it calls an auxiliary function to load the texture map image and create the texture map object from it. We'll look at how it does that in a moment, but first let's be clear about where the files need to be for this process to work. Because there is no path information in the object file for the texture map image files—only the file name—the texture map files must be in the same directory as the object file. Unfortunately, that's not the only problem. If you play with the sample applications, you'll notice that objects that have been loaded in previous sessions are added to the application's recent file list. If you select an object from the list to reload it, you might find that although the object itself loads, the texture maps do not. The reason for the failure is that the recent file list contains the full path of the object file but the object file only contains the filenames of the image files (no path information). Unless the object file happens to be in the application's current directory, the image files won't be found.

So how do we fix this? There are at least three solutions:

♦ You can modify the File Open code to change the current directory to where the object file is located before you attempt to load it.

♦ You can include the object file and its texture map images as resources in the application and load them from there.

♦ You can create your own file format that puts the object data and the image data into one file.

Let's see how the code that implements *C3dShape::Load* works. Here's the actual *Load* function in its entirety:

```
//Load a shape from a .X file.
//If no filename is given, show a File Open dialog box.
//Returns the filename or NULL if it fails.
const char* C3dShape::Load(const char* pszFileName)
{
    static CString strFile;

    if (!pszFileName || !strlen(pszFileName)) {

        // Show File Open dialog box
        CFileDialog dlg(TRUE,
                    NULL,
                    NULL,
                    OFN_HIDEREADONLY,
                    _3DOBJ_LOADFILTER,
                    NULL);
        if (dlg.DoModal() != IDOK) return NULL;

        // Get file path
        strFile = dlg.m_ofn.lpstrFile;

    } else {

        strFile = pszFileName;

    }

    // Remove any existing visual elements
    New();
```

(continued)

```
// Try to load file
ASSERT(m_pIMeshBld);
m_hr = m_pIMeshBld->Load((void*)(const char*)strFile,
                         NULL,
                         D3DRMLOAD_FROMFILE |
                         D3DRMLOAD_FIRST,
                         C3dLoadTextureCallback,
                         this);
if (FAILED(m_hr)) {
    return NULL;
}

AttachVisual(m_pIMeshBld);

m_strName = "File object: ";
m_strName += pszFileName;

return strFile;
}
```

The first part of the *Load* function deals with getting a filename. If a filename isn't supplied, a File Open dialog box is used to get one from the user. The shape object then has any existing visual elements removed, and the mesh builder interface is used to load the object from the named disk file. The fourth parameter to the load call, *C3dLoadTextureCallback*, is a pointer to the function that is called to load the texture images. The fifth parameter, *this*, is a user-defined value that gets passed to the function that loads the texture image. We use the *this* parameter to pass a pointer to the *C3dShape* object since the texture loading function is static and not part of the *C3dShape* class.

Let's look at the callback function that loads the textures:

```
static HRESULT C3dLoadTextureCallback(char* pszName,
                                      void* pArg,
                                      LPDIRECT3DRMTEXTURE*
                                      ppITex)
{
    C3dShape* pThis = (C3dShape*) pArg;
    ASSERT(pThis);
    ASSERT(pThis->IsKindOf(RUNTIME_CLASS(C3dShape)));
    ASSERT(pszName);

    // Load texture map
    ASSERT(ppITex);
    C3dTexture* pTex = new C3dTexture;
    if (!pTex->Load((const char*)pszName)) {
        delete pTex;
        return E_FAIL;
    }
    *ppITex = pTex->GetInterface();
```

```
// Add texture map to shape's image list
pThis->m_ImgList.Append(pTex);
return NOERROR;
}
```

We first cast the user-defined argument to be a *C3dShape* class pointer and validate it. A new *C3dTexture* object is then created, and its *Load* function is used to load the texture from the disk file. Once the texture object has been created from the image, the texture interface pointer is returned to the mesh builder so it can continue to load the object.

The problem with the story as told so far is that the texture we just created has to stay in memory for as long as the shape does. To ensure this, the *C3dTexture* object isn't destroyed and a pointer to it is added to a special image list in the shape. When the shape gets destroyed, any images (or textures) in the shape's image list are also destroyed:

```
C3dShape::~C3dShape()
{
    if (m_pIVisual) m_pIVisual->Release();
    if (m_pIMeshBld) m_pIMeshBld->Release();
    m_ImgList.DeleteAll();
}
```

If you're thinking, "Hey, wait a minute. Don't we already have an image list in the scene?" you're right. If the *C3dShape::Load* function included a pointer to the scene as one of its arguments, these images could simply have been added to the scene's image list. I thought that the implementation would be a bit untidy, however, and because the texture maps relate to only this shape, it seemed more sensible to keep track of them with the shape. If having an image list for every shape is more baggage than you care for, you can implement a better solution.

Loading from Resources

The easiest way to avoid disk file directory issues when loading objects is to build the objects and their texture maps right into the application as resources. As an example, I included the tank hull and the two texture maps used on the hull as resources in the Color sample. The Edit menu contains a Tank Hull (resource) menu item, which is implemented like this:

```
void CMainFrame::OnEditTank()
{
    C3dShape* pShape = new C3dShape;
    BOOL b = pShape->Load(IDX_TANK);
    ASSERT(b);
    ASSERT(m_pScene);
    m_pScene->AddChild(pShape);
    m_pScene->m_ShapeList.Append(pShape);
    MakeCurrent(pShape);
}
```

The resource ID for the tank object is all that's needed. So how do the texture maps get loaded? And how is all this stuff included in the application's resources?

The code below is almost exactly the same as the code that loads objects and their texture maps from disk files except that each component is in a resource rather than a file. Here's the code that loads the object from its resource:

```
//Load a shape from an XOF resource
BOOL C3dShape::Load(UINT uiResid)
{
    // Remove any existing visual
    New();

    // Try to load file
    ASSERT(m_pIMeshBld);
    D3DRMLOADRESOURCE info;
    info.hModule = AfxGetResourceHandle();
    info.lpName  = MAKEINTRESOURCE(uiResid);
    info.lpType  = "XOF";
    m_hr = m_pIMeshBld->Load(&info,
                             NULL,
                             D3DRMLOAD_FROMRESOURCE,
                             C3dLoadTextureResCallback,
                             this);
    ASSERT(SUCCEEDED(m_hr));
    if (FAILED(m_hr)) {
        return FALSE;
    }

    AttachVisual(m_pIMeshBld);

    m_strName = "Resource object";

    return TRUE;
}
```

Note that this function also uses a callback to load the texture maps. This time the texture maps are resources and need to be loaded from there:

```
static HRESULT C3dLoadTextureResCallback(char* pszName,
                                         void* pArg,
                                         LPDIRECT3DRMTEXTURE*
                                         ppITex)
{
    C3dShape* pThis = (C3dShape*) pArg;
    ASSERT(pThis);
    ASSERT(pThis->IsKindOf(RUNTIME_CLASS(C3dShape)));
    ASSERT(pszName);
```

```
// Load texture map
ASSERT(ppITex);
C3dTexture* pTex = new C3dTexture;
if (!pTex->LoadResource((const char*)pszName)) {
    delete pTex;
    return E_FAIL;
}
*ppITex = pTex->GetInterface();

// Add texture map to shape's image list
pThis->m_ImgList.Append(pTex);
return NOERROR;
}
```

Note that the name of the texture map image (the image filename, *pszName*, when the object file was created) is used to load the texture map image from the resource. To make this work, we have to add the texture map images to the application's resource file in a way that allows us to use the original image filename as the resource identifier for the image file.

Because we can't use a regular filename like Camo.bmp as a resource identifier in AppStudio, we can't simply add the texture map images as resources using AppStudio. Instead we must add them manually to the application's RC2 file in much the same way we have to add the .X file as a resource:

```
// Tank hull
IDX_TANK        XOF       res\t_hull.x
camo.bmp        BITMAP    res\camo.bmp
camousa.bmp     BITMAP    res\camousa.bmp
```

The files themselves are installed in the application project's *res* directory. Of course, if you're going to use the names as resource tags, you need to ensure that no two texture map image files use the same name.

As a final point: bitmaps are always big, and adding lots of them to the application makes the application very big. If this is an issue for you, you'll need to consider adding all the files for a scene to only one disk file that can be loaded when that scene is required.

So Much for Color

We've seen how to apply color and texture maps to our 3D shapes in various ways, but that's not quite the end of the story. There is a case that we haven't looked at yet that involves texture maps, transparency, and only two dimensions. We'll be looking at that in the next chapter.

sing 3D shapes for all the objects in an interactive application, such as a game, is a great way to create realistic looking characters and surroundings. However, having to render thousands of faces each time the scene changes is going to give you pretty poor performance. What we're going to look at in this chapter is a way to use two-dimensional shapes for the characters in an interactive 3D game. This technology doesn't apply only to games, of course, but games require absolutely the best performance, and this technique helps to achieve that. The sample for this chapter can be found in the Sprites directory.

Various works refer to two-dimensional, irregularly shaped images by different names. The DirectX 2 SDK documents, for example, call them *decals*, but I'm going to call them sprites. A *sprite* can be thought of as a cardboard cutout figure standing somewhere in a scene, somewhat like Figure 9-1.

Figure 9-1. *Cardboard cutout figures on a stage.*

In the interest of reality, Figure 9-1 shows the figures with feet. As any child will tell you, feet are required to make a figure stand up. Our sprites aren't going to have any feet, as such, but they'll stand just fine.

Let's consider what a scene built from the cardboard characters shown in Figure 9-1 looks like from the viewer's perspective. If the viewer has a fixed position at the front of the stage, the characters look quite solid and those further back on the stage look smaller than those in front. Figure 9-2 shows how the scene might look.

Figure 9-2. A front view of the scene shown in Figure 9-1.

Now consider what happens if the viewer moves around to the side of the stage. Because the cardboard shapes have no thickness, they seem to vanish. But what if we could make each shape rotate so that it always faced the viewer? The viewer could then move anywhere, and the shapes would still look solid.

But the images would always be the same, which isn't very realistic. For example, if I move behind a person, she doesn't look the same from behind as she does from in front. Well, how about if a person was trying to attack you? She certainly wouldn't stand still while you moved behind her—she would turn so she was facing you all the time.

OK, so if we make the cardboard shapes turn to face the viewer we could perhaps make some threatening hombres. Unfortunately, the average assailant isn't quite as static as cardboard figures tend to look. So as well as making the figure face the viewer, we also need the appearance of the figure to change so that it seems to move.

If we can create some images for a character, place one in a scene so that it rotates to face the viewer all the time, and provide a way to make the image change when we want it to, we'll have a viable alternative to building a complex 3D shape from individual faces.

How Sprites Are Implemented

Sprites are images that can be placed anywhere and scaled to any size, similar to texture maps. Texture maps need to be scaled and placed on arbitrary faces. If we could make irregularly shaped texture maps, we'd almost have a sprite. But in fact the shape doesn't need to be irregular at all. The shape of the texture map can be rectangular so long as we can define areas to be transparent. By defining a transparency color to use with a texture map, we can create what is effectively an irregularly shaped image.

We haven't considered transparency up till now because most 3D shapes are solid, and in coloring a solid object there isn't much use for transparency. Transparency is easy to implement in a renderer. Essentially one color is nominated as the transparency color, and all pixels that match the transparency color are simply not copied from the source image (typically a texture wrap) to the destination (the rendering buffer) when the destination is being rendered.

The only attribute missing from texture maps that is necessary to create sprites is that texture maps don't have any position associated with them. We can fix that problem by attaching the texture map to a frame. The frame provides the position information, and the texture map provides the visual component.

The rendering engine treats a texture map attached to a frame in a special way. The texture map is always rendered in the plane of the viewport—so it always faces the viewer. As an option, the texture map can be scaled according to its position along the z-axis, which gives the depth-scaling we need for sprites. The texture map is positioned so that an arbitrary point in the texture map is image-mapped to the location specified by the frame. By default the image origin is in the upper left corner, so the image gets positioned with its upper left corner located at the x, y, and z coordinates in the frame. As we'll see later, the origin can be moved to the bottom center of the image, for example, which is a more logical position when trying to place characters in a scene. Figure 9-3 shows the default configuration on the left and a more useful one on the right.

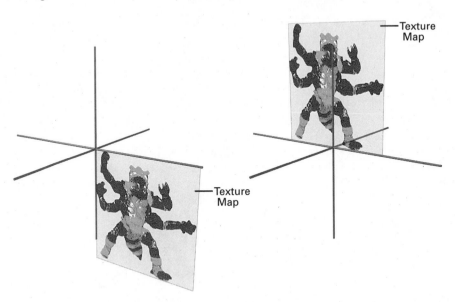

Figure 9-3. *Using different origins in the texture map for sprite placement.*

The default transparency color is black, which I don't think is particularly helpful when working with sprites because I find it hard to create images with black backgrounds. The texture map interface includes the *SetDecalTransparentColor* function to allow you to define a different transparency color. At the time of writing, this function was not working in any way that I could fathom so I was forced to leave all my images with black as the transparency color. Nonetheless, we need only one transparency color that works, and we have that.

Dealing with Multiple Images

Some sprites have only one image. For example, a chalice could easily be created using only one image. The sprite doesn't need to change shape, and a chalice looks much the same from whatever side it's viewed. Most sprites need more than one image, though, and we need an efficient way to create a sprite object from multiple images. I call these sub-images *phases,* because the image will appear to move as the phase of the image changes—exactly the same way the moon appears to change shape with its phases.

The Obvious Approach

The most obvious way to create a sprite that has multiple images is to create separate images for each phase, each in its own bitmap file, which are then loaded as an array of texture maps as shown in Figure 9-4.

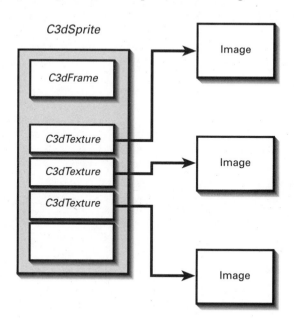

Figure 9-4. *Using multiple separate images for a sprite.*

This technique has the advantage of being easy to implement and, in fact, works quite well. The sprite keeps track of which image is currently attached to the frame as a visual. When you want to change the image of a sprite in a scene, you remove the current visual from the frame and attach the new one. Since all that's happening here is a bit of pointer juggling, it's actually very fast. In fact, I did implement a version of the *C3dSprite* class this way when my efforts to do something better were being hindered by my inability to read the documentation for the rendering engine—so I know this method works.

However, there are two important reasons why you shouldn't use separate images. First, you can waste a lot of memory using all the image and texture map data structures needed for a large set of images. Second, it's a pain to have to ensure a consistent palette for all the images, because the files are separate and can easily be edited individually.

A Better Solution

I prefer to create sprites from a single bitmap that contains all the possible states the sprite could be viewed in. Using a single bitmap is efficient in many cases because there is very little redundant data. Figure 9-5 shows the image used to create the phases of a running dog sprite, which was used in one of the sample applications I wrote for *Animation Techniques in Win32* (Microsoft Press, 1995).

Figure 9-5. *A strip of images in a single bitmap used to create a phased sprite.*

Each cell in the strip is exactly the same size and uses the same palette as all the other cells. This makes it difficult to lose a cell or get them out of order and also ensures color fidelity between the different phases of the sprite.

The strip could also have been seven dogs wide and one dog tall or a grid with a row of three and a row of four—whatever you fancy. So long as you know the location of each cell in the total image, you can write code to extract the one you want. The advantage of having all the cells in a vertical strip is that it simplifies the code slightly. Because it probably doesn't matter to you what formation the collection is in, I'd suggest you opt for the one that simplifies your job as a programmer.

CREATING TEXTURE MAPS FROM IMAGE STRIPS

So the next question is: "How do I make a texture map from a strip of images?"

A texture map is created by attaching an image to a data structure that describes how the image will be used when the texture map is rendered. The image consists of a header and the bits of the image itself. Figure 9-6 shows the relationships.

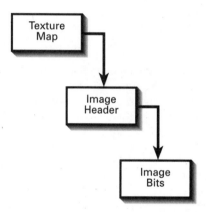

Figure 9-6. *Texture map architecture.*

It seemed to me that simply changing the pointer in the image header to point to a different chunk of image bits would be a great way to change the sprite phases. Unfortunately, at the time of writing, the implementation of the rendering engine required that the address of the image bits not change. So instead of changing the pointer, we have to change the bits. What this means in practice is that your strip of sprite images needs to have an extra cell to use as a work area. This cell is used to create the initial texture map. When we want to change the sprite's image we simply copy the correct cell bits into the working area and tell the rendering engine that the texture map bits have changed. Figure 9-7 on the next page shows how it works.

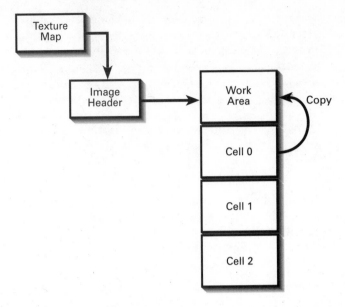

Figure 9-7. A multiple-image bitmap used to create a texture map.

When the texture map is created, the height field in the image header is altered to contain the height of one cell rather than the height of the whole image. Perhaps now you can see why a vertical strip is so handy: The image is trivial to subdivide if the width doesn't need to change, and copying the bits for any cell to the work area can be done with a call to *memcpy* or some other equivalent function.

> **NOTE**
>
> A later version of the rendering engine might let you manipulate the pointer to the image bit directly, thus avoiding the copy operation.

Creating the Images

Creating the images for a sprite requires some forethought. If you will run your application on a machine with a 256-color display, the primary consideration is color usage. If your target machine has more colors, you have more flexibility in creating the sprite images.

Because I have absolutely no artistic talent, I created the images by using a video camera and a video capture card to grab pictures of one of my children's plastic toys. Computer graphic artists have their own sets of favorite tools and can work wonders, but I have to rely on a few simple tools to get the job done. In case you find yourself without an artist to help you, I'll describe the process I used.

To create my set, I used a white cardboard scoop and a photographic modeling light. The toy figure was placed on the scoop and the camera set up as shown in Figure 9-8.

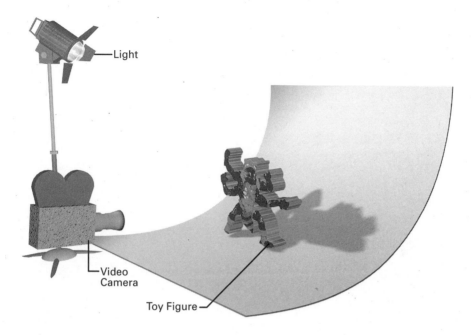

—Light

—Video
Camera

Toy Figure—

Figure 9-8. *The movie set.*

I set the toy into an aggressive stance and captured the image from the camera on the computer. I moved the toy to a new position and took a new shot. This was repeated until I had a set of frames of the toy waving its arms in a generally unfriendly way. The images were captured as 24-bit-per-pixel bitmaps at about 300-by-200 pixels.

I then cropped and resized each image to be exactly 256-by-256 pixels and then reduced the images to an 8-bit-per-pixel format (256 colors) with an arbitrary palette. When all the images had been converted, I copied one of them to use as a placeholder in the final image for the work area. I named the work area cell S00 and named the image cells S01, S02, and so on.

I then used a program I created for my animation book to take a series of images, map them all to the palette found in the first image, and construct a strip image containing all of them. This program is called Viewdib and can be found in the Tools directory. The result was like the image in Figure 9-5 except that the top cell in the image was a copy of one of the other cells.

Next I removed all the surrounding color (shadows, reflections, etc.) from the toys to leave a clean image. I filled the border with black, which becomes the transparency color. Obviously this means that you can't have other parts of the image black, too. If you want to use black as the transparency color and also have black parts of the image, change the image to use a different shade of black. (Use RGB: 0, 0, 1 instead of RGB: 0, 0, 0, for example.) Finally I used Microsoft Imager to reduce the colors from 256 to 8. The final result is shown in Figure 9-9.

Figure 9-9. *The composite sprite image.*

NOTE

The top cell is just a copy of the one below it. The top cell will become the work area in the texture map's image memory.

I must say that the process was rather tedious, and consequently, I tip my hat to those who do this for a living. All that remains now is to write the code.

The *C3dSprite* Class

Let's look now at the class that handles the frame and images that form a sprite, and then we can look at how the *C3dSprite* class can be used in an application. The implementation is partly in the *C3dImage* class and partly in the *C3dSprite* class. The *C3dImage* class provides the functionality to load a bitmap and divide it up into cells. The *C3dSprite* class uses the *C3dTexture* class, which is derived from *C3dImage*, to implement the texture map needed to make an animated sprite. I'm sure that made it sound way more complicated than it is, so let's have a look at how a sprite is created and fill in the details as we go. Here's how the class is defined in 3dPlus.h:

```
class C3dSprite : public C3dFrame
{
public:
    DECLARE_DYNAMIC(C3dSprite);
    C3dSprite();
    virtual ~C3dSprite();
    BOOL Create(C3dScene* pScene,
                double x, double y, double z,
                double scale,
                UINT uiIDBitmap,
                int iPhases = 1);
    BOOL SetPhase(int iPhase);
    int GetNumPhases() {return m_Tex.GetNumPhases();}
    int GetPhase() {return m_Tex.GetPhase();}

protected:
    C3dTexture m_Tex;
};
```

Note that *C3dSprite* is derived from *C3dFrame* and has a *C3dTexture* object as a data member. I want to look at two functions in detail, *Create* and *SetPhase*, because these provide most of the functionality of the sprite object. The *Create* function was designed to make adding a sprite to a scene as easy as possible. Let's walk through the code step by step:

```
BOOL C3dSprite::Create(C3dScene* pScene,
                       double x, double y, double z,
                       double scale,
                       UINT uiIDBitmap,
                       int iPhases)
{
    ASSERT(pScene);
    ASSERT(iPhases > 0);
    ASSERT(uiIDBitmap);
```

(continued)

```
// Create frame and add it to scene list
C3dFrame::Create(pScene);
pScene->m_ShapeList.Append(this);

// Put frame in requested position
SetPosition(x, y, z);

// Load texture map image
if (!m_Tex.C3dImage::Load(uiIDBitmap)) {
    TRACE("Failed to load texture image\n");
    return FALSE;
}

// Set number of phases
m_Tex.C3dImage::SetNumPhases(iPhases);

// Create texture map from image
m_Tex.Create();

// Set properties
IDirect3DRMTexture* pITex = m_Tex.GetInterface();
ASSERT(pITex);

// Enable depth-scaling
m_hr = pITex->SetDecalScale(TRUE);
ASSERT(SUCCEEDED(m_hr));

// Set initial size
double a = (double)m_Tex.GetWidth()
         / (double)m_Tex.GetHeight();
m_hr = pITex->SetDecalSize(scale * a, scale);
ASSERT(SUCCEEDED(m_hr));

// Turn on transparency
m_hr = pITex->SetDecalTransparency(TRUE);
ASSERT(SUCCEEDED(m_hr));

// Set the transparency color to black
m_hr = pITex->SetDecalTransparentColor(RGB_MAKE(
                                       0, 0, 0));
ASSERT(SUCCEEDED(m_hr));

// Set center bottom of image to map
// to frame origin
m_hr = pITex->SetDecalOrigin(m_Tex.GetWidth()/2,
                             m_Tex.GetHeight()-1);
ASSERT(SUCCEEDED(m_hr));

// Add texture as visual
return AddVisual(&m_Tex);
}
```

The first task is to create the *C3dFrame* object (from which *C3dSprite* is derived). The sprite is added to the scene, and the initial position of the frame in the scene is then set. The next step is to load the image for the texture map from its BITMAP resource, which was added to the application using AppStudio. Note that I'm calling the *C3dImage::Load* function from the base class and not a function in *C3dTexture* itself. I do this because I want to alter the image a bit before the actual texture map gets created from it.

Once the image is loaded, it is configured for the number of cells (*iPhases*). This number does not include the cell used for the work area. Once the image has been divided into cells, the texture map is created. (The way I've implemented this code isn't pretty, but it is quite efficient and allowed me to create multiphase sprites at almost no expense to the general image and texture map class code.)

After a pointer to the *IDirect3DRMTexture* interface has been obtained with a call to *GetInterface*, the depth-scaling option is turned on so that the image will change size according to its *z* position on the z-axis. The initial size of the image is set according to a scale factor provided as an argument to *Create*. The scale factor allows you to arbitrarily size your sprites independently of the size of the bitmaps. A little extra code ensures that the final sprite retains the aspect ratio of the original image. Because texture maps (and hence your sprites) are scalable in both directions, you can make short, fat characters out of tall, thin ones if you want. I think that most artwork is created the way it's intended to look on the screen, so keeping the aspect ratio correct is important.

Transparency is enabled for the texture map. I set the transparency color as the default black with a call to *SetDecalTransparentColor* just to give you an example of how the function should work. An alternative strategy that I have used in the past for determining the transparency color is to take the top-left pixel of the image and use that to define the transparency color. This gives you much greater flexibility when you create your images because any color can surround the image so long as that color isn't used in any other place in the image.

The final step in creating the texture map is to set the center of the bottom of the image as the point to map to the frame origin in the scene. I find this a convenient reference point to use, especially when the sprite is placed to appear standing on a ground surface, because the *y* value of the surface can then be used as the *y* value of the sprite to position it correctly.

Once the texture map is created, the last step in our sprite creation function is to add the texture map as a visual element of the frame. Now the sprite will be visible when the scene is rendered.

Changing the Phase

To alter the phase of the sprite, the *C3dSprite::SetPhase* function is called with the new phase number as the argument:

```
BOOL C3dSprite::SetPhase(int iPhase)
{
    return m_Tex.SetPhase(iPhase);
}
```

Which actually ends up as a call to *C3dImage::SetPhase*:

```
BOOL C3dImage::SetPhase(int iPhase)
{
    if ((iPhase < 0) || (iPhase >= m_iPhases)) {
        return FALSE;
    }
    m_iCurPhase = iPhase;

    // Copy bits for requested phase to work area
    int iBytes = m_rlimg.bytes_per_line * m_rlimg.height;
    memcpy(m_rlimg.buffer1,
            (BYTE*)m_rlimg.buffer1 + (m_iCurPhase + 1) *
            iBytes,
            iBytes);

    // Notify any derived class of change
    _OnImageChanged();
    return TRUE;
}
```

The code above implements the copy operation shown in Figure 9-7. The address of the requested cell is computed, then *memcpy* is used to copy the data for the cell to the work area. When the copy has been completed, *_OnImageChanged* is called. This virtual function in the *C3dImage* class does nothing in *C3dImage* itself, but it can be overridden in derived classes, such as *C3dTexture*, that might need to know if the image has changed. *C3dTexture* uses this function, located in 3dImage.cpp, to notify the renderer that the texture map bits have changed:

```
// virtual
void C3dTexture::_OnImageChanged()
{
    if (!m_pITexture) return; // Might not be created yet

    // Image has changed, so notify renderer
    // that pixels have changed but not palette
    m_hr = m_pITexture->Changed(TRUE, FALSE);
    ASSERT(SUCCEEDED(m_hr));
}
```

Notifying the rendering engine that the image bits have changed is vital because the renderer can be caching image data; simply changing the bits alone is not enough to guarantee that the rendered scene will also change.

The Sprites Sample

When I write sample code, I try to avoid adding anything that isn't absolutely essential to showing the features I'm talking about. In the case of the Sprites sample, I found that once I'd got the *C3dSprite* class to work, I wanted to add soooo much more. However, I did resist the temptation, and the result of my efforts can only loosely be described as a game.

The Sprites application is a DOOM-like game. If you haven't ever seen the game DOOM, I'm sure that the folks at Id Software would be only too happy to sign you up for a copy. (But please don't get it just yet, or you'll never finish reading this book.)

The idea of the game (mine, not DOOM) is to hunt down the bad guys and then make loud noises to simulate the weapons that you'd like to have with you in such a situation. The game takes place inside a maze of walls constructed of a lovely reddish substance. The walls are totally opaque and very solid looking, but you have magical powers and you can pass right through them, as you will quickly discover. The floor is covered in some cheap carpet that I found easy to put down.

You really need a joystick to play this game. I used my SideWinder PRO and coded the game so that button one (the trigger on the SideWinder) triggers the explosions. If you have only a mouse, you can still find the bad guys but you will have to imagine the explosions. Figure 9-10 shows the view at the start of the game—and is all the help you get.

Figure 9-10. *Looks like nobody is home.*

To create this application, I started with the floor plan shown in Figure 9-11 on the next page (which, for those of you not paying attention, is a *clue*).

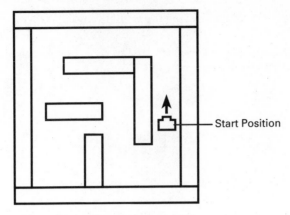

Start Position

Figure 9-11. *The floor plan.*

Each wall in the scene consists of four faces, each of which has the red texture map applied to it. I created a *CWall* class derived from *C3dShape* to build the walls, using code that is similar to what we've seen in the earlier chapters, so I won't include it here. Here is the code that uses the wall class to build the maze:

```
BOOL CMainFrame::NewScene()
{
    ⋮
    WALLINFO wi [] = {
        {-6,  5,  6,  6, 1},
        { 5, -5,  6,  5, 0.9},
        {-6, -6,  6, -5, 1.1},
        {-6, -5, -5,  5, 0.8},
        {-3,  2,  2,  3, 0.5},
        { 2, -3,  3,  3, 0.9},
        {-4, -1,  0,  0, 1},
        {-1, -5,  0, -2, 1.3}

    };
    int nWalls = sizeof(wi) / sizeof(WALLINFO);

    WALLINFO* pwi = wi;
    for (int i = 0; i < nWalls; i++) {
        CWall* pWall = new CWall(pwi);
        m_pScene->AddChild(pWall);
        m_pScene->m_ShapeList.Append(pWall);
        pwi++;
    }
    ⋮
}
```

The data for each wall consists of two corner *x* and *y* coordinate sets and the height. Each wall is created and added to the scene.

The floor is a single-faced object with a texture map applied to it. The scene background was set to blue to give the effect of sky above the walls.

```
m_pScene->SetBackground(0, 0, 1);

CFloor* pFloor = new CFloor(-6, -6, 6, 6);
m_pScene->AddChild(pFloor);
m_pScene->m_ShapeList.Append(pFloor);
```

I used another class for the floor, but, again, the code is exactly what we saw earlier in the color chapter when we created a single-faced object.

The last two things to add are the bad guys and the explosion. Again, I created classes for each of these. Both classes are derived from *C3dSprite*, and because they work similarly, we'll look at just one of them here. Here's the definition (found in maze.h) of the *CSoldier* class that is used to create the persons of bad intent:

```
class CSoldier : public C3dSprite
{
public:
    CSoldier(C3dScene* pScene, double x, double z);
    void Update();

};
```

As you can see, this isn't all that complicated: a constructor to create the object and an *Update* function that deals with movement. Here's the constructor code in maze.cpp:

```
CSoldier::CSoldier(C3dScene* pScene, double x, double z)
{
    Create(pScene, x, 0, z, 0.5, IDB_SOLDIER, 4);
}
```

This must rate as the simplest function we've looked at so far. The *C3dSprite::Create* function does the bulk of the work in creating the sprite object from the supplied bitmap ID value. The last argument value (*4*) is the number of cells in the sprite image (not counting the work area).

Because these sprites needed to move, I added an *Update* function to change the phase:

```
void CSoldier::Update()
{
    SetPhase((GetPhase() + 1) % GetNumPhases());
}
```

This function gets called in the application's idle time handler just before the scene is updated. The explosion class has a similar update handler to change the visual state as the explosion proceeds.

What explosion? Well, I'll leave that for you to encounter, along with the bad guys.

That's It for the Flat People

We have seen that sprites can be used to efficiently show characters or objects in a 3D scene without the expense of creating a multifaceted shape. Sprites can be used in a scene with other solid objects to provide the best balance between appearance and performance.

Creating a game involves rather more than placing a set of sprites in a 3D scene. I have made no attempt to show how movement should be constrained inside a scene or how to implement warnings of the presence of dangerous aliens in the vicinity. These are tasks for you. Go forth on your quest and implement.

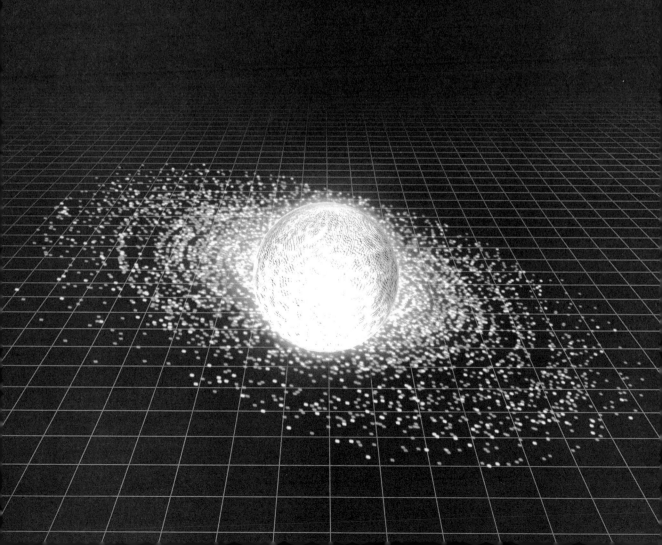

CHAPTER **10**

Lights
and Shadows

I n all the sample applications that we've seen in the previous chapters, the lighting model used in the scenes has been a low-level ambient background, augmented by a directional light to provide highlights. In this chapter we're going to look at all the different forms of light we can use, the properties of each one, and the cost of using each of them. We're also going to look at how you can generate shadow effects. The main sample for this chapter can be found in the Lights directory.

Color Models

Before we can start using lights to their full capacity, we need to back up just a little bit and look at how the rendering engine generates colors. To compute the final color of a pixel in the viewport, the engine must take into account the following:

◆ The color and material of the surface directly under the pixel

◆ The angle of the surface to each light in the scene

◆ The color, intensity, and position of each light

◆ The capabilities of the physical display device

Anything we can do to simplify the task of computing the final pixel color will speed up the operation, with a consequent increase in overall rendering speed.

We can simplify the task of computing the final color of a screen pixel in several ways. For example, we can ignore the color component of the lights and treat them all simply as sources of white light at some intensity. This simplifies the computation of the final color a lot and greatly improves rendering performance at very little cost to the fidelity of the scene. As another example, we can simplify how the properties of a material affect its color. We can do this by combining the specular and diffuse reflection properties of a material in a way that provides an index into a color table. The color table contains colors that vary from the object's fully diffuse color to its fully specular color. These examples provide a bit of an oversimplification, but they serve to illustrate the point that by applying a little ingenuity we can improve performance, albeit at the expense of the fidelity of the final image. Because performance is often the number-one priority, a slight loss in quality is often acceptable.

Judging by the examples above, we can skin this particular furry feline in many ways, and I suppose that the designers of the Direct3D rendering engine could have allowed us to choose which optimizations we wanted to use. That's not what they did, however. We get two choices: the mono mode and the RGB mode. The *mono mode,* sometimes referred to as the ramp mode, is so called because it uses monochromatic (white) light sources. The light source can vary in intensity but not in color. This characteristic simplifies the computation of color shades a great deal. The mono mode also computes material colors by using a table lookup mechanism to give an approximate result. The mono mode applies a lot of optimizations to produce the best possible speed solution. All the samples we've seen so far use the mono mode.

The *RGB mode* uses a much more complex computation than the mono mode to calculate the final color of a pixel on the screen. The RGB mode fully supports colored light sources and material properties. This mode attempts to produce the best possible quality result. Since we're going to be playing with colored lights in this chapter, we'll be setting up the rendering engine to work in the RGB mode. I'm sure you're thinking, "Oh no, there goes all the performance!" But hold on, the story's not that bad.

One final thing to consider when generating colors is the color depth of the physical display device, which has an effect on both image fidelity and performance.

◆ If you have a 24-bit-per-pixel display, it can show more or less any color for which the renderer wants to generate RGB values. Every pixel requires the transfer of 3 bytes of data, which might or might not be a factor that affects performance.

◆ If you have a 16-bit-per-pixel display, the renderer can display somewhere between 32,767 and 65,535 colors, depending on how the renderer is configured. To set a pixel the renderer has to provide only 2 bytes of data, but to create those 2 bytes it needs to shift the RGB components around a little, which takes a bit more effort.

◆ If you have an 8-bit-per-pixel display (still the most common), your display is limited to only 256 colors and the renderer has the additional problem of picking exactly which 256 colors it's going to use. It does have the advantage of having to transfer only 1 byte per pixel in this mode, though.

So here's the deal. If you have a 24-bit-per-pixel display, you get great images. If you have a 16-bit-per-pixel display, you get pretty good images and quite good performance. If you have an 8-bit-per-pixel display, you get average to good pictures and good performance. The problem with the 8-bit-per-pixel mode is that to get the vast range of colors the RGB color model requires from a 256-color palette, the image has to be dithered, which creates artifacts (unwanted images) in the picture and degrades the overall quality. In the mono color model on an 8-bit-per-pixel display, you can limit the number of colors used by the objects, making it possible for the palette to provide all the colors required to render the scene without any dithering. This actually gives great looking pictures and good performance, too. Do a little experimentation to determine which mode works best for you.

You set the color model when the 3D window is first created. Here's the part of the code that does the job when the application's main window is created:

```
int CMainFrame::OnCreate(LPCREATESTRUCT lpCreateStruct)
{
    ⋮
    // Create 3D window
    if (!m_wnd3d.Create(this, IDC_3DWND, D3DCOLOR_RGB)) {
        return -1;
    }

    ⋮
}
```

The *C3dWnd::Create* function defaults to D3DCOLOR_MONO if no value is supplied.

Well, we spent a bit longer than I intended on this subject, but I thought I'd mention why we're about to move to using the RGB mode instead of the mono mode that has served us so well thus far.

Choosing a Type of Light

The rendering engine supports five different types of light: ambient, directional, parallel point, point, and spot. Each light has different properties, affects a scene in different ways, and results in different computational costs. The table below shows the properties supported by each kind of light.

Light Type	Postion	Direction	Point Source	Range	Other
Ambient	no	no	no	no	no
Directional	no	yes	no	no	no
Parallel Point	yes	no	yes	no	no
Point	yes	no	yes	yes	no
Spot	yes	yes	yes	yes	yes

You can see from the table that there is a wide variety of property combinations. Each light can also be set to any RGB value, which provides a way to control both color and intensity. Let's take a look at each kind of light and what effect it has on a scene.

Ambient Light

The ambient light is the least computationally expensive to use. It provides a uniform level of illumination in a scene so that each face of an object is evenly illuminated. Figure 10-1 shows an example of a scene lit with a white ambient light.

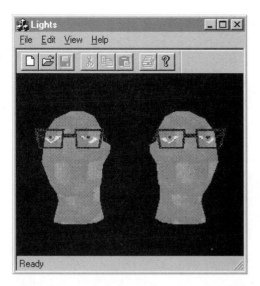

Figure 10-1. Scene lit by ambient light only.

Contrary to popular belief, these gentlemen are not about to rob a convenience store. The stocking mask effect is caused by a combination of the flat lighting and the dithering required to show the object's colors on my 256-color display. Using only an ambient light isn't very useful, but when used in combination with other lights, it helps eliminate very dark areas in a scene.

Directional Light

A directional light is the least expensive of the nonambient lights to use. It illuminates a scene with parallel rays that appear to come from a light an infinite distance from the scene. The direction of the light can be specified by setting the light's forward direction vector. Setting the light's position has no effect. Figure 10-2 on the next page shows a scene lit by a low-ambient background light and a directional light.

As you can see, the scene looks much better than it did with only the ambient light. The lighting in Figure 10-2 is very similar to the kind of lighting we see outdoors. The arrow in the scene shows the direction from which the light is coming. Figure 10-3, also on the next page, shows the same scene but without the ambient light.

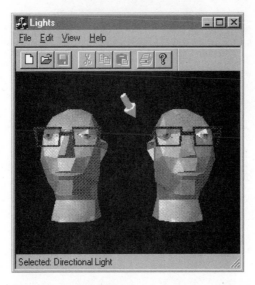

Figure 10-2. *A directional light used to provide highlights.*

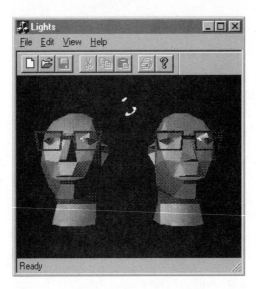

Figure 10-3. *A directional light used on its own.*

The effect in Figure 10-3 is rather harsh, and there are a lot of dark areas, making it hard to see any detail on some parts of the objects.

Parallel Point Light

If you need a light source to appear in a scene—a table lamp, for example—and you want to show the effects of that light on the scene, a parallel point light is the least expensive solution. This light comes from a fixed point, so moving its position affects the scene. The light is assumed, however, to have parallel rays, which simplifies the computation. Applying a parallel point light to the scene between the two heads gives the result shown in Figure 10-4.

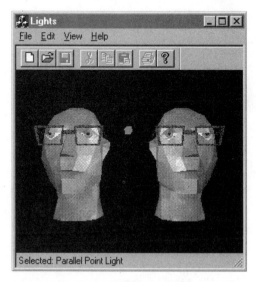

Figure 10-4. *A parallel point light.*

As you can see, the light (represented by the very small cube) illuminates the heads in a way that suggests the source of the light as coming from the position where the cube is. It's difficult to determine the depth of the light source in relation to the heads in Figure 10-4, but if you look at the code (which we'll do in part on page 224), you'll see that the light source is slightly behind the heads.

Point Light

The point light is much the same as the parallel point light except that the computation treats the rays from the light as diverging from the point of origin. This gives a slightly more realistic effect, as you can see in Figure 10-5 on the next page.

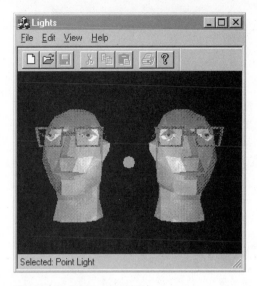

Figure 10-5. *A point light.*

I encourage you to play with the Lights sample to really see the difference between this light and the previous one. The increase in effect is quite costly, so I don't consider a point light to be as useful as a parallel point light.

Spot Light

The spot light is by far the most expensive light to use, but it has a very dramatic effect, as you can see in Figure 10-6. (Also take a look at the color version of this figure in the color insert.)

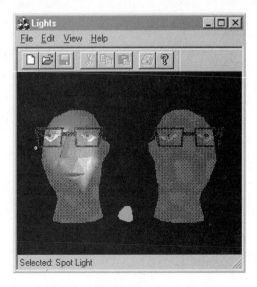

Figure 10-6. *A spot light.*

The spot light's position and direction affect how the scene is illuminated. In addition, the angle of the cone of light it emits can be altered using two parameters. The light cone is considered to consist of a central cone of full intensity and an outer cone of lesser intensity. You can control the angles of the central and outer cones, which are referred to as the *umbra* and *penumbra*, respectively, in the DirectX documentation. So if you want to create a prison yard or campfire scene, this is the light for you.

Time Out

Take a little time to play with the Lights sample and see how each type of light affects the scene. The application includes dialog boxes that allow you to control the ambient light level and most of the properties of the lights. You can also select and move the lights around in the scene as we have for other objects.

Range and Attenuation

Point lights and spot lights have two other properties that you can use to affect how they illuminate a scene. The simplest of these properties is the *range* value, which controls how far the light is effective. The default value is 256 model units, which would illuminate everything we've put into a scene so far. Setting this value to a very small number can result in some interesting effects. It also helps to improve rendering performance because objects that fall outside the light's range don't need to include that light in their shading computations.

The other property you can set is the *attenuation* characteristic of the light. This affects how the intensity of the light decreases with distance from the light source. Three parameters are used to control a quadratic equation that determines a light's intensity. The rendering engine documents refer to these parameters as the *constant, linear,* and *quadratic* components. The default values are *1, 0,* and *0,* respectively, which give a light with an intensity that doesn't vary with distance. The equation that determines the attenuation factor is

$$a = c + ld + qd^2$$

where *a* is the attenuation, *c* is the constant factor, *l* is the linear factor, *d* is the distance from the light, and *q* is the quadratic factor. You can use the *C3dLight::SetAttenuation* function to alter a light's attenuation parameters.

Enough Talk—Let's See the Code

I'm glad you stopped me there! I was really getting back to my physics roots for a moment, and that would never do. Before you would know it, I'd be rambling on about diffraction gratings and wave packets and how even an elephant gets deflected slightly if it rolls down a hill and through a line of trees.

Since the code required to implement a light is fairly simple and all of the lights require pretty much the same code to create them, I'll just show you the code that was used to create the parallel point light shown in Figure 10-4 on page 221:

```
void CMainFrame::OnEditParlight()
{
    C3dParPtLight* pLight = new C3dParPtLight;
    pLight->Create(1, 1, 1);
    m_pCurLight = pLight;

    // Make a shape to represent light source
    C3dShape* ps1 = new C3dShape;
    ps1->CreateCube(0.2);

    // Add light as child of the shape
    // so we can select the light
    ps1->AddChild(pLight);

    // Add light to scene
    m_pScene->AddChild(ps1);
    m_pScene->m_ShapeList.Append(ps1);
    m_pScene->m_ShapeList.Append(pLight);

    // Put light where it's easy to find
    ps1->SetPosition(0, 1, -2);
    ps1->SetName("Parallel Point Light");

    MakeCurrent(ps1);
}
```

Most of this code really has nothing to do with creating the light itself, but we'll take a look at it anyway. The first couple lines of the function create the actual light, in this case a *C3dParPtLight* object. To enable you to see where the light is in the scene, I created a shape and attached the light as a child of the shape so that the light moves with the shape. Both the shape and the light are derived from the *C3dFrame* class. This enables you to conveniently add them to the scene's shape list so they are destroyed when the scene is destroyed. The last step is to set the position of the light in the scene. If we were using a directional light, we'd be setting its direction; if we were using a spot light, we'd be setting both its position and its direction.

The C++ class code that implements the lights is very simple. Each specific light type is derived from the *C3dLight* class, and this class actually creates the light as follows:

```
BOOL C3dLight::Create(D3DRMLIGHTTYPE type,
                      double r, double g, double b)
{
    // Create frame that holds light
    if (!C3dFrame::Create(NULL)) return FALSE;

    // Create light object
    ASSERT(m_pILight == NULL);
```

```
        if (!the3dEngine.CreateLight(type, r, g, b, &m_pILight))
        {
            return FALSE;
        }
        ASSERT(m_pILight);

        // Add light to its frame
        ASSERT(m_pIFrame);
        m_hr = m_pIFrame->AddLight(m_pILight);
        if (FAILED(m_hr)) return FALSE;

        return TRUE;
    }
```

The light object is attached to a frame object so you can position it. The light object that the rendering engine creates doesn't have any sense of position or direction unless it's attached to a frame of some kind. Deriving the *C3dLight* class from *C3dFrame* gives you a more useful object to work with in your scenes.

Using Colored Lights

I wanted to find a really good example of using colored lights to improve the appearance of a scene, but for a long time I could only think of really simple examples that didn't have many practical applications. That all changed when I saw a pair of red and green 3D glasses in someone's office. So I present here Nigel's silly example of using colored lights—a 3D object viewer. The Stereo directory contains the application. You'll need to be wearing your supercool 3D glasses to get the best effect. Figure 10-7 shows what the sample looks like if you've lost your 3D glasses.

Figure 10-7. *A non-3D picture of a 3D object in green.*

Those of you experienced with printed 3D pictures on Cornflakes packages and the like might wonder why the image in Figure 10-7 doesn't show the customary red and green overlapped images. The reason is that I implemented the viewer to render the scene in red and then to render it in green after moving the camera a bit. The camera then gets moved back again, and the cycle repeats. So a screen shot gets either the green half or the red half of the cycle. To view the glorious full effect, you need to run the Stereo application while wearing your glasses, and it's best if you do it in a dark room with the lights off.

I'm not sure that this is a practical use for colored lights, but it was a lot of fun to create. The core of the application is the part that moves the camera, sets the lighting, and renders the scene, so I thought we'd spend a few minutes looking at how all that was done. Just before we look at the code, though, let's look at Figure 10-8, which shows the mechanics of how the 3D viewer works.

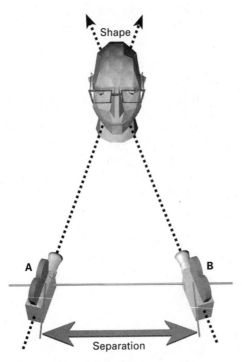

Figure 10-8. Constructing a stereo image.

The scene is illuminated with red light, and the camera is placed at *A* to take the picture your left eye sees. The scene is then illuminated with green light, and the camera moves to *B*, where it takes the right-eye picture. By viewing the scene with a red filter over the left eye and a green filter over the right eye, the left eye sees only the image as viewed from position *A* and the right eye sees only the image as viewed from position *B*. Here's the code from the application's idle loop that implements it:

```
BOOL CMainFrame::Update()
{
    ⋮
    m_bPhase = !m_bPhase;
    double d = 1.0;      // Separation
    double cz = 10;      // Camera z position
    C3dVector vo;
    if (m_pCurShape) {
        m_pCurShape->GetPosition(vo);
    } else {
        vo = C3dVector(0, 0, 0);
    }
    C3dVector cv;
    if (m_pDirLight && m_pScene) {
        if (m_bPhase) {
            m_pDirLight->SetColor(1, 0, 0);
            cv = C3dVector(-d, 0, -cz);
        } else {
            m_pDirLight->SetColor(0, 1, 0);
            cv = C3dVector(d, 0, -cz);
        }
        m_pScene->SetCameraPosition(cv);
        C3dVector vl = vo - cv;
        m_pScene->SetCameraDirection(vl);
    }

    // Update 3D window
    if (m_wnd3d.Update(1)) {
        bMore = TRUE;
    }
    return bMore;
}
```

The object's current position vector (*vo*) is used to compute the look vector (*vl*) for the camera so that the left and right views of the object converge at its center.

There are three flaws to implementing a stereo viewer this way.

◆ Because the left and right views are presented separately, the image tends to flicker noticeably.

◆ It is not possible to capture the stereo scene, so although the scene might not change, the application must constantly draw it.

◆ A new scene position effectively takes twice as long to draw to the screen as any other kind of scene because you need to render the scene once with a red light, then again with a green light to view a single frame.

All of these problems would be solved if both the left and right views could be rendered at once. What this means in practice is that the left picture, which consists entirely of red pixels, would be rendered to a buffer. The right picture, which consists entirely of green pixels, would then be *added* to the image in the buffer. The resulting composition could then be drawn to the screen. Unfortunately, this version of the rendering engine doesn't have any image mixing capabilities, so there is no way to combine the images in one buffer.

Shadows

Back at the start of this book I mentioned that the rendering technique that this engine uses doesn't cast shadows. However, we can simulate shadows for a few cases where they would be effective by creating a visual object that is the shape of the shadow we want and placing it approximately in the scene. Figure 10-9 shows the example in the Lights sample, created by choosing File-New from the menu followed by Edit-Insert Shape. Click OK on the Sphere tab, then Edit-Shadow.

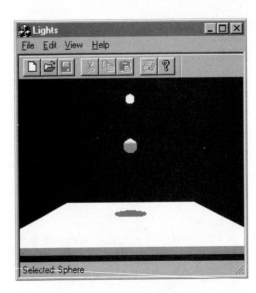

Figure 10-9. A simulated shadow.

The shadow is a visual object created by projecting the shape of the obscuring object onto a plane, using the light source position as a parameter. To make the shadow appear in the scene, it needs to be attached to a frame. Attaching the shadow to the obscuring object's frame makes the shadow move when the obscuring object moves. As a bonus, if you move the light, the shadow moves too. The plane the shadow will be cast onto is defined using a point that lies in the plane and the plane's normal vector. Here's the code fragment that creates the sphere in Figure 10-9 that's casting the shadow, and the code that attaches the shadow to the sphere:

```
void CMainFrame::OnEditShadow()
{
    :
    C3dShape* pCast = new C3dShape;
    pCast->CreateSphere(0.3);
    m_pScene->AddChild(pCast);
    m_pScene->m_ShapeList.Append(pCast);
    pCast->SetPosition(0, 1, 0);
    MakeCurrent(pCast);

    // Create a shadow object slightly above the plane
    C3dVector pt(0, -1.9, 0);        // Point in plane
    C3dVector normal(0, 1, 0);       // Normal to plane
    pCast->CreateShadow(pLight, pt, normal);
}
```

The *C3dShape::CreateShadow* function uses the current light, a point in the plane the shadow is to be cast onto, and the normal of the plane to create the shadow visual:

```
BOOL C3dShape::CreateShadow(C3dLight* pLight,
                            D3DVECTOR& vPt,
                            D3DVECTOR& vN)
{

    IDirect3DRMVisual* pIVisual = NULL;
    m_hr =
      the3dEngine.GetInterface()->CreateShadow(GetVisual(),
                                    pLight->GetLight(),
                                    vPt.x, vPt.y, vPt.z,
                                    vN.x, vN.y, vN.z,
                                    &pIVisual);
    ASSERT(SUCCEEDED(m_hr));

    // Attach shadow to frame
    ASSERT(m_pIFrame);
    m_hr = m_pIFrame->AddVisual(pIVisual);

    return SUCCEEDED(m_hr);
}
```

Because the shadow is a visual object just like any other shape in the scene, you must be careful when you specify the plane it is to be projected onto. Make sure that the plane is slightly above the surface the shadow is to apparently fall on. If you specify the actual plane of an object's face, the shadow pixels get mixed up with the face pixels at rendering time and the result is a bit random. Raising the shadow slightly above the surface gives it a clean appearance.

You should note that the shadow can only be projected onto a single plane. You can't have it bend around corners or over the edge of a cube. The projection plane is also considered to be infinite. If you run the demonstration shown in

Figure 10-9 on page 228, you'll find that by moving either the light or the shape, you can make the shadow slide out beyond the face of the plane it's being projected onto. It's also possible to drag the shape through the plane, and the shadow object will remain on top of the plane.

Obviously shadows give you some additional realism, but you must be careful how you employ them if you don't want to break the illusion. Figure 10-10 shows a screen shot from the Globe application, which we'll be looking at in Chapter 13, that uses a shadow to improve the scene's overall appearance. (Also see the color rendition of this figure in the color insert.)

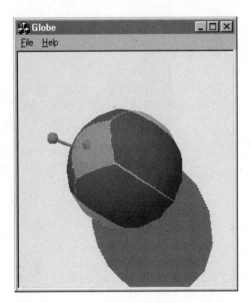

Figure 10-10. *The Globe application that uses a shadow.*

Summary

Using lights of various types can greatly improve the appearance of the scene. Because some lights are computationally more expensive than others, choose wisely if the performance of your application is important. Colored lights can be used for special effects, but remember that you must use the RGB color model. Shadows can also be used for realistic effects, but keep in mind that they are limited to a single plane.

y now you've learned most of what you need to make your own 3D applications. A few minor points remain to cover, but a lot of what we'll do in this chapter will be to apply what we've learned to a new application.

In this chapter we're going to look at a couple of ways to make movies. The first involves capturing the scene frame by frame, and the second involves capturing the position and orientation of a shape as it moves. Each method has its merits and drawbacks, so I'll present both and you can choose the one that suits your needs. The sample code for this chapter can be found in the Movie directory.

Using Frame Capture

This topic reminds me of a joke from my childhood that I will share with you whether you want to hear it or not: Cecil B. DeMille was out in the desert making a cowboy movie. The scene involved thousands of extras who were all waiting out in the hot sun. Three cameras were set up to record the take from various hilltops. The director called for action and the cast blazed off down the trail. After the take was complete, Mr. DeMille asked the cameramen if everything had gone OK. The first replied that his film had jammed and he had missed everything. The second replied that he had been enveloped in a cloud of dust and had seen only the first few seconds. The third was silent. Mr. DeMille shouted, "Hey you. Camera Three. How did it go?" This reply came back: "Ready, Mr. DeMille."

The concept of frame capture is quite simple: Each time the scene is moved and rendered, we want to grab the rendered image of the scene and save the image in a list. We can then play back the movie by copying the images in the list to the screen one after the other. If we like what we've captured, we can save all the images in the list to a disk file in a form that can be used elsewhere. The complete sequence of events is as follows:

1. Set up an empty image list.

2. Capture the current palette (if the display is 256 colors).

3. Save the current size of the 3D window.

4. Move any objects in the scene to new positions.

5. Render the scene to the back buffer.

6. Grab the image in the back buffer.

7. Add the image to the list.

8. Repeat from Step 4 as many times as needed.

Before we look at the code that does this, I want to warn you that this technique really eats system memory. For example, let's say you have a 320-by-240-pixel window on a 256-color display. That's 76,800 bytes per image. If we can record at 10 frames per second (fps), in 10 seconds we'll have used up 7,680,000 bytes of memory (ignoring the overhead required to manage the list, image headers, and so on). If you run the sample application, be aware that your disk is going to get a big thrashing once the available RAM is used up. Obviously there are some things we could do to improve the situation, such as compressing the image data or writing directly to a disk file, but we'll come to some of that later in this chapter. For now I want to take the simplistic approach and see what's involved in simply capturing frames.

The Movie Classes

I set up three classes in the 3dPlus library to support recording movies. I use a *CMovieFrame* object to hold the image for a single frame, a *CMovieTake* object to hold a palette and a list of frames (one take), and a *CMovie* object to hold an entire movie that could theoretically be several takes. However, unlike Mr. DeMille, we're going to get it right the first time, so the *CMovie* object will contain only one *CMovieTake*.

The interesting bits of code in the Movie application are those that capture the current palette on a 256-color display and those that capture the image from the rendering buffer.

Capturing the Palette

If your display uses more than 8 bits per pixel, you don't have a palette and you can skip this section. However, because a 256-color display is still the most common, it's quite likely you'll need to know how to capture a palette.

To speed up the frame capture process, I'm assuming that the palette doesn't change during the time we're capturing frames. This is true if you run the rendering engine in RGB mode where it uses a fixed color-cube palette but is not true in mono mode, where the engine dynamically modifies the palette entries according to what colors are needed. For a simple sequence, however, the set of objects doesn't change much and the palette is fairly stable. Therefore, grabbing the palette once isn't so unreasonable. OK, that's not a great argument. But as it turns out, to play back any sort of movie with acceptable performance, we can't afford to have a separate palette for each frame. Realizing a new palette in Microsoft Windows takes way too long and is, incidentally, rather ugly visually.

In addition to using only one palette, we actually need a special kind of palette, called an *identity palette,* that exactly matches the current system palette. Using an identity palette ensures that bitmap memory can be copied directly to video memory without color conversion. Converting the color index of each pixel from the bitmap to the color index in the physical palette is very slow. For a more in-depth discussion of this issue, refer to *Animation Techniques in Win32* (Thompson, Microsoft Press, 1995).

Given that we can have only one palette, grabbing the current palette at the start of a frame-recording session seems reasonable. Let's see how we do that. We'll start by viewing the object hierarchy in Figure 11-1, which shows how the movie object relates to the palette object.

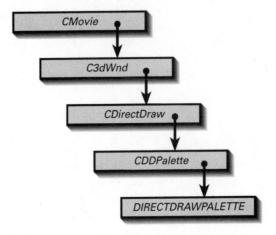

Figure 11-1. *The path from movie to palette.*

If you recall from way back in Chapter 2, the *C3dWnd* class is built on top of a *CDirectDraw* object. The *CDirectDraw* object includes a *CDDPalette* object. These classes all provide wrappers for the Direct3D interfaces and structures that manage the underlying video memory and the physical palette in the video adapter. Grabbing the palette requires getting access to the interface that controls the physical palette and asking it for the current set of colors. Here's the code from 3dDirGrb.cpp which does that:

```
CPalette* CDirectDraw::GrabPalette()
{
    if (!m_pPalette) return NULL;
    LOGPALETTE* plp = (LOGPALETTE*)new
      BYTE[sizeof(LOGPALETTE) + 256 * sizeof(PALETTEENTRY)];
    plp->palVersion    = 0x300;
    plp->palNumEntries = 256;
    m_pPalette->GetInterface()->GetEntries
                              (0,
                               0,
                               256,
                               plp->palPalEntry);

    // Initialize palette entry flags
    for (int i = 0; i < 256; i++)
        plp->palPalEntry[i].peFlags = 0;
```

```
    // Create palette from color set
    CPalette* pPal = new CPalette;
    pPal->CreatePalette(plp);
    delete plp;

    return pPal;
}
```

A *LOGPALETTE* structure is used to receive the palette colors, and a *CPalette* object is created to return them to the application. *CPalette* is an MFC class, and it is a convenient container for the colors, as we'll see when we look at how to play a movie back to the application's window.

The *CMovie* object code that requests the palette from the *DirectDraw* object at the start of each recording looks like this:

```
BOOL CMovie::Record()
{
    Stop();

    // Delete any existing recording
    m_Take.DeleteAll();
    m_iCurFrame = 0;

    // Grab current palette
    ASSERT(m_p3dWnd);
    CDirectDraw* pDD = m_p3dWnd->GetDD();
    ASSERT(pDD);
    m_Take.SetPalette(pDD->GrabPalette());

    // Save frame size
    CRect rc;
    m_p3dWnd->GetClientRect(&rc);
    m_Take.SetSize(rc.Width(), rc.Height());

    // Start recording
    m_bIsRecording = TRUE;
    return TRUE;
}
```

As you can see, the palette is saved in the current (only) *CMovieTake* object by calling *CMovieTake::SetPalette*. The current window's client area size is also saved. The actual recording of the frames takes place in the application's idle loop.

Capturing the Images from the Rendering Buffer

Capturing the rendered image from the rendering buffer is a complicated task because of the level of details involved, as we'll see on page 237. The fragment of code from the *CMovie::Update* function that is called in the application's idle loop to record the frames from the rendered images appears on the next page.

```
        ⋮
        // Get a pointer to DirectDraw object in 3D window
        ASSERT(m_p3dWnd);
        CDirectDraw* pDD = m_p3dWnd->GetDD();
        ASSERT(pDD);

        // Grab current image
        BITMAPINFO* pBMI = NULL;
        BYTE* pBits = NULL;
        HBITMAP hBmp = pDD->GrabImage(&pBMI,
                                      (void**)&pBits);
        ASSERT(hBmp);
        ASSERT(pBMI);
        ASSERT(pBits);

        // Create movie frame
        CMovieFrame* pFrame = new CMovieFrame(hBmp, pBMI,
                                              pBits);

        // Add this frame to the take
        m_Take.AddTail(pFrame);

        m_iCurFrame++;
        ⋮
```

The code above essentially consists of asking the *DirectDraw* object to grab the image, creating a new *CMovieFrame* object to encapsulate the grabbed image, and adding the *CMovieFrame* object to the end of the list of frames in the current take.

Each frame object containing a grabbed image is actually a chunk of memory called a device independent bitmap (DIB) section. This handy item can be used as a Windows bitmap (via an HBITMAP handle associated with it) and can also be directly written to using a pointer. We'll see how it gets created in just a minute, but it's worth noting that in the code above, the *hBmp*, *pBMI*, and *pBits* variables all relate to the grabbed image in one way or another. This can be very confusing when you want to delete the memory associated with the DIB section. It's important that you call *::DeleteObject* on the HBITMAP handle (*hBmp*) and that you do not try to delete the data using the *pBits* pointer. The *pBMI* variable points to a header block, which is deleted separately from the bits. It might seem ridiculously complex, but a DIB section can be accessed in several ways, and all these variables are required to manage it effectively.

The *CDirectDraw::GrabImage* function is significantly more complicated because it deals with a variety of possible buffer formats. The general process involves getting a description of the type of the composition buffer, creating a *BITMAPINFO* structure for a DIB section, creating a DIB section, creating a set of shift masks, and, finally, copying the bits. Some of the complexity arises because the pixel formats used for DirectDraw surfaces do not exactly match in every case the formats used in a DIB section, which means that the color components of the pixels need to be masked and shifted to match the format required in the DIB section.

I think that's prepared you enough. Here's the code that actually grabs the image from the rendering buffer:

```
// Grab current back buffer image.
// If bitmap info header or bits are returned, the caller
// must free the associated memory, using delete pBMI and
// ::DeleteObject(hBmp). Don't try to delete the bits, as
// they belong to the bitmap object.
HBITMAP CDirectDraw::GrabImage(BITMAPINFO** ppBMI,
                                void** ppBits)
{
    // Set initial return results
    if (ppBMI) *ppBMI= NULL;
    if (ppBits) *ppBits = NULL;
    if (!m_pBackBuffer) return NULL;

    // Lock back buffer to get its description.
    // WARNING: You can't step through this code with the
    // debugger - the GDI surface will be locked.
    LPDIRECTDRAWSURFACE iS = m_pBackBuffer->GetInterface();
    ASSERT(iS);
    DDSURFACEDESC ds;
    ds.dwSize = sizeof(ds);
    m_hr = iS->Lock(NULL,
                    &ds,
                    DDLOCK_WAIT,
                    NULL);
    if (m_hr != DD_OK) {
        TRACE("Failed to lock surface\n");
        return NULL; // Failed to lock surface
    }

    // Unlock surface again to use debugger
    // and also exit if needed
    m_hr = m_pBackBuffer->GetInterface()->
                        Unlock(ds.lpSurface);

    // Make sure surface is of a type we can deal with.
    // Note: We handle only 8-bpp pal, 16-bpp RGB, and 24-
    // bpp RGB here.
    if (!(ds.ddpfPixelFormat.dwFlags & DDPF_PALETTEINDEXED8)
        && !(ds.ddpfPixelFormat.dwFlags & DDPF_RGB)) {
        return NULL; // Don't handle this format
    }
    int iBitCount;
    if (ds.ddpfPixelFormat.dwFlags & DDPF_PALETTEINDEXED8) {
        iBitCount = 8;
```

(continued)

```
    } else if (ds.ddpfPixelFormat.dwFlags & DDPF_RGB) {
        // Check surface type is a bit depth we can deal
        // with
        iBitCount = ds.ddpfPixelFormat.dwRGBBitCount;
        if ((iBitCount != 16) && (iBitCount != 24)) {
            return NULL; // Not handled
        }
    }

    ASSERT(ds.dwFlags & DDSD_WIDTH);
    int iWidth = ds.dwWidth;
    ASSERT(ds.dwFlags & DDSD_HEIGHT);
    int iHeight = ds.dwHeight;

    // See if creating a color table is necessary
    int iClrTabEntries = 0;
    if (ds.ddpfPixelFormat.dwFlags & DDPF_PALETTEINDEXED8) {

        // Build a color table
        iClrTabEntries = 256;
        iBitCount = 8;
    }

    // Create BITMAPINFO structure to describe bitmap
    int iSize = sizeof(BITMAPINFO) + iClrTabEntries *
                sizeof(RGBQUAD);
    BITMAPINFO* pBMI = (BITMAPINFO*)new BYTE[iSize];
    memset(pBMI, 0, iSize);
    pBMI->bmiHeader.biSize = sizeof(BITMAPINFOHEADER);
    pBMI->bmiHeader.biWidth = iWidth;
    pBMI->bmiHeader.biHeight = iHeight;
    pBMI->bmiHeader.biPlanes = 1;
    pBMI->bmiHeader.biBitCount = iBitCount;
    pBMI->bmiHeader.biClrUsed = iClrTabEntries;

    HDC hdcScreen = ::GetDC(NULL);
    // Create color table if needed
    if (iClrTabEntries > 0) {
        ASSERT(iClrTabEntries <= 256);
        PALETTEENTRY pe[256];
        ASSERT(m_pPalette);
        m_pPalette->GetInterface()->GetEntries
                                    (0,
                                     0,
                                     iClrTabEntries,
                                     pe);
        for (int i = 0; i < iClrTabEntries; i++) {
            pBMI->bmiColors[i].rgbRed = pe[i].peRed;
            pBMI->bmiColors[i].rgbGreen = pe[i].peGreen;
            pBMI->bmiColors[i].rgbBlue = pe[i].peBlue;
        }
    }
```

```
// Create DIB section same size as back buffer
BYTE* pBits = NULL;
HBITMAP hBmp = ::CreateDIBSection(hdcScreen,
                                  pBMI,
                                  DIB_RGB_COLORS,
                                  (VOID**)&pBits,
                                  NULL,
                                  0);
::ReleaseDC(NULL, hdcScreen);
if (!hBmp) {
    delete pBMI;
    return NULL;
}
ASSERT(pBits);

// Copy bits to DIB surface

int iDIBScan =
    (((pBMI->bmiHeader.biWidth
        * pBMI->bmiHeader.biBitCount) + 31) & ~31) >> 3;
int iSurfScan = ds.lPitch;
BYTE* pDIBLine = pBits + (iHeight - 1) * iDIBScan;
BYTE* pSurfLine = (BYTE*)ds.lpSurface;

// Build shift masks.
// Shift down until the lsb of the source maps to the
// lsb of the destination.
// Shift again until we have only 5 bits of precision.
DWORD dwRShift = 0;
DWORD dwGShift = 0;
DWORD dwBShift = 0;
DWORD dwNotMask;
if ((ds.ddpfPixelFormat.dwFlags & DDPF_RGB) &&
    (iBitCount >= 16)) {
    if (iBitCount == 16) {
        dwNotMask = 0xFFFFFFE0;
    } else {
        dwNotMask = 0xFFFFFF00;
    }
    DWORD dwMask = ds.ddpfPixelFormat.dwRBitMask;
    ASSERT(dwMask);
    while ((dwMask & 0x01) == 0) {
        dwRShift++;
        dwMask = dwMask >> 1;
    }
    while ((dwMask & dwNotMask) != 0) {
        dwRShift++;
        dwMask = dwMask >> 1;
    }
    dwMask = ds.ddpfPixelFormat.dwGBitMask;
```

(continued)

```
        ASSERT(dwMask);
        while ((dwMask & 0x01) == 0) {
            dwGShift++;
            dwMask = dwMask >> 1;
        }
        while ((dwMask & dwNotMask) != 0) {
            dwGShift++;
            dwMask = dwMask >> 1;
        }
        dwMask = ds.ddpfPixelFormat.dwBBitMask;
        ASSERT(dwMask);
        while ((dwMask & 0x01) == 0) {
            dwBShift++;
            dwMask = dwMask >> 1;
        }
        while ((dwMask & dwNotMask) != 0) {
            dwBShift++;
            dwMask = dwMask >> 1;
        }
}

// Lock surface again to get bits
m_hr = iS->Lock(NULL,
                &ds,
                DDLOCK_SURFACEMEMORYPTR | DDLOCK_WAIT,
                NULL);
ASSERT(m_hr == DD_OK);

for (int y = 0; y < iHeight; y++) {
    switch (iBitCount) {
    case 8:     {
        BYTE* pDIBPix = pDIBLine;
        BYTE* pSurfPix = pSurfLine;
        for (int x = 0; x < iWidth; x++) {
            *pDIBPix++ = *pSurfPix++;
        }
        } break;

    case 16: {
        WORD* pDIBPix = (WORD*)pDIBLine;
        WORD* pSurfPix = (WORD*)pSurfLine;
        WORD r, g, b;
        for (int x = 0; x < iWidth; x++) {
            r = (*pSurfPix & (WORD)
                ds.ddpfPixelFormat.dwRBitMask)
                >> dwRShift;
            g = (*pSurfPix & (WORD)
                ds.ddpfPixelFormat.dwGBitMask)
                >> dwGShift;
            b = (*pSurfPix & (WORD)
                ds.ddpfPixelFormat.dwBBitMask)
                >> dwBShift;
```

```
                *pDIBPix++ = ((r & 0x1F) << 10)
                           | ((g & 0x1F) << 5)
                           | (b & 0x1F);
            pSurfPix++;
        }
        } break;

    case 24: {
        BYTE* pDIBPix = pDIBLine;
        BYTE* pSurfPix = pSurfLine;

        for (int x = 0; x < iWidth; x++) {
            // WARNING: I'm assuming the same RGB masks
            // for surface and DIB, which is not really
            // valid. We should look at
            // ds.ddpfPixelFormat.dwRGBBitMask.
            *pDIBPix++ = *pSurfPix++;
            *pDIBPix++ = *pSurfPix++;
            *pDIBPix++ = *pSurfPix++;
        }
        } break;

    default:
        // Shouldn't be able to get here
        break;
    }
    pDIBLine -= iDIBScan;
    pSurfLine += iSurfScan;
}

// Unlock buffer
m_hr = m_pBackBuffer->GetInterface()->
                    Unlock(ds.lpSurface);

// See if bitmap info header is returned
if (ppBMI) {
    *ppBMI = pBMI;
} else {
    delete pBMI;
}

// See if bits pointer is returned
if (ppBits) *ppBits = pBits;

// Return bitmap handle
return hBmp;
}
```

If this has put you off wanting to make movies, remember that this code exists! I wrote it, so all you need to do is call it. A detailed description of this function is beyond the scope of this chapter and really beyond the scope of this book.

I created this code by referring to the Direct3D documentation on the subject of Immediate Mode and by using some of the sample code that ships with the DirectX 2 SDK. You can read more about Immediate Mode in Chapter 13.

Given that we have grabbed the currently rendered scene's image, what happens next? A *CMovieFrame* object is created to hold the image, and the frame is added to the list of frames in the *CMovieTake* object.

Playing Back the Movie

Playing a captured set of frames is relatively easy. In fact, if you have just waded through the *GrabImage* code above, you'll think it's trivial. The code does, however, have a few small points that are important to performance. Just before we play back a set of frames, the *CMovie::Stop* function is called to halt the recording process. This might seem like an irrelevant detail, but the function includes one extremely important line (can you spot it?):

```
void CMovie::Stop()
{
    if (m_bIsPlaying) {
        m_bIsPlaying = FALSE;

        // Remap colors
        m_Take.Optimize();
    }
    if (m_bIsRecording) {
        m_bIsRecording = FALSE;
    }
}
```

So what does *Optimize* do? It makes the captured palette into an identity palette and maps the colors of all the frames to the new palette. At least that's what it should do. In practice, I've found that I can cheat a bit and shorten the optimization time considerably by omitting the step that maps the image colors. In other words, I'm optimizing playback by creating a new palette (an identity palette) but I'm not bothering to map the image's colors to the new palette. How can the resultant screen colors display correctly if the images were created using a different palette from the one we're using to display them?

Because the identity palette is very similar to the original palette, and in some cases it will be exactly the same. The only colors in the palette that are likely to change are the 20 reserved system colors, of which 10 are at the start of the palette and 10 are at the end. These colors aren't used by the renderer and don't affect the final image if we change them. In any case, any change is usually insignificant to the image. Perhaps this explanation doesn't convince you; I won't be surprised if it doesn't. *Animation Techniques in Win32* covers this icky subject in detail if you'd like to know more. I'll leave you to browse the code for *Optimize* at your leisure.

So now we're ready to play back the movie. Because we obviously can't render the scene *and* play back the movie in the same window simultaneously, the idle time handler in the application that normally updates and renders the scene is disabled during playback. Given that the renderer has been temporarily suspended, the following code gets called in *CMovie::Update* during playback mode to draw the next frame of the recording to the window:

```
BOOL CMovie::Update()
{
    if (m_bIsPlaying) {

        // Show next frame
        if (m_Take.IsEmpty()) {
            m_bIsPlaying = FALSE;
            return FALSE;
        }

        // Find current frame
        POSITION pos = m_Take.FindIndex(m_iCurFrame);
        if (!pos) {
            m_bIsPlaying = FALSE;
            return FALSE;
        }
        CMovieFrame* pFrame = m_Take.GetAt(pos);
        ASSERT(pFrame);

        // Get window device context (DC)
        ASSERT(m_p3dWnd);
        CDC* pdc = m_p3dWnd->GetDC();

        // Set up palette
        CPalette* pOldPal = NULL;
        CPalette* pPal = m_Take.GetPalette();
        if (pPal) {
            pOldPal = pdc->SelectPalette(pPal, FALSE);
            pdc->RealizePalette();
        }

        // Create memory DC for bitmap
        CDC dcMem;
        dcMem.CreateCompatibleDC(pdc);

        // Select palette and place into memory DC
        CPalette* pOldMemPal = NULL;
        if (pPal) {
            pOldMemPal = dcMem.SelectPalette(pPal, FALSE);
            dcMem.RealizePalette();
        }
```

(continued)

```
// Select bitmap and place into memory DC
HBITMAP hOldBmp = (HBITMAP) ::SelectObject(dcMem,
                                           pFrame->m_hBmp);

// Copy bitmap to window
pdc->BitBlt(0, 0,
            m_Take.GetWidth(), m_Take.GetHeight(),
            &dcMem,
            0, 0,
            SRCCOPY);

// Tidy up
if (pOldMemPal) {
    dcMem.SelectPalette(pOldMemPal, FALSE);
}
::SelectObject(dcMem, hOldBmp);
if (pOldPal) {
    pdc->SelectPalette(pOldPal, FALSE);
}
m_p3dWnd->ReleaseDC(pdc);

m_iCurFrame++;
return TRUE; // More frames
    ⋮
}
```

The sequence of events in the code above is as follows:

1. Find the next frame to play.

2. Get a device context (DC) for the window.

3. Select the palette, and place it in the window DC.

4. Create a memory DC.

5. Select the palette, and place it in the memory DC.

6. Select the bitmap handle in the *CMovieFrame* object, and place it in the memory DC.

7. Call *BitBlt* to copy the image from the memory DC to the window DC.

8. Tidy up the DCs, and release them.

Veteran Windows programmers will recognize this horrendous task list as necessary in drawing any bitmap to a window.

If you haven't traveled this road before, you might think that selecting and realizing the palette so many times is bound to be slow. But Windows knows to take no action if you do this repeatedly with the same palette, so the only expense is calling *BitBlt*.

Astute readers might now be wondering why we are using *BitBlt*. After all, we have DirectDraw installed and, in fact, we're sitting on top of a DirectDraw surface. Surely we can reverse the process we used to grab the image and send the image back to the DirectDraw surface, achieving the same result. This is what we generally refer to as an exercise for the student. And why is that? Look back at the huge wad of code used to grab the image on page 237, and imagine reversing that process. Now you know why you're doing it and not me! In practice it doesn't matter how you perform this task, so I chose a way that is familiar to me. You can, of course, experiment with any technique you want.

Is It Worth It?

To summarize what we've discussed so far: The code is vast, and it uses lots of memory. That's not usually a good indicator. In fact, given that you generally don't have enough memory to keep an entire movie in real memory (rather than swapped out to the paging file), the playback process is slowed by the disk data transfer rate in most cases. So capturing frames is a somewhat brutal technique for making a movie sequence. We can take the process a bit further, though, and that next step is worth exploring.

Making an AVI File

We can take the list of captured frames and build an AVI file that the Microsoft Video for Windows components can play on almost any Windows machine, whether it has Direct3D installed or not. If you have a video compressor and expander (CODEC) installed on your Windows machine, you can compress the data by a factor that depends on the CODEC. An MPEG (Motion Picture Expert Group) compressed movie can actually be quite small. The code I'm about to show you doesn't do any compression but simply writes the sequence of frames to an AVI file. You'll need to write extra code or use third-party tools to compress the file it creates.

Once again, I have to punt on explaining this code because the subject requires more space and time than I have available. The Microsoft Development Library is the best resource for documentation on Video for Windows. Here's the *CMovie::Save* function that creates the AVI file from the image list:

```
BOOL CMovie::Save()
{
    if (GetNumFrames() <= 0) return FALSE;

    // Get file name
    ASSERT(m_p3dWnd);
    CFileDialog dlg(FALSE,
                    "avi",
```

(continued)

```
                        NULL,
                        OFN_OVERWRITEPROMPT,
                        "AVI Files (*.avi)|*.avi||",
                        m_p3dWnd);
    if (dlg.DoModal() != IDOK) return FALSE;

    // Open AVI file
    HRESULT hr;
    PAVIFILE pfile = NULL;
    hr = ::AVIFileOpen(&pfile,
                       dlg.GetFileName(),
                       OF_CREATE | OF_WRITE,
                       NULL);
    if (FAILED(hr)) return FALSE;

    // Create video stream in file
    PAVISTREAM pstream = NULL;
    AVISTREAMINFO si;
    memset(&si, 0, sizeof(si));
    si.fccType = streamtypeVIDEO;
    si.fccHandler = mmioFOURCC('M','S','V','C');
    si.dwRate = 100; // Fps
    si.dwScale = 1;
    si.dwLength = 0;
    si.dwQuality = (DWORD) -1;
    si.rcFrame.top = 0;
    si.rcFrame.left = 0;
    si.rcFrame.bottom = m_Take.GetHeight();
    si.rcFrame.right = m_Take.GetWidth();
    strcpy(si.szName, "3dPlus Movie");

    hr = ::AVIFileCreateStream(pfile, &pstream, &si);
    ASSERT(SUCCEEDED(hr));

    // Set format
    CMovieFrame* pFrame = m_Take.GetHead();
    ASSERT(pFrame);
    int iSize = sizeof(BITMAPINFOHEADER)
            + DIBColorEntries((BITMAPINFOHEADER*)
            (pFrame->m_pBMI))
            * sizeof(RGBQUAD);
    hr = ::AVIStreamSetFormat(pstream,
                              0,
                              pFrame->m_pBMI,
                              iSize);
    ASSERT(SUCCEEDED(hr));

    // Write out frames
    POSITION pos = m_Take.GetHeadPosition();
    int iSample = 0;
```

```
    while (pos) {

        CMovieFrame* pFrame = m_Take.GetNext(pos);
        BITMAPINFOHEADER* pBIH = (BITMAPINFOHEADER*)
                            &(pFrame->m_pBMI->bmiHeader);
        int iBits = DIBStorageWidth(pBIH) * pBIH->biHeight;
        hr = ::AVIStreamWrite(pstream,
                        iSample, // This sample
                        1, // Just the one, thank you
                        pFrame->m_pBits, // The data
                        iBits, // Size of the buffer
                        0,
                        NULL,
                        NULL);
        ASSERT(SUCCEEDED(hr));
        iSample++;
    }

    // Release stream
    ::AVIStreamRelease(pstream);

    // Release AVI stream and file
    ::AVIFileRelease(pfile);

    return TRUE;
}
```

The short story is that a new AVI file is created and a video stream created in it. The type of the video stream is set using an image BITMAPINFOHEADER, and the image's frame is written out to the stream. The stream and the file are then closed. The file can be played by either the Windows 95 Media Viewer or another similar tool.

Grabbing Just One Frame

You might like to try grabbing just one frame. Why? Because if you spend a lot of time setting up a wonderful 3D scene, you might like to save what it looks like. The Save sample on the companion CD uses the image capture code we saw on page 237 to grab just one image and then write it out as a Windows device independent bitmap (DIB) file. I'll leave you to explore the code if you're interested.

Using Shape Data Capture

So, grabbing frames for a movie is expensive in code and memory usage, and playback is limited by the disk data transfer rate (or network, CD, or whatever). Movies also are not interactive, which prohibits their use in a lot of applications. If we want to have some objects busily flying around in a window, perhaps we'd better explore another technique.

In Chapter 6 we created some objects that zipped along very nicely, but their movement was limited to circular paths. At the time, I mentioned that the paths don't need to be circular but could, in fact, be any shape you wanted. What we're going to look at now is a way to create a path by placing an object at points along the path and recording the object's position and orientation at each point. We can then play back the path, interpolating between the recorded point positions to make a smooth trajectory. To be consistent with the Direct3D documentation, I'll refer to this technique as *creating an animation*. As you'll see when you try it out, the performance of the rendering engine is such that this technique makes the frame capture type of movie almost redundant.

Quaternions

The Direct3D engine uses quaternions to define rotation in its animation sequences. I want to own up right now and tell you that before I wrote the Movie sample for this chapter, I had no idea what a *quaternion* is. After reading a lot of reference material, I can now tell you that a quaternion is yet another tricky mathematical function that does something cute with very little data. It is also completely impossible to explain in English. (That's being a bit unfair, actually, since the inventor of quaternions, a Mr. W. R. Hamilton, managed to write rather a lot about them in 1843 for the Royal Irish Academy.) But for your benefit, I will take a stab at defining them. A quaternion is a mathematical means of describing an object's rotation in space using a minimal number of variables. For our 3D world, it takes only four values to define a quaternion. The final rotation of an object can be described by a quaternion that is the product of all the quaternions that describe individual rotations along the object's path. So the short story is that quaternions are a very data-efficient way to describe an object's rotation.

I tried for a considerable period of time to get a *C3dQuaternion* class to perform exactly the way I wanted it to. I could not, however, get it right, and because time was running out, I abandoned quaternions and the animation sequence support that is built into the Direct3D engine in favor of my own animation sequence recorder and a few *C3dVector* objects. If you *do* know how to make a quaternion, I really don't mind if you throw out my solution. Of course, I'd love to see your class if you get it working.

There is one other reason I chose not to use quaternions, which has nothing to do with how hard they are to construct: In practice, using quaternions to control object motion can have undesirable side effects. A quaternion describes the overall effect of a rotation, but it doesn't describe which way you got there. So if you interpolate between quaternions as a means of determining intermediate positions along a flight path, it's possible that your object will exhibit "unrealistic" behavior in the way it moves from one position to another. You can adjust for this problem by including more control points, but those additional points defeat the advantage of the quaternion's data compactness.

Recording an Object's Path

In the absence of quaternions, I decided that to faithfully record a *C3dShape*'s position in a scene I needed to save its position, direction, and up vector values. (The direction and up vectors require six values for the quaternion's four, so there is a little waste here.) I created a *C3dAnimKey* object to hold the data:

```
class C3dAnimKey : public C3dObject
{
public:
    C3dAnimKey(double time,
               const D3DVECTOR& pos,
               const D3DVECTOR& dir,
               const D3DVECTOR& up)
      : m_vPos(pos), m_vDir(dir), m_vUp(up), m_dTime(time)
    {
    }

public:
    C3dVector m_vPos;
    C3dVector m_vDir;
    C3dVector m_vUp;
    double m_dTime;
};
```

As you can see, it's essentially a structure with a simple constructor to initialize it. The animation itself is based on the MFC *CObList* class and consists of a list of *C3dAnimKey* objects, a pointer to the frame of the shape that's being controlled, and a variable to hold the current time along the path. The units of time are arbitrary. You record points, specifying a time value for each. The points are inserted into the list in chronological order, and the playback interpolates linearly between them to give you any position along the path.

NOTE

At the time of writing, the Direct3D animation support included only linear interpolation. By the time you get this book, it might also include spline-based path interpolation, which would make figuring out the quaternions a more valuable goal. (Of course, you can always do your own spline code, too.)

Recording is done by clearing the list, placing the object in the scene, and adding a key point for each position of the object that you want to use to define the animation path. Playback then moves along the path in 0.1 time unit increments. I made the recording process in the Movie sample add points at 1.0 time unit intervals for simplicity, so the motion during playback is not particularly easy to predict while you're recording. The Movie sample includes a Demonstration menu option under the Edit menu that records a sequence and plays it back continuously until you stop it.

To simplify the sample code, I added a global *C3dAnimation* object to the application that allows you to animate only one object in the sample at a time.

The implementation is so simple that it's almost pointless to include it here, but, in the spirit of completeness, we'll look briefly at the key functions in the

C3dAnimation class. Let's start by seeing how a new key point is added to the list. I'll assume that a shape is already associated with the animation from an earlier call to *C3dAnimation::Attach*:

```
BOOL C3dAnimation::AddKey(double time)
{
    if (!m_pFrame) return FALSE;

    // Get frame's position and orientation
    C3dVector p, d, u;
    m_pFrame->GetPosition(p);
    m_pFrame->GetDirection(d, u);

    // Create new key
    C3dAnimKey* pKey = new C3dAnimKey(time, p, d, u);

    // Add key to list
    return AddKey(pKey);
}
```

This function takes the frame's current position and orientation and creates a new *C3dAnimKey* object. The key is then added to the list:

```
BOOL C3dAnimation::AddKey(C3dAnimKey* pNewKey)
{
    if (!pNewKey) return FALSE;

    // Update current time
    m_dCurTime = pNewKey->m_dTime;

    // Insert key into list
    if (IsEmpty()) {

        AddTail(pNewKey);
        return TRUE;

    }

    // Step through list backward
    POSITION pos = GetTailPosition();
    ASSERT(pos);
    do {
        POSITION thispos = pos;
        C3dAnimKey* pKey = (C3dAnimKey*) GetPrev(pos);
        if (pKey->m_dTime <= pNewKey->m_dTime) {

            // Insert new key after this one
            InsertAfter(thispos, pNewKey);
            return TRUE;

        }
    } while (pos);
```

```
    // Put new key in at start
    AddHead(pNewKey);

    return TRUE;
}
```

New keys are added by searching the list backward from the end, because the
search is generally shorter that way.

Having built a list, playback consists of sitting in a loop and setting the time
of the animation, which causes the object to be moved according to the time in
the animation sequence. Here's the playback code fragment from the application's
idle loop:

```
BOOL CMainFrame::Update()
{
    ⋮
    if (m_bPlayAnimation) {

        double l = m_Anim.GetLength();
        double t = m_Anim.GetCurTime();
        t += 0.1;
        if (t > l) {
            if (m_bLoopAnim) {
                m_Anim.SetTime(0.0);
            } else {
                m_bPlayAnimation = FALSE;
                Status("End of animation");
            }
        } else {
            m_Anim.SetTime(t);
        }
    }
    ⋮
}
```

The animation time is advanced by 0.1 unit. If the end is reached, the animation is either stopped or restarted, depending on the state of *m_bLoopAnim*. The
C3dAnimation::SetTime function that sets the frame's position is shown on the
next page.

```
BOOL C3dAnimation::SetTime(double time)
{
    m_dCurTime = time;

    if (!m_pFrame) return FALSE;
    if (IsEmpty()) return FALSE;

    // Step through list looking for pair of keys that
    // bracket this value (or an exact match)
    POSITION pos = GetHeadPosition();
    ASSERT(pos);
    C3dAnimKey* pBefore = (C3dAnimKey*) GetNext(pos);
    ASSERT(pBefore);
    if (pBefore->m_dTime > time) return FALSE; // No key
                                               // that early

    C3dAnimKey* pAfter = NULL;
    while (pos) {

        pAfter = (C3dAnimKey*) GetNext(pos);
        ASSERT(pAfter);
        if ((pBefore->m_dTime <= time) &&
            (pAfter->m_dTime >= time)) break;
        pBefore = pAfter;
    }

    // Compute interpolated values
    C3dVector p, d, u;
    double dt;
    if (pAfterh!= NULL) {
        dt = pAfter->m_dTime - pBefore->m_dTime;
    } else {
        dt = pBefore->m_dTime;
    }
    if ((pAfter == NULL) || (dt == 0)) {
        p = pBefore->m_vPos;
        d = pBefore->m_vDir;
        u = pBefore->m_vUp;
    } else {
        double r = (time - pBefore->m_dTime) / dt;
        p = pBefore->m_vPos + (pAfter->m_vPos -
            pBefore->m_vPos) * r;
        d = pBefore->m_vDir + (pAfter->m_vDir -
            pBefore->m_vDir) * r;
        u = pBefore->m_vUp + (pAfter->m_vUp -
            pBefore->m_vUp) * r;
    }

    // Set new position and direction
    m_pFrame->SetPosition(p);
    m_pFrame->SetDirection(d, u);
```

```
        return TRUE;
    }
```

The list is searched for two points spanning the requested time, and the position, direction, and up vectors are linearly interpolated from the values at the two points. This code shows just how wonderful the *C3dVector* class is at keeping the code readable. Imagine having to do the computations on all the individual vector components in here!

The *AddKey* and *SetTime* functions were named so as to be similar to names used in the Direct3D animation interface. If you do fancy your chances with the quaternion, you won't need to make too many changes to the application code to use it.

Exercises for You

Hang on, don't stop reading yet! I've got a few things you might like to try out. Before we get into them, however, I want to point out that this chapter had nothing much to do with 3D graphics. Everything that we looked at here is also applicable to 2D sprite-based graphics. We've passed the point where you're learning *how* to do the 3D techniques; instead, we're now concentrating on *what* you can do with them. So, really, you've graduated, and in the spirit of graduation, you get a few postgraduate tasks to try out.

1. Create a list class for animations, and create a scene with many objects all in motion at the same time. Model the solar system, for example.

2. Try attaching the animation sequence directly to an object derived from *C3dShape* so that each object has its own path. Create the scene for Problem 1 again. Is this better than the solution for Problem 1?

3. Modify the *C3dAnimation::SetTime* function to use splines instead of linear interpolation.

4. Do a comparison of the frame capture and point animation techniques. Are there applications where the choice of which one to use is clear cut?

12

The DirectDraw Interface

Welcome to the Engine Room. In this chapter we're going to look at the DirectDraw interface, which provides very low-level access to the video hardware. We'll look at what it does, how it is built, and what you can do with it. The sample application for this chapter can be found in the DDEval directory.

What Is DirectDraw?

DirectDraw is a software component that provides a consistent interface to a variety of video hardware. If you're thinking that we've already got one of those, the Microsoft Windows Graphics Device Interface (GDI), you're right. The difference between DirectDraw and GDI is that DirectDraw is designed to let you access the video hardware as directly as possible and GDI is designed to keep you away from it! That's perhaps a little unfair to GDI, but the truth is that Windows GDI was designed to enable application developers to create portable applications, and you don't get portability by letting everyone party on the video chip set.

Creating portable applications is all very well, but if the software layers that provide the portability are too thick or inefficient, the performance of the applications suffers and they might be too slow for the purpose for which they were designed. Games are a class of application in which a slight performance edge can mean the difference between heavy sales and heavy losses.

Even though Windows GDI has improved over the years, there has always been a case for avoiding it altogether and going straight to the hardware—for example, when the target application is going to run full-screen. After all, if the application is using the entire screen, who cares how it draws to the hardware? No matter what your point of view, the release of the DirectDraw interfaces gives us nearly direct hardware access in any Windows application. The only decision remaining is, should you use it?

To help you answer this question, we'll take a brief tour of the most interesting features of DirectDraw and look at a simple application that makes use of them. This should provide you with enough tools to experiment with DirectDraw on your own.

DirectDraw Architecture

Figure 12-1 shows a slightly simplified view of both the GDI and the DirectDraw architectures from the perspective of an application that might want to draw some 3D objects.

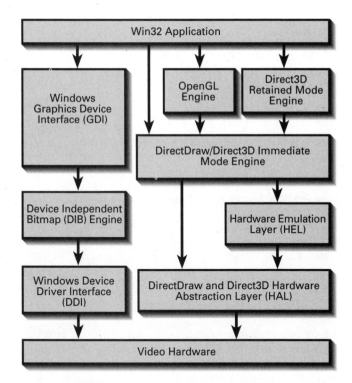

Figure 12-1. *The GDI and DirectDraw architectures.*

As you can see, the application has four different ways it can draw a 3D object onto the video hardware:

◆ GDI

◆ OpenGL

◆ Direct3D Retained Mode

◆ DirectDraw

Drawing with GDI

The path we're most familiar with as Windows programmers is shown on the left in Figure 12-1. The application calls functions in GDI, which translate to calls into the DIB engine. The DIB engine calls a video device driver, which writes to the video hardware. To implement a 3D application using this path, you need to do all your own coordinate transformations, depth computations, clipping, and so on. The result of all that work should be an application that can be compiled to run on a wide variety of platforms.

Drawing with OpenGL

I've included the OpenGL rendering engine in this discussion to provide a complete picture. OpenGL is an integral part of Win32 and provides a way for you to create fairly portable 3D applications without having to do your own depth computations and so on. The OpenGL language is supported on a wide variety of systems, making your application, in principle, very portable. The quality of implementation of OpenGL varies quite a bit from platform to platform, so performance can also vary. Because the implementation in Microsoft Windows 95 takes advantage of the Direct3D layer, the performance is better than on some other systems.

Drawing with Direct3D Retained Mode

We've been using the Direct3D Retained Mode so far. The Retained Mode engine is in many ways similar to OpenGL. The primary difference is that the Retained Mode engine is highly tuned for the Direct3D layer to give absolutely the best possible performance.

Drawing with DirectDraw

The path we're going to look at now is the one that goes from the application directly to the DirectDraw/Direct3D engine layer. In particular, we're interested in the DirectDraw part of the path that winds down through the Hardware Abstraction Layer (HAL) and the Hardware Emulation Layer (HEL) to the hardware. In some ways, choosing to use only the DirectDraw services is a bit like using GDI because you have to do a lot of the work yourself. If you know what you're doing, however, this route potentially gives you the best possible performance because you have virtually direct access to the video hardware. If you're considering porting an existing rendering engine to Windows, this is the path to follow.

The diagram in Figure 12-1 shows the DirectDraw and Direct3D components in one box. The two components are similar in many ways, so one box describes them well in an architectural picture. However, they are distinct, and we're going to look at only DirectDraw in this chapter. We'll cover Direct3D in Chapter 13.

The Hardware Abstraction Layer (HAL)

I don't like either "abstraction" or "layer" because both words imply fat and slow software, and the HAL is neither of those. The HAL exists to provide a consistent way of talking to the video hardware. In many cases, you could consider it simply a table of which bits can be found where. For example, the HAL needs to know where the video memory starts if it's mapped into the main memory address space. It also needs to know which port the color lookup table (hardware palette) is accessed through and so on. In principle, the HAL is extremely thin.

Most video cards have their memory arranged in one large, contiguous block, so you can get a pointer to the video memory and draw directly to it. Some older VGA-era cards use a bank-switching technology to map chunks of the video memory into a small window in the processor's address space. This means that you can get a pointer to only a part of the memory, which is where the HAL comes to the rescue. The HAL can simulate a large, flat video-memory buffer by giving you an address to read from and write to that doesn't physically exist. When you attempt to read or write to that address range, the processor then generates an exception that the HAL traps and uses to map in the correct chunk of video memory. By employing a virtual memory scheme such as this for video memory, practically all video cards can be made to look as if they have a single, flat video-address space.

So to summarize, the HAL is generally a thin code layer that tracks where a particular video card has its memory and operating registers. In some cases, it provides an emulation mechanism to simulate a flat memory address space.

The Hardware Emulation Layer (HEL)

The HEL exists to provide services not supported by a given piece of video hardware. Many video cards contain hardware to perform bit block transfers (bitblts) from one piece of video memory to another. Some cards include blitters that can transfer to and from main memory as well as video memory. In your code, you want to bitblt a sprite from one place to another without regard for where it's stored. That means that some piece of code outside your application needs to keep track of the separate capabilities of hardware and software. The HEL provides this functionality through bitblt functions that help out when the hardware isn't capable of a particular operation.

The DirectDraw Components

We can view the architecture from a slightly different viewpoint, as shown in Figure 12-2 on the next page.

From this point of view, DirectDraw provides an interface for a big chunk of video memory and a palette. I've shown a palette here because 256-color palletized displays are still the most common. If your display runs at 16, 24, or 32 bits per pixel, you don't need a palette and the picture is a little simpler. Ignoring the palette for a moment, we see that the application needs access to the video memory and the ability to move bits of the video memory around.

In a typical animated application, we use several video memory buffers. A front buffer contains the scene that's actually being presented by the video hardware to the user. A back buffer composes the next scene for display. In a typical 2D animation, we'd also have several sprites for the characters in the current scene. Ideally we'd like these sprites to be cached in buffers that the video blitter can get at efficiently, which is generally somewhere in the video memory.

If you consider that the HEL will provide bitblt capabilities even if the hardware doesn't directly support them, you can see why we don't need to include the hardware blitter in the picture in Figure 12-2. The application's view consists of various pieces of video memory and, maybe, a palette.

The picture in Figure 12-2 might be a little more complex if the application were 3D rather than just 2D, but we'll address those differences in the next chapter. Now we're going to discuss the DirectDraw components and ways to control them.

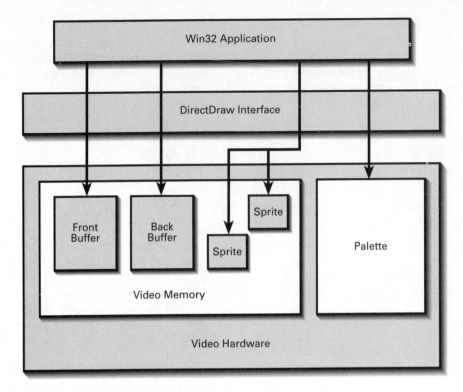

Figure 12-2. *The DirectDraw components.*

Video Memory Surfaces

DirectDraw divides the video memory up into *surfaces*. Because each surface can be as big as the largest free block of memory, you can have one surface that uses all of the memory or many smaller surfaces. Surfaces can also be created in main memory, so when you've used up all the available video memory, you don't need to change your programming model. Of course, drawing to surfaces in main memory might not be as efficient as drawing to surfaces in video memory, so you do need to keep track of how you use them.

Surfaces can also have other surfaces attached to them. Consider the arrangement in Figure 12-2. The back buffer could be an attached surface of the front buffer and might make them simpler to keep track of because you then need maintain a pointer only to the front buffer. The back buffer pointer can always be obtained from the front buffer's attached surface list. When working in 3D you might need to use a surface as a Z buffer, and this, too, can be conveniently attached to your front buffer. You can also use a surface as an alpha buffer and attach that to another surface.

A surface is described by a *DDSURFACEDESC* structure that contains fields for the height, width, and so on. This structure also contains a *DDPIXELFORMAT* structure, which describes the individual pixels of the surface. A pixel might be an RGB value, a palette index, a YUV value, or some other format your hardware supports. The number of bits per pixel can vary from 1 through 32. For surfaces with 16 or more bits per pixel, the individual color components (red, green, and blue, for example) are described by mask values that are ANDed with the pixel value to extract them.

Access to a surface is obtained by locking it, which returns a pointer. When you're done with the surface, you unlock it. The locks control who can read and/or write to a surface and also help to control interaction with the blitter hardware and so on. Therefore, you need to be aware of who is using a surface before you attempt to gain access to it. We'll be looking at an example of how this is done a little later in the section "Testing Direct Pixel Access" on page 277.

It is possible for you to lose a surface that you have been working with if another application that uses DirectDraw is also running. If you attempt to perform an operation on a surface that has been lost, the operation will generally return the DDERR_SURFACELOST code. You can recover the lost surface by calling the surface's *IDirectDrawSurface::Restore* function. (Windows is a sharing environment—you get used to it eventually.)

Surfaces can also include a single color or range of colors that can be used as a color key. The support for color keys is quite varied and can be used to define source areas of a surface not to be copied or areas of a destination surface not to be written to. The *IDirectDrawSurface::Blt* function also includes a flag to control color key use during copy operations.

Palettes

Surfaces of 1, 4, or 8 bits per pixel need a palette to describe their colors. DirectDraw supports 4-bit and 8-bit palettes, which gives you up to 16 or 256 colors. A palette can also be a set of indices into another palette. If you've used palettes in Windows, you'll find using the DirectDraw palettes very similar. If you're used to playing with the video hardware color lookup tables, you'll probably like the flexibility the DirectDraw palettes have. We'll see how a palette is created later on page 279.

Most video hardware supports only one palette, but DirectDraw allows you to associate an arbitrary palette with a surface. You should be aware, though, that the bitblt operations do not support color conversion; if you bitblt from one surface to another with a different palette, the results won't be pretty.

You can actually control how much of a palette DirectDraw is allowed to use when you set up the palette. If you are running in a windowed mode, you typically reserve the 20 Windows system colors (10 at each end of the palette) and let DirectDraw use the remaining 236 entries. If you run in full-screen mode, no other applications are visible, so you don't need to reserve the system colors for them to use and you can let DirectDraw use all of the palette. DirectDraw defines some new palette entry flags (in addition to the existing Windows flags) that control palette entry use. Use the D3DRMPALETTE_FREE flag to allow DirectDraw to use an entry, use D3DRMPALETTE_READONLY to allow DirectDraw to read (and use) the entry but not to alter it (use this for the system color entries in the windowed case), and use D3DRMPALETTE_RESERVED to reserve a palette entry for your own use. DirectDraw won't alter or use entries marked with the D3DRMPALETTE_RESERVED flag.

Video Memory Clippers

You can use DirectDraw in one of two modes. The one that excites most ex–DOS games programmers is the full-screen mode. Once you're in full-screen mode, you have total control over the video presented to the user. You typically have two buffers, as shown in Figure 12-3.

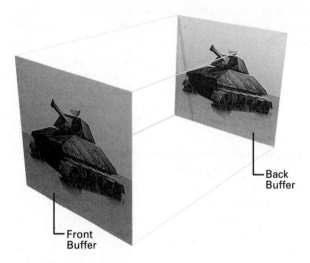

Figure 12-3. *Full-screen buffering.*

The front buffer and the back buffer are the same size. In this mode, you can actually flip buffers by telling the video hardware to use the back buffer for the live buffer instead of the front buffer. This gives you a page flip with zero overhead. You can, of course, also use the blitter functions to bitblt bits of the back buffer to the front buffer if you want to.

The second mode is more in keeping with a general Windows application. In windowed mode, you have a conventional window area on the desktop, as shown in Figure 12-4.

Windowed mode is a bit more challenging because the surface you use for the front buffer is shared with GDI. Because you can write directly to the video memory, you need to be careful not to write outside your window area. To help you with this clipping task, DirectDraw provides a *DirectDrawClipper* object that you can attach to your front buffer. The clipper keeps track of the window created on the desktop, determining where the boundary is in the front buffer memory. In windowed mode, you usually can't flip pages as you can in full-screen mode and your back buffer is generally only the size of your window. Some video hardware supports complex overlays, which do allow you to flip pages as though you were in full-screen mode; DirectDraw allows you to call the *Flip* function on a surface in windowed mode if this hardware support is available.

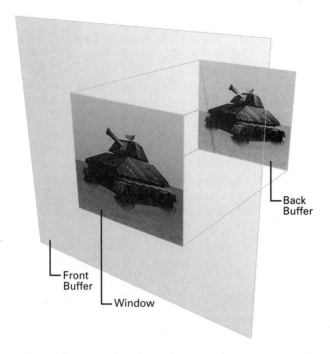

Figure 12-4. *Windowed mode.*

The clipper does a bit more than just ensure you don't write outside the window rectangle. It also ensures that if another window partially obscures yours, you don't write over the parts of the overlapping window.

Surfaces and GDI

You might think that once you've committed to using DirectDraw, GDI would no longer be a part of your life. You'd be wrong on two counts. First, GDI doesn't go away but, in fact, shares the video memory with you. Second, you can use GDI to draw to DirectDraw surfaces. This capability might seem obscure, but it can be handy if you want to write out some text, for example.

It's important to know that GDI doesn't disappear just because you have access to the video memory. GDI is still active and working on the surface it was using before your application got started. If your application gains exclusive control and changes to full-screen mode, GDI can still write to the buffer it was using, which could potentially damage what you render to your buffers. You can prevent GDI from interfering by creating a window that occupies the entire desktop before going to full-screen mode. GDI then knows that your window is on top and doesn't attempt to draw anything to what it thinks is still the screen area.

You can take advantage of GDI for some operations on your own surfaces. DirectDraw allows you to get a device context (DC) to any surface you create. You can then use GDI calls on the DC to draw to your surface. We'll look at an example of this later, beginning on page 272. GDI handles certain operations very well, such as area fills and writing text. Don't dismiss it completely just because the main part of your application uses direct video memory access. When in doubt, don't guess— try it, measure it, and evaluate the results for yourself.

You might encounter an interesting side effect of GDI's use of video memory if you try to debug code that does direct pixel manipulation with a graphical debugger, such as the debugger in Microsoft Visual C++. Before you can access a surface, you need to lock it. When you do this, DirectDraw grabs a lock on the Win16 subsystem, which is used to guarantee serial access to the User and GDI parts of Windows. Once DirectDraw has the Win16 lock, GDI can't run, so your debugger can't write to the screen, and you lock up and die.

The workaround is either to use a non-GUI debugger such as WDEB386 or to use a second machine and run Visual C++ in the remote debugging mode with either a serial or TCP/IP net connection to the target machine. Instructions for setting up a remote debugging session are included in "Books Online" with Visual C++.

Using DirectDraw

Having had a brief look at the DirectDraw Engine Room, let's turn our attention now to how you can use the DirectDraw interface in your own applications. The sample code we're going to look at comes from the sample in the DDEval directory, which I wrote to experiment with DirectDraw. This is very much a test and evaluation tool rather than an application, so it has a somewhat limited user interface. DDEval doesn't do anything very ambitious, but it does show you how to use GDI with a surface, how to run in full-screen or windowed mode, and how to perform direct pixel access to a surface. The tests also include a measurement of performance expressed as frames per second (fps), so you can get a real idea of how well the code is performing.

> **NOTE**
>
> Remember that different video hardware can result in massive performance differences in the code, depending on which acceleration features the hardware has to offer. If you make performance tests on your code, be sure to test the same code with a variety of video hardware.

DDEval Architecture

I created the DDEval sample using the Visual C++ AppWizard. I chose to create it as a Dialog rather than an SDI or MDI application. The dialog box is shown in Figure 12-5.

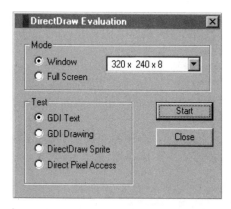

Figure 12-5. *The DDEval application.*

DDEval contains four tests, and each of these can be run either in a window or full-screen. The windowed option includes a variety of window sizes to choose from, ranging from 320 by 240 through 1024 by 768. The bit depth is always the same as the bit depth your machine is currently running in. To try different bit depths in windowed mode, you need to use the Windows Control Panel to change your display settings.

If you select the full-screen option, the code enumerates the currently available full-screen modes and fills the list box with them. My Dell machine showed 17 different modes, so you get quite a bit of variety. Full-screen modes are not limited to the current screen's bit depth. If you're running 8 bits per pixel on the desktop, you can opt to run the tests in 16-bit-per-pixel mode full-screen, if that's what you want.

The code we're going to look at uses classes from the 3dPlus library that wrap the DirectDraw interfaces with a very thin C++ class. Where appropriate, I'll show both the call to the C++ class and the interface code in the class member function.

DDEval Code

Let's begin with some simple stuff: how to set up a *CDirectDraw* object and enumerate the available full-screen modes. Here is how the *CDirectDraw* control object is initially created:

```
void CDDEvalDlg::SetInitialState()
{
    ⋮
    // Create a DirectDraw object to play with
    m_pDD = new CDirectDraw;
    BOOL b = m_pDD->Create();
    ⋮
}
```

This simple piece of code hides a lot of code that actually creates a front and a back buffer and an associated palette. We'll look at that code in just a moment.

Once the *CDirectDraw* object has been created, we can enumerate the supported modes. Here's the code that fills the list box in the DirectDraw Evaluation dialog box with the full-screen mode list:

```
void CDDEvalDlg::ShowModes()
{
        ⋮
        int iModes = m_pDD->GetNumModes();
        DDSURFACEDESC dds;
        for (int i = 0; i < iModes; i++) {
            m_pDD->GetModeInfo(i, &dds);
            sprintf(buf,
                    "%4lu x %4lu x %2lu",
                    dds.dwWidth,
                    dds.dwHeight,
                    dds.ddpfPixelFormat.dwRGBBitCount);
            m_cbModes.AddString(buf);
        }
        ⋮
```

As you can see, the number of modes is retrieved and then the surface description for each mode is obtained. A string describing each mode is then created and added to the list box. The code in the *CDirectDraw* object is a bit more complicated, though, because DirectDraw uses a callback function to enumerate modes. I used a single enumeration callback function, located in 3dDirDrw.cpp, to implement the *CDirectDraw::GetNumModes* and *CDirectDraw::GetModeInfo* functions:

```
// Mode enumeration info structure
typedef struct _EnumModeInfo {
    int iModeCount;
    int iMode;
    DDSURFACEDESC ddSurf;
} EnumModeInfo;

// Callback function for device mode enumeration
static HRESULT FAR PASCAL EnumModesFn(LPDDSURFACEDESC psd,
                                      LPVOID pArg)
{
    EnumModeInfo* pInfo = (EnumModeInfo*) pArg;
    ASSERT(pInfo);

    // See if it's the correct mode
    if (pInfo->iMode == pInfo->iModeCount) {
        pInfo->ddSurf = *psd;
        return DDENUMRET_CANCEL; // Stop enumerating
    }

    pInfo->iModeCount++;
    return DDENUMRET_OK;
}

// Get number of supported display modes
int CDirectDraw::GetNumModes()
```

```
    {
        ASSERT(m_pIDD);
        EnumModeInfo mi;
        mi.iModeCount = 0;
        mi.iMode = -1;
        m_hr = m_pIDD->EnumDisplayModes(0, NULL, &mi,
                                        EnumModesFn);
        ASSERT(SUCCEEDED(m_hr));
        return mi.iModeCount;
    }


    // Get data for a given mode
    BOOL CDirectDraw::GetModeInfo(int iMode,
                                  DDSURFACEDESC* pDesc)
    {
        int iModes =  GetNumModes();
        if (iMode >= iModes) return FALSE;
        ASSERT(m_pIDD);
        EnumModeInfo mi;
        mi.iModeCount = 0;
        mi.iMode = iMode;
        m_hr = m_pIDD->EnumDisplayModes(0, NULL, &mi,
                                        EnumModesFn);
        ASSERT(SUCCEEDED(m_hr));
        *pDesc = mi.ddSurf;
        return TRUE;
    }
```

The enumeration function uses an *EnumModeInfo* structure to control its operation and return its results. When counting the number of modes, the return data is not used. When obtaining data on a specific mode, the enumeration function gets called repeatedly until the mode number returned by the DirectDraw interface matches the requested one.

When you select a test to run, the test function fills a structure with the selected size and mode information and creates a test window to run the test. Let's look at each of the four tests in turn to see what they do and how the code works.

SETTING UP THE TEST WINDOW

For each test, a window is created, the appropriate DirectDraw mode is set, and the test is run. Each test runs for about 100 frames, reports the results, and tests to see if any key has been hit to terminate the test. Here's the code that creates the window, sets the mode, and starts each test:

```
    BOOL CTestWnd::Create(TESTINFO* pti)
    {
        // Save test info
        m_pTI = pti;
        ASSERT(m_pTI);
```

(continued)

```
// Create a DirectDraw object
m_pDD = new CDirectDraw;
BOOL b = m_pDD->Create();
ASSERT(b);

// Register a class
CString strClass =
    AfxRegisterWndClass(CS_HREDRAW | CS_VREDRAW,
                        ::LoadCursor(NULL, IDC_ARROW),
                        (HBRUSH)
                        ::GetStockObject(GRAY_BRUSH));

// Define window style and size
DWORD dwStyle = WS_VISIBLE | WS_POPUP;
RECT rc;
if (m_pTI->bFullScreen) {
    rc.top = 0;
    rc.left = 0;
    rc.right = ::GetSystemMetrics(SM_CXSCREEN);
    rc.bottom = ::GetSystemMetrics(SM_CYSCREEN);
} else { // Windowed
    dwStyle |= WS_CAPTION | WS_SYSMENU;
    rc.top = 50;
    rc.left = 50;
    rc.bottom = rc.top + m_pTI->iHeight;
    rc.right = rc.left + m_pTI->iWidth;
    ::AdjustWindowRect(&rc, dwStyle, FALSE);
}

if (!CreateEx(0,
              strClass,
              "DirectDraw Window",
              dwStyle,
              rc.left, rc.top,
              rc.right - rc.left, rc.bottom - rc.top,
              m_pTI->pParent->GetSafeHwnd(),
              NULL)) {
    return FALSE;
}

// Ensure window is visible
UpdateWindow();

// Set mode for window
ASSERT(m_pTI);
if (m_pTI->bFullScreen) {
    b = m_pDD->SetFullScreenMode(GetSafeHwnd(),
                                 m_pTI->iWidth,
                                 m_pTI->iHeight,
                                 m_pTI->iBpp);
```

```
    } else {
        b = m_pDD->SetWindowedMode(GetSafeHwnd(),
                                   m_pTI->iWidth,
                                   m_pTI->iHeight);
    }
    ASSERT(b);

    // Run tests
    SetTimer(1, 100, NULL);
    return TRUE;
}
```

The first half of the previous function is concerned with creating a *CDirect-Draw* object and the window that we will see on the screen. For the most part, this is straightforward Windows code. Once the window has been created, the *CDirectDraw* object is set to either windowed or full-screen mode. This last step is the most complicated. The *SetFullScreenMode* and *SetWindowedMode* functions both map directly to *CDirectDraw::_SetMode*, which does all the work of creating a pair of front and back buffers and an associated palette. There are three main steps to set the mode:

1. Set the cooperative level, which determines what we are allowed to do with DirectDraw. If we want to run in a window, we select normal mode. If we want to run full-screen, we have to request exclusive mode. Setting the cooperative level helps resolve contention for resources between the system and DirectDraw applications.

2. Create the front and back buffers. These buffers are DirectDraw surfaces. If we want to run full-screen, we create what DirectDraw calls a *complex flipping surface* consisting of two similar buffers. If we want to run in a window, we create two separate buffers: a front buffer that we share with GDI and a private back buffer.

3. Determine if a clipper is needed, and if so, create one.

Here's the code for setting the mode:

```
BOOL CDirectDraw::_SetMode(HWND hWnd, int cx, int cy,
                           int bpp, BOOL bFullScreen)
{
    ASSERT(m_pIDD);

    // Release any existing buffers
    _ReleaseAll();

    // Set cooperative level
    if (bFullScreen) {
        if (!SetCooperativeLevel(hWnd, DDSCL_EXCLUSIVE |
                                 DDSCL_FULLSCREEN)) {
            return FALSE;
        }
    }
```

(continued)

```
        m_hr = m_pIDD->SetDisplayMode(cx, cy, bpp);
        if (FAILED(m_hr)) {
            return FALSE;
        }
        m_bRestore = TRUE;
    } else {            // Windowed
        if (!SetCooperativeLevel(hWnd, DDSCL_NORMAL)) {
            return FALSE;
        }
    }
}

// Create front and back buffer surfaces

m_iWidth = cx;
m_iHeight = cy;

DDSURFACEDESC sd;
memset(&sd, 0, sizeof(sd));
sd.dwSize = sizeof(sd);

if (bFullScreen) {

    // Create a complex flipping surface with front
    // and back buffers
    sd.dwFlags = DDSD_CAPS
                | DDSD_BACKBUFFERCOUNT;
    sd.ddsCaps.dwCaps = DDSCAPS_PRIMARYSURFACE
                    | DDSCAPS_FLIP
                    | DDSCAPS_COMPLEX
                    | DDSCAPS_3DDEVICE;
    sd.dwBackBufferCount = 1;

    // Create front and back buffer surfaces
    m_pFrontBuffer = new CDDSurface;
    if (!m_pFrontBuffer->Create(this, &sd)) {
        return FALSE;
    }
    ASSERT(m_pFrontBuffer);

    // Get pointer to attached back buffer
    DDSCAPS caps;
    memset(&caps, 0, sizeof(caps));
    caps.dwCaps = DDSCAPS_BACKBUFFER;
    m_pBackBuffer =
            m_pFrontBuffer->GetAttachedSurface(&caps);
    if (!m_pBackBuffer) {
        delete m_pFrontBuffer;
        m_pFrontBuffer = NULL;
        return FALSE;
    }
```

```
} else {          //Windowed

    // Create two surfaces for windowed case,
    // a primary surface to share with GDI and
    // a back buffer to render into.

    // Create the front buffer surface.
    // Note: Because the front buffer is the primary
    // (existing) surface, don't specify height and
    // width.
    sd.dwFlags = DDSD_CAPS;
    sd.ddsCaps.dwCaps = DDSCAPS_PRIMARYSURFACE;
    m_pFrontBuffer = new CDDSurface;
    if (!m_pFrontBuffer->Create(this, &sd)) {
        return FALSE;
    }


    // Create back buffer surface
    sd.dwFlags = DDSD_WIDTH
               | DDSD_HEIGHT
               | DDSD_CAPS;
    sd.dwWidth = cx;
    sd.dwHeight = cy;
    sd.ddsCaps.dwCaps = DDSCAPS_OFFSCREENPLAIN
                      | DDSCAPS_3DDEVICE;
    m_pBackBuffer = new CDDSurface;
    if (!m_pBackBuffer->Create(this, &sd)) {
        delete m_pFrontBuffer;
        m_pFrontBuffer = NULL;
        return FALSE;
    }

    // Create a clipper object for front buffer
    // so drawing is clipped to the window
    m_pClipper = new CDDClipper;
    if (!m_pClipper->Create(this, hWnd)) {
        return FALSE;
    }

    // Attach clipper to front buffer
    if (!m_pFrontBuffer->SetClipper(m_pClipper)) {
        return FALSE;
    }

}
⋮
```

Although many of the calls here refer to 3dPlus class member functions, I'm not going to show the DirectDraw interface calls that implement those functions because the functions, by and large, simply pass the incoming parameters down to the encapsulated DirectDraw interfaces.

There are a lot of details in this code that I'm not going to explain here. You can read more about the DirectDraw interfaces in the DirectX SDK documentation. The code here should serve well for many experiments you might want to try.

RUNNING THE TESTS

A timer is used to run each test cycle. The timer message handler, shown below, actually calls the test function:

```
void CTestWnd::OnTimer(UINT nIDEvent)
{
    // Run next test
    switch (m_pTI->iTest) {
    case 1:
        TestGDIText();
        break;
    case 2:
        TestGDIGfx();
        break;
    case 3:
        TestDDSprite();
        break;
    case 4:
        TestDirectPixels();
        break;
    default:
        ASSERT(0);
        break;
    }
}
```

TESTING GDI TEXT PERFORMANCE

I wanted to use GDI to write some text to the window. The first thing to evaluate was how slowly GDI would be doing this task and whether it would be invasive in the other tests. I was happy with the results I obtained on my Dell machine, which reported frame rates over 200 fps for a 320-by-240 window running this test. The framework for this test was used to construct all the others, so we'll go through it step by step.

```
void CTestWnd::TestGDIText()
{
    ASSERT(m_pTI);

    // Get front and back buffers
    CDDSurface* pBB = m_pDD->GetBackBuffer();
    ASSERT(pBB);
```

```
CDDSurface* pFB = m_pDD->GetFrontBuffer();
ASSERT(pFB);

// Get rectangle that describes front buffer
RECT rcFront;
if (m_pTI->bFullScreen) {
    pFB->GetRect(rcFront);
} else {
    GetClientRect(&rcFront);
    ClientToScreen(&rcFront);
}

RECT rcBack;
pBB->GetRect(rcBack);

DWORD dwStart = timeGetTime();
int nFrames = 100;
for (int iFrame = 0; iFrame < nFrames; iFrame++) {

    DWORD dwNow = timeGetTime();
    double fps;
    if (dwNow == dwStart) {
        fps = 0;
    } else {
        fps = iFrame * 1000.0 /
                (double)(dwNow - dwStart);
    }

    // Make up some text
    char buf[64];
    sprintf(buf, "Frame %d  (%3.1f fps)", iFrame, fps);

    // Get a DC to back buffer
    CDC* pdc = pBB->GetDC();
    ASSERT(pdc);

    // Fill buffer with white
    pdc->PatBlt(rcBack.left,
                rcBack.top,
                rcBack.right - rcBack.left,
                rcBack.bottom - rcBack.top,
                WHITENESS);

    // Draw text
    pdc->DrawText(buf,
                  -1,
                  &rcBack,
                  DT_CENTER | DT_BOTTOM |
                  DT_SINGLELINE);
```

(continued)

CHAPTER 12 The DirectDraw Interface   **273**

```
        // Release DC
        pBB->ReleaseDC(pdc);

        // Swap buffers
        if (m_pTI->bFullScreen) {
            pFB->Flip();
        } else {
            pFB->Blt(&rcFront, pBB, &rcBack);
        }
    }
}
```

The test starts by obtaining pointers to the front and back buffers and setting up a rectangle to describe each buffer. Note that the front buffer rectangle is different, depending on whether we're running in full-screen or windowed mode. In windowed mode, we share the front buffer surface with the other applications running on the system.

Each test cycle in the *TestGDIText* function consists of the following steps:

1. Get the current time, and compute the current frame rate.

2. Create the text to display.

3. Get a device context for the back buffer.

4. Erase the entire back buffer by using a GDI call to fill it with white.

5. Use another GDI call to render the text to the back buffer.

6. Release the device context.

7. Swap the front and back buffers to display the results.

Once we've obtained a DC, the code consists of regular Windows GDI calls, and it's easy to forget that we're working with a DirectDraw surface and not just a window DC.

Swapping the front and back buffers isn't necessarily a *swap,* of course. If we're running in full-screen mode, the call to *CDDSurface::Flip* really does swap the buffers. If we're in windowed mode, calling *Blt* copies the back buffer to the front buffer. When a buffer is actually flipped, we don't need to worry about changing the sense of our back and front buffers because DirectDraw manages that task so that when we ask for a pointer to the back buffer, we always get the right pointer.

So that wasn't really any big deal was it? That's what I thought, too, and since the performance using GDI to render some text was so good, my next test was to see how fast GDI could *draw* to a surface.

TESTING GDI DRAWING PERFORMANCE

To test GDI's drawing performance, I added some code to the framework used for the text test to have GDI draw a rectangle that bounces around the window. The code involves adding only the line below in the *CTestWnd::TestGDIGfx* function and managing the rectangle position in the window for each cycle:

```
// Draw picture
pdc->Rectangle(x, y, x+cx, y+cy);
```

You can run the test yourself to see how well GDI draws rectangles.

TESTING A DIRECTDRAW SURFACE SPRITE

This test was the really interesting one for me. I wanted to use a surface in video memory to create a simple sprite, using a color key to define transparent areas, and then see how quickly I could move the sprite around in the window. To implement this test, I used the text test framework and added two chunks of additional code. The first addition creates the sprite, and the second draws it to the back buffer each cycle. For a while, I agonized over how to create the sprite and then gave in and used some GDI calls:

```
void TestWnd::TestDDSprite()
{
    ⋮
    DDSURFACEDESC sd;
    memset(&sd, 0, sizeof(sd));
    sd.dwSize = sizeof(sd);
    sd.dwFlags = DDSD_WIDTH
               | DDSD_HEIGHT
               | DDSD_CAPS;
    sd.dwWidth = cx;
    sd.dwHeight = cy;
    sd.ddsCaps.dwCaps = DDSCAPS_OFFSCREENPLAIN;
    CDDSurface sprite;
    BOOL b = sprite.Create(m_pDD, &sd);
    ASSERT(b);

    // Get DC to sprite surface and draw sprite
    // as a red circle on a black background
    CDC* pdc = sprite.GetDC();
    ASSERT(pdc);
    pdc->PatBlt(0, 0, cx, cy, BLACKNESS);
    CBrush br;
    br.CreateSolidBrush(RGB(255, 0, 0));
    CBrush* pbrOld = pdc->SelectObject(&br);
    pdc->Ellipse(0, 0, cx, cy);
    pdc->SelectObject(pbrOld);
    sprite.ReleaseDC(pdc);

    // Set color key as black
    DDCOLORKEY ck;
    ck.dwColorSpaceLowValue = 0; // Black
    ck.dwColorSpaceHighValue = 0;
    sprite.SetColorKey(DDCKEY_SRCBLT, &ck);
    ⋮
```

I created a surface the same size as the sprite (*cx* × *cy*) and then used GDI to fill the surface with black and draw a red circle. Because the surface color key is set to black, only the red circle will be drawn when the sprite is rendered. I confess I cheated here a bit. I chose black as the color key because the value 0 is black whether you consider it as an RGB value or as a palette index.

Having built my simple sprite, I added the following code to draw it in place on the back buffer:

```
    ⋮
// Fill buffer with white
CDC* pdc = pBB->GetDC();
ASSERT(pdc);
pdc->PatBlt(rcBack.left,
            rcBack.top,
            rcBack.right - rcBack.left,
            rcBack.bottom - rcBack.top,
            WHITENESS);

// Draw text
pdc->DrawText(buf,
              -1,
              &rcBack,
              DT_CENTER | DT_BOTTOM |
              DT_SINGLELINE);

pBB->ReleaseDC(pdc);

// Draw sprite
RECT rcDst;
rcDst.left = x;
rcDst.top = y;
rcDst.right = rcDst.left + cx;
rcDst.bottom = rcDst.top + cy;
RECT rcSrc;
rcSrc.left = 0;
rcSrc.top = 0;
rcSrc.right = rcSrc.left + cx;
rcSrc.bottom = rcSrc.top + cy;

// Call Blt using a color key
pBB->Blt(&rcDst, &sprite, &rcSrc,
         DDBLT_WAIT|DDBLT_KEYSRC);
    ⋮
```

I used GDI calls again to fill the back buffer with white and draw the frame rate text before blitting the sprite to the buffer. Note that the arguments to the *Blt* call include the DDBLT_KEYSRC flag, which tells the *Blt* function to use the color key defined in the source surface. For transparency to work, you need to set the color key in the source surface *and* you must set this flag. I spent five or six hours discovering that I needed the DDBLT_KEYSRC flag in the call to *Blt*. What can I say? I'm a slow learner.

Because a screen shot of this test would show only a red circle in a window, you really need to run the test yourself to see just how fast it is. I think you'll be impressed.

TESTING DIRECT PIXEL ACCESS

I nearly canned this test because, after spending an entire day rebooting my machine every five minutes, I thought that I could spend the rest of my days happily using GDI for my drawing. I spent the day struggling with the code to lock and unlock the buffer so that I could write to it. Every time I locked the buffer, I also locked the machine and had to reboot. Then I went to bed, and in the true tradition of the nerd, the solution came to me in my sleep. I had to remove only *one character* from my code to make it work. Here are the before and after versions of my *CDDSurface-::Unlock* routine, contained in the 3dDirDrw.cpp file, that caused me so much grief:

```
void CDDSurface::Unlock()
{
    if (!m_SurfDesc.lpSurface) return; // Not locked
    m_hr = m_pISurf->Unlock(&m_SurfDesc.lpSurface);
    ASSERT(SUCCEEDED(m_hr));
    m_SurfDesc.lpSurface = NULL;
}


void CDDSurface::Unlock()
{
    if (!m_SurfDesc.lpSurface) return; // Not locked
    m_hr = m_pISurf->Unlock(m_SurfDesc.lpSurface);
    ASSERT(SUCCEEDED(m_hr));
    m_SurfDesc.lpSurface = NULL;
}
```

Can you spot the difference? Can you say "void *"? One pointer is much like another until you need to use it!

With the lesson of the pointers behind me, I completed the code for the direct pixel test. This test erases the back buffer, writes the frame rate text, and draws a series of horizontal colored lines using direct pixel access.

Before you can draw anything, you need to do two things. First you must lock the buffer and obtain a pointer to the buffer memory. Then you must use the pixel format information for the surface to determine how to write the pixels. In a real application, you'd probably pick one buffer format and stick with it, but in the test I check the format every time.

Once you have the number of bits that each pixel uses and the masks used to define the red, green, and blue components (or the palette index), you can start drawing pixels. To determine where in the buffer you need to write a pixel, multiply the pitch of each buffer line by the line number you want. The pitch of a surface is always expressed in bytes and might well be different from the number of pixels multiplied by the number of bytes per pixel because line ends are often padded to make the overall buffer line an exact multiple of 4 bytes (32-bit aligned).

Here is the code that obtains the pixel format information for the back buffer:

```
void CTestWnd::TestDirectPixels()
{
    ⋮
    // Get some info about back buffer
    int iBpp = pBB->GetBitsPerPixel();
    ASSERT(iBpp >= 8);
    int iWidth = pBB->GetWidth();
    int iHeight = pBB->GetHeight();
    int iPitch = pBB->GetPitch();

    // Get RGB masks
    DWORD dwRMask, dwGMask, dwBMask;
    pBB->GetRGBMasks(dwRMask, dwGMask, dwBMask);

    // For each mask, check its width in bits
    // and see how many bits from the LSB (least significant
    // bit) end it's shifted
    DWORD dwRShift, dwGShift, dwBShift;
    DWORD dwRBits, dwGBits, dwBBits;
    dwRShift = dwRBits = 0;
    dwGShift = dwGBits = 0;
    dwBShift = dwBBits = 0;
    if (iBpp > 8) {
        DWORD d = dwRMask;
        while ((d & 0x1) == 0) {
            d = d >> 1;
            dwRShift++;
        }
        while (d & 0x01) {
            d = d >> 1;
            dwRBits++;
        }
        d = dwGMask;
        while ((d & 0x1) == 0) {
            d = d >> 1;
            dwGShift++;
        }
        while (d & 0x01) {
            d = d >> 1;
            dwGBits++;
        }
        d = dwBMask;
```

```
        while ((d & 0x1) == 0) {
            d = d >> 1;
            dwBShift++;
        }
        while (d & 0x01) {
            d = d >> 1;
            dwBBits++;
        }
    }
    ⋮
```

Note that you need the pixel color masks only if the surface has more than 8 bits per pixel. Also, I've assumed that the surface is RGB rather than YUV or another format. If the buffer is 8 bits per pixel, we need to create a palette:

```
    ⋮
// If buffer is 8bpp, get palette entries
// and set them to color values we want to use
PALETTEENTRY pe[256];
BYTE r, g, b;
CDDPalette* pPal = pBB->GetPalette();
if (pPal) {
    pPal->GetEntries(0, 256, pe);

    // Set color values we want to use.
    // We'll create a small color cube using 2 bits for
    // R, G and B.
    for (r = 0; r < 4; r++) {
        for (g = 0; g < 4; g++) {
            for (b = 0; b < 4; b++) {
                int index = 10 + r * 16 + g * 4 + b;
                pe[index].peRed = r * 85;
                pe[index].peGreen = g * 85;
                pe[index].peBlue = b * 85;
            }
        }
    }

    // Fill remainder of palette entries with gray just
    // so we can see them while debugging
    for (int i = 10 + 4*4*4; i < 246; i++) {
        pe[i].peRed = 192;
        pe[i].peGreen = 192;
        pe[i].peBlue = 192;
    }

    // Update palette
    pPal->SetEntries(0, 256, pe);

    // Delete palette
    delete pPal;
}
    ⋮
```

I filled the palette entries with gray so that I could watch the rendering engine allocate the colors it was using.

Here is how the lines are drawn to the buffer memory:

```
    ⋮
// Lock buffer and get pointer.
// WARNING: Don't try stepping until Unlock.
BYTE* pBuf = (BYTE*) pBB->Lock();
if (pBuf) {

    for (int y = 0; y < iHeight; y++) {

        // Compute where line segment starts
        int n = iWidth;
        DWORD dwOffset = y * iPitch; // In bytes

        // Get color
        int ir = GetRValue(clrLine);
        int ig = GetGValue(clrLine);
        int ib = GetBValue(clrLine);

        // Draw pixels directly to buffer
        switch (iBpp) {
        case 8: {
            // Find index into color cube for this
            // color
            int index = 10 + (ir / 85) * 16 +
                        (ig / 85) * 4 + (ib / 85);

            BYTE* p = pBuf + dwOffset;
            while (n--) {
                *p++ = (BYTE) index;
            }
            } break;

        case 16: {
            // Build color
            DWORD dw = (ir >> (8 - dwRBits)) <<
                    dwRShift
                | (ig >> (8 - dwGBits)) <<
                    dwGShift
                | (ib >> (8 - dwBBits)) <<
                    dwBShift;
            WORD w = (WORD)dw;
            WORD* p = (WORD*)(pBuf + dwOffset);
            while (n--) *p++ = w;
            } break;

        case 24:
            // Student exercise :)
            break;
```

```
case 32: {
    DWORD dw = (ir >> (8 - dwRBits)) <<
                dwRShift
            | (ig >> (8 - dwGBits)) <<
                dwGShift
            | (ib >> (8 - dwBBits)) <<
                dwBShift;
    DWORD* p = (DWORD*)(pBuf + dwOffset);
    while (n--) *p++ = dw;
    } break;

default:
    break;
}

// Move on to next color
NextColor(clrLine);

}
pBB->Unlock();
// You can debug again now
}
NextColor(clrStart);
⋮
```

The code is slightly different for each color depth because of the different number of bytes used by each pixel and the different RGB masks required. Please be careful when you're performing the pointer arithmetic. It's easy to mix up byte pointers with DWORD pointers and get the math wrong as the compiler adds 2 or 4 instead of 1, or vice versa.

You can make the test generate different line patterns by altering the *NextColor* function, which determines the color in which each line will be drawn.

You'll no doubt have spotted that I omitted the 24-bit-per-pixel code. My display adapter would only run in 8-, 16-, and 32-bit-per-pixel modes, so I had no way to test the 24-bit-per-pixel case. That's my excuse anyway. (Turn to the color insert to see the results of the Direct Pixel Access test.)

Party On, Dudes

Somehow I can't quite see Bill and Ted working on a DirectDraw application, if their approach to rock music is anything to go by. If you have no idea what I'm talking about, take time out to drive to your local video store and rent *Bill and Ted's Excellent Adventure*. It has nothing to do with coding down to the bone, but it's lots of fun and great preparation for a day of rebooting when you do get around to trying out some of the techniques I've shown you here.

If reading this chapter has you all fired up to do your own rendering engine, then read on. The next chapter covers the Direct3D layer, which you'll also want to know about before you start banging the keys.

n Chapter 12 we looked at the DirectDraw interface that provides access to video memory and support for blitting and page flipping. In this chapter we're going to look at the Direct3D Immediate Mode engine, which is the layer above DirectDraw that provides services to render points, lines, and triangles.

The Direct3D Immediate Mode engine could use a small book of its own, but my goal is to give you some understanding of what goes on and a code framework, which will let you experiment on your own. The sample code for this chapter can be found in the D3DEval directory.

The Direct3D Immediate Mode Engine

Figure 13-1 shows the DirectDraw and Direct3D components in a single box because applications that use Direct3D are always involved in some way with DirectDraw, too. (If we put them in separate boxes, there would just be more arrows on the diagram.)

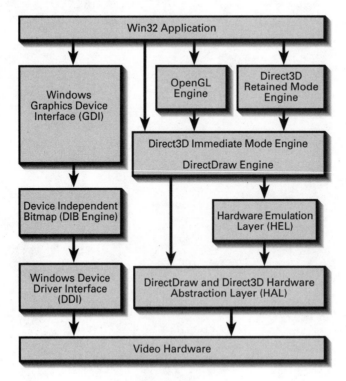

Figure 13-1. *The DirectDraw architecture.*

Because the DirectDraw and Direct3D engines do offer different functionality, it might be better to look at a diagram that represents the services provided by each. Figure 13-2 shows some of the services we'll be using when we create an application that uses the Direct3D Immediate Mode engine.

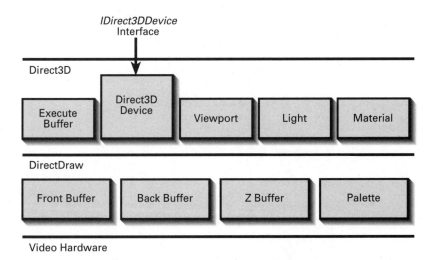

Figure 13-2. *Services provided by the DirectDraw and Direct3D engines.*

Figure 13-2 is a slightly simplistic view of what we might do with Direct3D, but it provides a good starting point. As you can see, the DirectDraw layer is really concerned only with managing the video hardware memory and palette. In a typical animation system, we might divide the video memory up to provide a front and back buffer pair, a Z buffer, and maybe some sprites (not shown) if there is still free memory.

If we want to draw a 3D scene, we need a lot more things, such as a definition of the view of the scene, how the scene is lit, where the objects are located, and how they reflect light. All of these can be defined using the Direct3D Immediate Mode services.

Referring to Figure 13-2 again, we see a large box labeled *Direct3D Device*. This device provides much of the interface to the DirectDraw layer below. Also in this box is the rendering engine, which takes all the data and generates the colored pixels that form the final 3D scene we see on the screen. To the right of the device box is a viewport. The viewport defines how we see the scene in the window—scale factors, perspective projection, and so on. The light box represents one of many possible lights there might be in the scene, and the material box represents one of many materials used to define how the surfaces of shapes reflect light. The last box is the execute buffer (see the bottom of the next page for more information on this buffer) shown on the left, and this is the most complicated element as far as we are concerned. I've used a bit of license here in placing this box where it is because in practice, the actual "buffer" is often located in video memory for performance reasons (but let's not worry about that right now).

The Rendering Pipeline

The most interesting part of the entire Immediate Mode engine is the actual *rendering pipeline,* which takes the descriptions of the objects in a scene, the lighting data, and some 4-by-4 matrices and creates the final picture we see. Figure 13-3 shows a simplified diagram of the rendering pipeline.

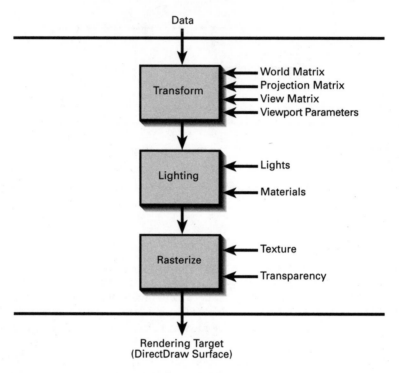

Figure 13-3 shows the following flow:

Data

Transform ← World Matrix, Projection Matrix, View Matrix, Viewport Parameters

Lighting ← Lights, Materials

Rasterize ← Texture, Transparency

Rendering Target (DirectDraw Surface)

Figure 13-3. *The rendering pipeline.*

The transform module converts input coordinates into world coordinates according to an overall transform matrix. You can influence the transform by setting the world, projection, and view matrices. The lighting module uses the current set of lights and the materials attached to the vertices of each object to calculate the actual color of each vertex. Whichever lighting module is used, mono or RGB, the output to the rasterizer is a set of vertices that have defined colors.

The final step is to use the rasterizer module to generate the picture in the rendering buffer. There are several different rasterizer modules, and the one you get depends on the type of fill and shading you select. The fill mode can be set to draw only points, draw a wire frame, or use a solid fill. Shading varies from none to Gouraud.

To use the rendering pipeline, you typically package a set of vertices, materials, matrix instructions, lights, and so on into what is called an *execute buffer*. You then pass the execute buffer through the rendering pipeline. You can pass the same buffer through the pipeline multiple times, which can be very useful, as we shall see later.

If you want to do your own world coordinate transforms, you can enter the pipeline at the lighting step. If you want to do your own transforms and your own lighting, you can enter the pipeline at the rasterizer. (I should point out that if you want to do your own transforms, lighting, and rasterization, you should ignore this chapter and go back to Chapter 12.)

Execute Buffers

Data is passed to the rendering pipeline via execute buffers. These buffers typically contain a set of vertices and a series of commands that dictate what happens to those vertices. Figure 13-4 shows a simplified view of a typical execute buffer.

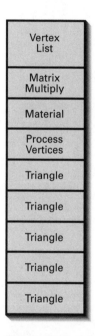

Figure 13-4. *A typical execute buffer.*

In the example buffer in Figure 13-4, we have a list of vertices that describe one or more shapes in model coordinates. Following the vertex list is a matrix multiply operation, which could be used to rotate the scene a few degrees, for example. The next item in the list is a material, and this is followed by a command to process the vertex list (typically to transform and light the vertices). The remainder of the list is filled with commands to draw individual triangles. Each triangle is described by three index values. Each index is an entry in the vertex list at the beginning of the buffer. It doesn't take much imagination to see that the execute buffer is mostly filled with vertex and shape data.

Because the execute buffer command set also includes commands to draw single points and lines, you can use the same basic buffer configuration to draw a wire-frame model by replacing the triangle commands with line commands. If you want to do your own transformations with or without lighting, your execute buffer looks much the same except that the type of vertex in the vertex list is different and, of course, you won't have any matrix operations in the buffer (or materials, if you're doing your own lighting). Figure 13-5 shows the structure of a command in the execute buffer.

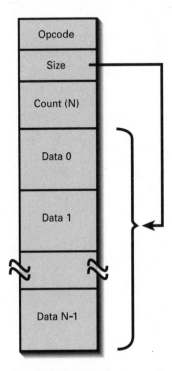

Figure 13-5. *The structure of an execution command.*

Each execution command consists of an operation code (opcode) that describes which command is to be executed, a size value that describes the total size of the accompanying data block, and a count field that gives the number of commands of this type that follow. The count field is very useful when specifying a series of triangles, for example.

This is an oversimplified view of what execute buffers do. However, we'll be looking at some code shortly that uses them (on page 296) to give you a feel for how you might want to use them in practice. If you want to know more of the details, refer to the DirectX 2 SDK documentation.

Using Immediate Mode in Practice

If you read the DirectX 2 SDK documentation, you'll find that many Immediate Mode objects (such as lights) have some sort of data structure defined, a handle value that you can access, and a COM interface for manipulating the object. These might seem like overkill, but once you've considered how objects are implemented, it makes a bit more sense.

The whole mission for Direct3D is to enable hardware acceleration of as many operations as possible, which is where the handle values come in. Let's say we want to define a material to be used. We fill out a data structure with a definition of the material and ask the rendering engine to create the material object. The rendering engine finds that the hardware has special capabilities for materials, so after the hardware creates the material object, the hardware driver returns a handle value for the new material. We need the handle to be able to manipulate the material object in the hardware because it's probably in video hardware memory and we can't access it directly. Because we started with a data structure in our address space, it would be nice to be able to use the same structure to alter the material in the hardware. The COM interface for the object provides a way to take information from the data structure and apply it to the object. The handle value is also what we put into an execute buffer that requires access to the material because the execute buffer might be handled directly by the hardware. Figure 13-6 shows the relationships between the various components.

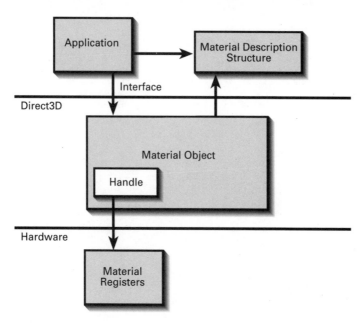

Figure 13-6. *The location of various parts of a material.*

The need for data structures, interfaces, and handles for each object makes for some very messy code, so I stuffed everything into a tidy C++ class. The class provides a cast operator to return the handle value and implements any member functions the object's COM interface might have that we find useful.

I created a C++ class for each object I wanted to use and for the execute buffer. These classes are not in the 3dPlus library because they are used only in the D3DEval example. You'll find them in the Direct.cpp and Direct.h files, which are in the D3DEval directory. If you look at the classes, you'll see that they are hardly complete but contain only what I needed to make the sample work.

A Better Execute Buffer

The class that I tried to make the most useful is the one that implements the execute buffer. Because the vertex lists and commands in an execute buffer are all of variable lengths, it's hard to determine how much buffer space you'll need ahead of time. The execute buffer class allocates a chunk of memory and adds items to it until it runs out of space. At that point it dies. (You thought I'd say that it reallocated the memory and made more space, didn't you? Instead, I made the buffer size bigger than I needed for the example and added an *ASSERT* statement to trap the case where you run out of buffer space.) Here's the function from the Direct.cpp file that adds one byte to the execute buffer:

```
BOOL CExecute::AddByte(BYTE b)
{
    // See if pointer to buffer exists
    if (m_Desc.lpData == NULL) {
        LockBuffer();
    }

    BYTE* pBuf = m_dwOffset + (BYTE*)m_Desc.lpData;
    *pBuf++ = b;
    m_dwOffset++;

    // Check that space remains in buffer
    ASSERT(m_dwOffset < m_Desc.dwBufferSize);

    // Append an exit code
    *pBuf = D3DOP_EXIT;

    return TRUE;
}
```

This function is used to add all structures to the execute buffer. By modifying this function to extend the buffer when it's full, you'll have a much more flexible system.

Despite its wimpy implementation, the execute buffer class makes building and using an execute buffer much easier than the Direct3D macros do.

Matrices

You need three matrices to define the world, projection, and view transforms. I created a simple matrix class (*CMatrix*), which is not unlike the *C3dMatrix* class in the 3dPlus library, to handle the three Immediate Mode matrices. The class makes it easy to create and use a matrix, but you do need to be a little careful because I've been a bit lax on the encapsulation front. Essentially, I let you play with the matrix elements directly and then I require you to call the class's *Update* function, shown in the following code, to apply the data to the actual matrix object.

```
void CMatrix::Update()
{
    if(m_hMatrix && m_pID3D) {
        HRESULT hr = m_pID3D->SetMatrix(m_hMatrix, this);
        ASSERT(SUCCEEDED(hr));
    }
}
```

Although this code might look unwieldy, it's reasonably efficient and avoids updating the objects needlessly if you're setting multiple values.

The three Immediate Mode matrices need a little explanation. The world matrix starts out as an identity matrix and is likely to stay that way if your scene doesn't move. Moving the scene can be done by altering the world matrix, and this is what the D3DEval sample does, as we'll see shortly on page 300. Here's the initial world matrix:

$$\begin{bmatrix} 1 & 0 & 0 & 0 \\ 0 & 1 & 0 & 0 \\ 0 & 0 & 1 & 0 \\ 0 & 0 & 0 & 1 \end{bmatrix}$$

The view matrix controls the camera position and usually consists of a simple translation along the *z*-axis in the initial state. I set up the sample to more or less mimic what the earlier samples have done. The camera is set a short distance out on the *z*-axis (a negative *z* value). Here's the view matrix I use in the example, which puts the camera at 0, 0, −2:

$$\begin{bmatrix} 1 & 0 & 0 & 0 \\ 0 & 1 & 0 & 0 \\ 0 & 0 & 1 & 0 \\ 0 & 0 & 2 & 1 \end{bmatrix}$$

The projection matrix is much more fun. To add perspective to the picture and map 3D coordinates to 2D screen pixel values, we need to use a matrix that converts *x* and *y* values by dividing them by the *z* value. The projection matrix also sets the scale factor—this determines how many screen pixels we move an object for a given model distance when the object is projected onto the screen. Here's the projection matrix used in the example:

$$\begin{bmatrix} 2 & 0 & 0 & 0 \\ 0 & 2 & 0 & 0 \\ 0 & 0 & 1 & 1 \\ 0 & 0 & -1 & 0 \end{bmatrix}$$

If this looks obvious to you, you have my undying respect. To see how this works, I took an imaginary input point (x, y, z, w) and multiplied it by the matrix. Here's the result:

```
x' = 2x
y' = 2y
z' = z - w
w' = z
```

Now we normalize the result by dividing by z:

```
x' = 2x / z
y' = 2y / z
z' = (z - w) / z
w' = 1
```

If we assume the input point was normalized ($w = 1$), we can simplify a bit more:

```
x' = 2x / z
y' = 2y / z
z' = (z - 1) / z
w' = 1
```

Terrific, Nigel. That's much clearer. OK, so it's not obvious, but you can see that both x and y get divided by z, which is what gives us the perspective transformation we need. You can also see that both x and y get scaled by a factor of 2, which was also a design goal (although I didn't mention it).

If you want to do a different projection of some kind, then you'll need to dive into some reference texts for help.

The D3DEval Sample Application

The D3DEval sample demonstrates how to display a simple 3D shape in a window or full-screen, using either the MONO or RGB driver. (Look in the color insert to see what the D3DEval sample looks like when you run it.) You can select the window size or, when in full-screen mode, the screen resolution. The setup code is very similar to the DDEval example from Chapter 12, so I'm going to concentrate only on the code that deals with the Direct3D engine.

To explore as much of Direct3D Immediate Mode as possible with as little code as possible, I decided to use a single 3D object in a scene with one light (in addition to the ambient light), one material for the background, and one material for the object. I use a rotation matrix to modify the world transform each cycle so that the scene rotates. As for the DDEval sample, the frame rate is displayed each time the scene is rendered.

The code includes a few *#if* ... statements that you can use to set up different options, such as drawing a wire frame instead of a solid object.

The object I display consists of four vertices, which is the least number of vertices I could use to get a solid object. A single material is used for the object, so it's nominally one color. The background is a single color, too. Restricting the colors is interesting, because on a 256-color display you can watch the system palette (using the Syspal tool on the companion CD, in the Tools directory) and see which entries get allocated.

The code consists of two major pieces. The first piece sets up the rendering engine, viewport, lighting, and background. The second piece renders the object in the scene. Because both pieces of code are rather long, I've broken them up into small steps and explained each step in turn. This code uses the classes in the Direct.cpp module. Most of the member functions are very simple, so I'll skip the explanation of the class member functions and focus on the overall flow.

Setting Up

Let's start by briefly looking at the code that creates the window and the DirectDraw surfaces and sets the mode to windowed or full-screen:

```
BOOL CTestWnd::Create(TESTINFO* pti)
{
    ⋮
    // Create a DirectDraw object
    m_pDD = new CDirectDraw;
    BOOL b = m_pDD->Create();
    ASSERT(b);

    // Register window class for test window
    CString strClass =
        AfxRegisterWndClass(CS_HREDRAW | CS_VREDRAW,
                            ::LoadCursor(NULL, IDC_ARROW),
                            (HBRUSH)::GetStockObject
                            (GRAY_BRUSH));

    // Define window style and size
    DWORD dwStyle = WS_VISIBLE | WS_POPUP;
    RECT rc;
    if (m_pTI->bFullScreen) {
        rc.top = 0;
        rc.left = 0;
        rc.right = ::GetSystemMetrics(SM_CXSCREEN);
        rc.bottom = ::GetSystemMetrics(SM_CYSCREEN);
    } else { // Windowed
        dwStyle |= WS_CAPTION | WS_SYSMENU;
        rc.top = 50;
        rc.left = 50;
        rc.bottom = rc.top + m_pTI->iHeight;
        rc.right = rc.left + m_pTI->iWidth;
```

(continued)

```
        // Adjust window size so its client area is
        // requested size
        ::AdjustWindowRect(&rc, dwStyle, FALSE);
    }


    // Create window.
    // We have no WM_CREATE handler, so not much happens
    // here.
    if (!CreateEx(0,
                  strClass,
                  "Direct3D Window",
                  dwStyle,
                  rc.left, rc.top,
                  rc.right - rc.left, rc.bottom - rc.top,
                  m_pTI->pParent->GetSafeHwnd(),
                  NULL)) {
        return FALSE;
    }


    // Ensure window is visible
    UpdateWindow();

    // Set mode for window in DirectDraw object,
    // which creates front and back buffers and palette
    // if one is required
    if (m_pTI->bFullScreen) {
        b = m_pDD->SetFullScreenMode(GetSafeHwnd(),
                                     m_pTI->iWidth,
                                     m_pTI->iHeight,
                                     m_pTI->iBpp);
    } else {
        b = m_pDD->SetWindowedMode(GetSafeHwnd(),
                                   m_pTI->iWidth,
                                   m_pTI->iHeight);
    }
    ASSERT(b);
```

This is the same as the code that was used in the DDEval sample. It creates the front and back buffers and the palette if one is needed. Now let's look at the rest of the setup.

```
        // Create Direct3D object on top of DirectDraw surfaces
        m_pD3D = new CDirect3D();
        b = m_pD3D->Create(m_pDD);
        ASSERT(b);

        // Set lighting model, which selects either hardware or
        // software driver and also creates Z buffer
        if (pti->iLightMode == 1) {
            b = m_pD3D->SetMode(D3DCOLOR_MONO);
        } else {
            b = m_pD3D->SetMode(D3DCOLOR_RGB);
        }
```

```
ASSERT(b);

// Get the D3D engine and device interface pointers
m_pIEngine = m_pD3D->GetD3DEngine();
ASSERT(m_pIEngine);
m_pIDevice = m_pD3D->GetD3DDevice();
ASSERT(m_pIDevice);
```

A Direct3D object is created based on the DirectDraw buffers. The lighting mode is used to determine which lighting module will be used; and the interfaces for the chosen Direct3D engine and device are obtained. We'll be using these interfaces to create and manage all the other objects we need.

```
// Create viewport
HRESULT hr = m_pIEngine->CreateViewport(&m_pIViewport,
                                        NULL);
ASSERT(SUCCEEDED(hr));
ASSERT(m_pIViewport);

// Attach viewport to device
hr = m_pIDevice->AddViewport(m_pIViewport);
ASSERT(SUCCEEDED(hr));
```

A viewport object is created and attached to the device object. A device can have many viewports, but we'll be using only one here.

```
// Configure viewport.
// Note: Some details here relate to scale factors and
// so on, which will get set again later when we set up
// projection matrix.
D3DVIEWPORT vd;
memset(&vd, 0, sizeof(vd));
vd.dwSize = sizeof(vd);        // Structure size

// Define viewport area on device
vd.dwX = 0;     // Left side
vd.dwY = 0;     // Top
vd.dwWidth = m_pTI->iWidth;    // Width
vd.dwHeight = m_pTI->iHeight;  // Height

// Set scale so that viewport is 2-by-2 model units
vd.dvScaleX = D3DVAL(m_pTI->iWidth) / D3DVAL(2.0);
vd.dvScaleY = D3DVAL(m_pTI->iHeight) / D3DVAL(2.0);

// Set maximum x and y values to 1 so origin is
// in the center and x and y ranges vary from -1 to +1,
// i.e., -range/2 to +range/2
vd.dvMaxX = D3DVAL(1.0);
vd.dvMaxY = D3DVAL(1.0);
```

(continued)

```
// Set Z range
vd.dvMinZ = D3DVAL(-5.0);
vd.dvMaxZ = D3DVAL(100.0);

// Apply settings to viewport
hr = m_pIViewport->SetViewport(&vd);
ASSERT(SUCCEEDED(hr));
```

A *D3DVIEWPORT* structure is filled out to define the initial state of the viewport. The viewport needs to know the physical area of the device it will use and what the *x* and *y* scale factors will be. I chose to use a scale of 2 units by 2 units and set the origin in the middle so the range of *x* and *y* values can vary from −1 to +1. The range of *z* values is also set, which is very important as it determines which objects will be visible. Objects behind the maximum *z* value or in front of the minimum *z* value are not rendered. Be sensible here: Choose values that bracket your scene objects as closely as you can, because this gives the most precision to the Z buffer values and avoids funny rendering artifacts when objects are positioned near the camera.

Once the data structure is complete, the viewport is updated with the new parameters.

```
// Set rendering characteristics.
// Create an execute buffer.
CExecute ex1 (m_pIDevice, m_pIViewport);

// Set a shade mode and fill mode. Direct3D selects the
// drivers it will use based on these values, and it
// has no default.
ex1.AddRenderState(D3DRENDERSTATE_FILLMODE,
                   D3DFILL_SOLID);
ex1.AddRenderState(D3DRENDERSTATE_SHADEMODE,
                   D3DSHADE_GOURAUD);
ex1.AddRenderState(D3DRENDERSTATE_DITHERENABLE, 1);

// Enable Z buffer
ex1.AddRenderState(D3DRENDERSTATE_ZENABLE, 1);
```

An execute buffer is created, to which the subsequent commands will be added.

The next step is to determine how each scene will be rendered. I chose to use solid fills with Gouraud shading, and I enabled dithering for use with RGB mode. There are many other possible factors to alter, but these were the most critical to how I wanted my scenes to look. You can refer to the DirectX 2 SDK documentation for a complete list of what you can alter. I also enabled the use of the Z buffer that was created earlier.

```
// Create matrix for world transform (identity)
m_mWorld.Create(m_pIDevice);
ex1.AddState(D3DTRANSFORMSTATE_WORLD, m_mWorld);

// Create matrix for projection.
```

```
// Note: We did this when we set up the viewport
// earlier, but when we selected the fill mode and
// shading mode the viewport data was reset.
m_mProjection.Create(m_pIDevice);
m_mProjection._11 = D3DVAL(2);
m_mProjection._22 = D3DVAL(2);
m_mProjection._34 = D3DVAL(1);
m_mProjection._43 = D3DVAL(-1);
m_mProjection._44 = D3DVAL(0);
m_mProjection.Update();
ex1.AddState(D3DTRANSFORMSTATE_PROJECTION,
             m_mProjection);

// Create matrix for view
// (the effective camera position)
m_mView.Create(m_pIDevice);
m_mView._43 = D3DVAL(2); // Camera Z = -2;
m_mView.Update();
ex1.AddState(D3DTRANSFORMSTATE_VIEW, m_mView);
```

The matrices for the world, projection, and view are created and set. Note that the constructor sets the matrix to an identity matrix to start with, making it necessary to alter only the cells that differ from the identity case. The member data names, _43 and so on, come from the Direct3D structure *D3DMATRIX* from which the *CMatrix* class is derived.

```
// Add command to set ambient light level
ex1.AddAmbLight(RGB_MAKE(64, 64, 64));
```

The ambient light level is set to some mid-low level. Note that the units here for RGB vary from 0 through 255. In some other cases we'll be using color values that vary from 0.0 to 1.0—watch out for this.

```
// Execute command list
b = ex1.Execute();
ASSERT(b);
```

The execute buffer is sent to the rendering pipeline to set up the conditions we want. This is a kind of death-or-glory call. If it fails, the machine usually locks up, so be sure you set the command parameters correctly before you run *Execute* on the buffer.

```
// Add light source to viewport
m_Light1.Create(m_pIEngine);
m_Light1.SetColor(0.8, 0.8, 0.8);
m_Light1.SetType(D3DLIGHT_DIRECTIONAL);
m_Light1.SetDirection(1, -1, 1);
m_Light1.Update();
hr = m_pIViewport->AddLight(m_Light1);
ASSERT(SUCCEEDED(hr));
```

A directional light is added to the lighting module. Note the use of the *Update* member function, which updates the physical object with the parameters set in the earlier calls. The light color is white (OK, gray), and the light is set to point down and inward from the top left corner.

```
// Create material for background.
// Note: We must set the number of shades to 1, or the
// MONO driver sets the color to black.
// Of course, we need only one shade for the background
// color, so this avoids wasted palette space.
m_matBkgnd.Create(m_pIEngine, m_pIDevice);
m_matBkgnd.SetColor(0.0, 0.0, 0.5);    // Dark blue
m_matBkgnd.SetShades(1); // Only one shade
hr = m_pIViewport->SetBackground(m_matBkgnd);
ASSERT(SUCCEEDED(hr));
    ⋮
}
```

The final step is to create a material for the background. If you omit this step, the background will be black. The material used for the background must have only *one* color shade. If you specify more than one shade (or use the class default, which is 16), the MONO driver will give you a black background. Because the color of the background isn't affected by lighting, you need only one shade and using more wastes palette space.

Now we have a scene set up with a background, some lighting, a camera position, and a projection frustum. All we need now is an object.

Executing the Tests

The D3DEval sample includes two tests. One test uses unlit vertices and the rendering pipeline to perform the transformation and lighting. The other test uses pretransformed and lit vertices and uses just the rasterizer. We'll look in detail at the first test, because it is the most common, and then we'll briefly look at what's different about skipping the transform and lighting steps in the rendering pipeline.

Each test cycle consists of establishing an execute buffer and then executing the buffer multiple times. Tests are initiated by a timer, so the whole process ends up looking continuous. Let's start by looking at the setup code, step by step.

```
void CTestWnd::Test1()
{
    ⋮
    // Get pointers to front and back buffers
    CDDSurface* pBB = m_pDD->GetBackBuffer();
    ASSERT(pBB);
    CDDSurface* pFB = m_pDD->GetFrontBuffer();
    ASSERT(pFB);

    // Get rectangle that describes front buffer
    RECT rcFront;
    if (m_pTI->bFullScreen) {
        pFB->GetRect(rcFront);
```

```
    } else {
        GetClientRect(&rcFront);
        ClientToScreen(&rcFront);
    }

    // Get rectangle that describes back buffer
    RECT rcBack;
    pBB->GetRect(rcBack);
```

We obtain pointers to the front and back buffers and the sizes of the buffers. This is the same as the setup code used in the DDEval example.

```
    // Create vertex list for shape (a pyramid of sorts)
    D3DVERTEX vShape [] = {
        {   // Vertex xyz
            D3DVAL(-0.3), D3DVAL(-0.1), D3DVAL( 0.1),
            // Normal xyz
            D3DVAL(-1.0), D3DVAL(-1.0), D3DVAL(-1.0),
            // Texture uv
            D3DVAL( 0.0), D3DVAL( 0.0)
        },
        {   D3DVAL( 0.3), D3DVAL(-0.1), D3DVAL( 0.2),
            D3DVAL( 1.0), D3DVAL(-1.0), D3DVAL(-1.0),
            D3DVAL( 0.0), D3DVAL( 0.0)
        },
        {   D3DVAL( 0.0), D3DVAL(-0.3), D3DVAL( 0.3),
            D3DVAL( 0.0), D3DVAL(-1.0), D3DVAL( 1.0),
            D3DVAL( 0.0), D3DVAL( 0.0)
        },
        {   D3DVAL( 0.1), D3DVAL( 0.4), D3DVAL( 0.3),
            D3DVAL( 0.0), D3DVAL( 1.0), D3DVAL( 0.0),
            D3DVAL( 0.0), D3DVAL( 0.0)
        }
    };
    int nVerts = sizeof(vShape) / sizeof(D3DVERTEX);
```

A vertex list is created for the object. The object here has four vertices, and each vertex has a normal vector. The normal vector is used by the lighting module and the two texture mapping coordinates that are not used in this example.

```
    // Create material for shape
    CMaterial mShape;
    mShape.Create(m_pIEngine, m_pIDevice);
    mShape.SetColor(0.0, 1.0, 0.0);    // Bright green
```

Remember that the material consists of data in the application's memory space and also an object on the hardware side that is represented by a handle value.

```
    // Create execute buffer
    CExecute ex (m_pIDevice, m_pIViewport);

    // Add vertex data to buffer
    ex.AddVertices(vShape, nVerts);
```

My implementation of the execute buffer class (*CExecute*) requires that the vertices are the first thing added to an execute buffer.

```
// Create matrix for world rotation
CMatrix mRot(m_pIDevice);
double ry = 1; // Degrees about y axis
double siny = sin(ry * D2R);
double cosy = cos(ry * D2R);
mRot._11 = D3DVAL(cosy);
mRot._13 = D3DVAL(-siny);
mRot._31 = D3DVAL(siny);
mRot._33 = D3DVAL(cosy);
mRot.Update();

// Add command to multiply world matrix by rotation
// matrix
ex.AddMatMul(m_mWorld, m_mWorld, mRot);
```

The matrix is added to the execute buffer as part of a command to multiply the world matrix by the new matrix and return the result to the world matrix. When this is executed, the scene rotates by one degree about the *y*-axis.

```
// Add shape material to execute buffer
ex.AddMaterial(mShape);

// Add processing command for vertices so
// each is transformed and lit
ex.AddProcess(nVerts, 0,
                  D3DPROCESSVERTICES_TRANSFORMLIGHT|
                  D3DPROCESSVERTICES_UPDATEEXTENTS);
```

Note that the transformation command above is added after the world matrix has been updated so that the transformation will include the result of the world matrix rotation.

```
// Add a set of commands to draw shape
ex.AddTriangle(0, 3, 1);
ex.AddTriangle(1, 3, 2);
ex.AddTriangle(2, 3, 0);
ex.AddTriangle(0, 1, 2);
```

The triangles above must be defined using clockwise vertex order, or they will not be rendered correctly. The triangle parameters are index values into the vertex list.

That completes the setup phase. The next step is to enter a loop that repeatedly renders the scene to the back buffer, computes the frame rate, and flips the back and front buffers so that we can see the results:

```
DWORD dwStart = timeGetTime();
int nFrames = 360;
for (int iFrame = 0; iFrame < nFrames; iFrame++) {

    DWORD dwNow = timeGetTime();
    double fps;
```

```
        if (dwNow == dwStart) {
            fps = 0;
        } else {
            fps = iFrame * 1000.0 /
                    (double)(dwNow - dwStart);
        }

        // Clear viewport (to current background material)
        D3DRECT r;
        r.x1 = 0;
        r.y1 = 0; // Top-left
        r.x2 = m_pTI->iWidth;
        r.y2 = m_pTI->iHeight; // Bottom-right
        hr = m_pIViewport->Clear(1, &r, D3DCLEAR_TARGET |
                                    D3DCLEAR_ZBUFFER);
        ASSERT(SUCCEEDED(hr));

#if 1 // Set to zero to remove frame rate text.
        // Draw frame rate text to back buffer.
        char buf[64];
        sprintf(buf, "Frame %2d  (%3.1f fps)", iFrame, fps);
        CDC* pdc = pBB->GetDC();
        ASSERT(pdc);
        pdc->DrawText(buf, -1, &rcBack, DT_CENTER |
                    DT_BOTTOM | DT_SINGLELINE);
        pBB->ReleaseDC(pdc);
#endif

        // Execute buffer
        BOOL b = ex.Execute();
        ASSERT(b);

        // Swap buffers
        if (m_pTI->bFullScreen) {
            pFB->Flip();
        } else {
            pFB->Blt(&rcFront, pBB, &rcBack);
        }
    }
}
```

Apart from the execution of the execute buffer, this is the same code we used in the DDEval sample.

Doing Your Own Transformation and Lighting

If you want to do your own transformation and lighting, the rendering code becomes much simpler. Of course, the transformation and lighting code you have to write is pretty significant, so I wouldn't exactly call this a gain!

You need to write slightly different code for the RGB rasterizer and the Mono rasterizer. The RGB rasterizer interpolates the individual RGB elements of colors; the Mono rasterizer interpolates only the shade of a single color, which varies from black to white with the color shades in between. If you use the RGB rasterizer, you specify the colors of the vertices directly as RGB values and you can use any values you want. For the test, I made one vertex red, one green, and the last one blue. The test shows how the RGB rasterizer interpolates between the colors. Here's the definition of the vertices used with the RGB rasterizer:

```
void CTestWnd::Test2RGB()
{
    ⋮
    D3DTLVERTEX vShape [] = {
        {   // x, y, z, 1/w
            D3DVAL(10), D3DVAL(10), D3DVAL(2), D3DVAL(1),
            // Color, specular color
            RGBA_MAKE(255, 0, 0, 255),
            RGBA_MAKE(255, 255, 255, 255),
            // Texture u, v
            D3DVAL(0), D3DVAL(0)
        },
        {   D3DVAL(m_pTI->iWidth - 10), D3DVAL( 10),
            D3DVAL(2), D3DVAL(1),
            RGBA_MAKE(0, 0, 255, 255),
            RGBA_MAKE(255, 255, 255, 255),
            D3DVAL(0), D3DVAL(0)
        },
        {   D3DVAL( 10), D3DVAL(m_pTI->iHeight - 10),
            D3DVAL(2), D3DVAL(1),
            RGBA_MAKE(0, 255, 0, 255),
            RGBA_MAKE(255, 255, 255, 255),
            D3DVAL(0), D3DVAL(0)
        }
    };
    int nVerts = sizeof(vShape) / sizeof(D3DTLVERTEX);
```

Each vertex consists of screen coordinates expressed as x, y, z, and 1/w followed by the color and specular color of the vertex and then the texture u and v values, which are not used in this example.

The execution buffer setup is very simple:

```
// Create execute buffer
CExecute ex (m_pIDevice, m_pIViewport);

// Add vertex data to buffer
ex.AddVertices(vShape, nVerts);

// Add processing command for vertices so
// each gets transformed and lit
ex.AddProcess(nVerts, 0, D3DPROCESSVERTICES_COPY|
              D3DPROCESSVERTICES_UPDATEEXTENTS);
```

```
// Add commands to draw shape
ex.AddTriangle(0, 1, 2);
  ⋮
```

There isn't a screen shot here because a grayscale graphic doesn't do it justice. You'll need to run the sample yourself to see what it comes out like. The remainder of the code is the same as the Test1 example that starts on page 298.

If we're using the Mono rasterizer, we need to define the color of the face using a material:

```
void CTestWnd::Test2MONO()
{
    ⋮
    CMaterial mShape;
    mShape.Create(m_pIEngine, m_pIDevice);
    mShape.SetColor(0.0, 1.0, 0.0);     // Bright green
```

Now we can specify the vertices. The colors for the vertices are defined using only the blue channel of the color structures. The value provides the shade of the material color to use. I set my vertices to show as much variation as I could:

```
D3DTLVERTEX vShape [] = {
    {   // x, y, z, 1/w
        D3DVAL(10), D3DVAL(10), D3DVAL(2), D3DVAL(1),
        // Color, specular color
        RGBA_MAKE(0, 0, 64, 0), RGBA_MAKE(0, 0, 64, 0),
        // Texture u, v
        D3DVAL(0), D3DVAL(0)
    },
    {   D3DVAL(m_pTI->iWidth - 10), D3DVAL( 10),
        D3DVAL(2), D3DVAL(1),
        RGBA_MAKE(0, 0, 255, 0),
        RGBA_MAKE(0, 0, 255, 0),
        D3DVAL(0), D3DVAL(0)
    },
    {   D3DVAL( 10), D3DVAL(m_pTI->iHeight - 10),
        D3DVAL(2), D3DVAL(1),
        RGBA_MAKE(0, 0, 0, 0), RGBA_MAKE(0, 0, 0, 0),
        D3DVAL(0), D3DVAL(0)
    }
};
```

The material needs to be added to the execute buffer before the vertices are processed:

```
// Create execute buffer
CExecute ex (m_pIDevice, m_pIViewport);

// Add vertex data to buffer
ex.AddVertices(vShape, nVerts);
```

(continued)

```
// Add shape material to execute buffer
ex.AddMaterial(mShape);

// Add processing command for vertices so
// each gets transformed and lit
ex.AddProcess(nVerts, 0, D3DPROCESSVERTICES_COPY|
            D3DPROCESSVERTICES_UPDATEEXTENTS);
```
⋮

The remainder of the code is the same as for the RGB test.

You can see that the RGB rasterizer is very simple to work with. The Mono rasterizer requires a little more work because you have to consider each face having only a single color. In order to get adequate performance, you need to group all the faces of an object that are the same color in one execute buffer.

What's Missing?

This brief look at the Direct3D Immediate Mode engine shows you essentially how it works and how you use execute buffers to drive it. I skipped over a lot of the capabilities and avoided some large areas, such as how texture maps are used. As I mentioned at the beginning of this chapter, Direct3D is a pretty big subject. However, if you're interested, the code I've provided here gives you a good place to start your own experiments.

You've probably also noticed by now that the number of pages in your right hand is getting pretty small, and, in fact, this is the last chapter of the book. I'm sure you're thinking that it can't be the last chapter because we didn't cover multiplayer Internet virtual worlds or how to create a side, end, and plan view of your house in one window, or how to do constrained motion in a robot arm, or many other things. If you've read the entire book and given the DirectX 2 SDK documentation a once-over, you're now equipped to play on your own. I really can't help you much more because now you know what I know.

Party on.

Appendix: Debugging

f you decide that you need to debug code that locks a rendering buffer (or after a *GetDC* call has locked a rendering buffer for you), you'll need to use a debugger that doesn't use the same display as your application. This appendix includes some notes on using the Microsoft Visual C++ debugger remotely and also provides an introduction to the Microsoft Windows kernel debugger, Wdeb386, provided with the Win32 SDK. There are many other debuggers that you can use, of course, but these are the two I used in preparing the code for this book.

Remote Debugging with Visual C++

The following instructions assume that you have Microsoft Windows 95 installed on both your development machine (the host) and your test machine (the target). They also assume that you have Visual C++ installed on the host machine and that both machines are connected to a network and have the TCP/IP protocol stack installed. Substitute your machine names where you see the *host* and *target* placeholder names.

1. On the target machine, create a TEST directory and share it as TEST with full access and no password.

2. Copy the following list of files from the appropriate directory, either Msdev\bin or Windows\System, of the host to \\TARGET\TEST: Msvcmon.exe, Msvcrt40.dll, Tln0com.dll, Tln0t.dll, Dmn0.dll. These files are required to run the debugging session on the target machine.

3. Copy the EXE for the code you want to debug and any DLLs it requires to \\TARGET\TEST.

4. On the host, run Visual C++ and choose Remote Connection from the Tools menu. In the Remote Connection dialog box, select the TCP/IP connection item, and click the Settings button.

5. In the Win32 Network (TCP/IP) Settings dialog box, enter the name of your target machine or its IP address (for example, 199.99.99.9) and enter a password (for example, DEBUG). You *must* include an entry in the password field. Click OK in each dialog box.

6. On the target machine, run Msvcmon.exe, select the Network (TCP/IP) option, and click the Settings button.

7. In the Win32 Network (TCP/IP) Settings dialog box, enter the name of your target machine and the password that you used in Step 5. Click OK.

8. Click the Connect button to start the debugging session on the target machine. The Connecting dialog box appears while the target machine waits for a connection from the host machine.

9. On the host machine, choose Settings from the Visual C++ Build menu. In the Project Settings dialog box, click the Debug tab. In the Remote Executable Path and File Name field, enter the path to the target executable that you copied in Step 3 to the target machine. (For example, \TEST\D3DEval.exe.) Click OK.

10. Click the Go button in Visual C++ to start the debugging session. You will probably see the Find Local Module dialog box, which asks for the location of local DLLs. Enter the path for each one, or uncheck the box that asks if you want to look for more of them.

The target machine should now run your application, and you can debug it from the host. When you are finished, exit the application and click the Disconnect button in the Connecting dialog box on your target machine. Be sure to reset your Remote Connection to Local on your host machine.

The Visual C++ documentation covers the debugger in detail if you haven't used it before.

Debugging with Wdeb386

If you want total control over your debugging environment, you need to use the kernel debugger, Wdeb386. This debugger enables you to debug anything in a Windows 95 system, including applications, DLLs, device drivers, VxDs, and so on. The debugger is shipped with the Win32 SDK, which is a part of the Microsoft Developer Network Level II Platform.

The advantage of using Wdeb386 over WinDbg (also included with the Win32 SDK) or the Visual C++ debugger is that Wdeb386 runs on a separate terminal and doesn't involve the Windows GUI layer at all. The Win32 SDK includes debug versions of all the important Windows system DLLs and their symbol files. The DirectX 2 SDK also includes debug versions of its DLLs and their symbol files.

To use Wdeb386, follow these steps. More details and the Wdeb386 command set are documented in the Win32 SDK.

1. Use an RS232 terminal or another PC. Configure the terminal for 9600 or 19200 baud. I usually set mine to be 8 data bits, no parity, and 1 stop bit.

2. Connect the terminal to one of your main machine's COM ports using a null-modem cable. (Details of the cable connections are included in the Wdeb386 installation notes.)

3. Run a terminal application such as HyperTerminal on the main machine, and verify that you can send text to the terminal. Type on the terminal, and verify that you see the correct text on the main machine. This confirms that your hardware setup is OK.

4. On your main machine, copy all the DLLs and symbol files from the Mstools\debug directory to the Windows\System directory. You'll probably have to boot to a DOS session to do this because you can't overwrite a file such as Gdi32.dll while it's in use. (To boot to DOS, press F8 when you see the Starting Windows message at boot time and select Command Prompt Only from the menu, or select Shut Down from the Windows 95 Start menu and choose the option to Restart The Computer In MS-DOS Mode.)

5. To run a debugging session, boot to a DOS prompt and then run Wdeb386 from the DOS prompt. A typical command line might be *wdeb386 /c:1 /r:9600 /s:myfile.sym /s:gdi.sym \windows\win.com.*

Once the debugger is started, Windows will load and you can run your application. You can enter the debugger at any time by typing *Ctrl-C* on the terminal or by pressing Ctrl-Alt-SysRq on the main machine. If you have a Non-Maskable Interrupt (NMI) switch on your machine, it too can be used to force an entry into the debugger. Once you have entered the debugger, your main machine locks up until you execute a command in the debugger. (Try *g* for *go,* if you get stuck.)

To load lots of symbol files, it's easiest to make up the set of commands in a text file like this:

```
/s:DDRAW16.SYM
/s:D3DRAMPF.SYM
/s:D3DRGBF.SYM
/s:KRNL386.SYM
/s:D3DRM8F.SYM
/s:GDI.SYM
/s:D3DRM16F.SYM
/s:D3DRG8F.SYM
/s:D3DRG16F.SYM
/s:D3DHALF.SYM
```

Save the file—as Debug.inf, for example. You can then create a simple batch file to start a debug session or just type the following command line:

```
wdeb386 /c:1 /r:9600 /f:debug.inf \windows\win.com
```

Refer to the Wdeb386 user guide in the Win32 SDK for instructions on using the debugger once it's installed and running.

Glossary

Alpha Buffer   An array of values that determine how pixels of a source image are merged with a destination image. Alpha buffers can be used to implement transparency, soft edges, and fading.

Back Buffer   A video buffer used to render the next frame. When this buffer is complete, it is exchanged with the front buffer to become visible.

Bit Block Transfer (bitblt)   A graphics operation that moves a rectangle of pixels from one place to another.

Blitter   A piece of hardware used to copy images from one buffer location to another.

Cooperative Level   In a Direct3D application, the cooperative level determines what an application will be allowed to do. If the application requests exclusive use of the screen, it can then run full-screen and change the video mode.

Deadband   In a control mechanism, the deadband is a range of input values between which the output is not affected—that is, the output appears "dead" if the input lies in this range. It is used to prevent hunting or drift in servo-mechanisms.

Decal   In the context of Direct3D, refers to what is more commonly known as a *sprite.*

Direction Vector   A vector that indicates a direction in 3D space.

Diffuse Reflection   The light scattered by an object, which is colored largely by the natural color of the object.

Double Buffer   A technique of using two (or sometimes more) image buffers to enable a moving scene to be updated without flickering. New data is written to the buffer that is not currently being displayed. The buffers are then swapped to show the new data.

Frame   A structure used to hold a set of visual elements and other (child) frames in a scene. Each frame includes a transform matrix that describes the world transform for the frame.

Front Buffer   The video buffer containing the currently visible scene. In a windowed application, this buffer is shared with other Windows-based applications.

Frustum   A pyramid truncated by a plane parallel to its base. Used to represent what is viewable in a 3D scene. The top of the frustum is the front clipping plane. The base is the back clipping plane.

Identity Matrix   A matrix that, when multiplied by any other matrix, leaves the original matrix unchanged.

Identity Palette   A logical Windows palette that corresponds exactly to the current state of the physical palette in the video hardware.

Immediate Mode   The Direct3D mode that allows a programmer to work more directly with the rendering hardware and software than does the Retained Mode.

Mesh   A collection of vertex and face descriptions (lists) that describe a 3D object.

Model Units   Arbitrary units that are used to describe the positions of object vertices in the 3D model you are building. These can be miles, meters, inches, or whatever you like, since the model is infinitely scalable.

Orthographic   A type of projection that essentially flattens an object against the projection surface. Typical of technical or construction drawings used in manufacturing and building.

Perspective   A type of projection that gives an illusion of depth. Faces that are relatively far away from the viewer are smaller than faces that are close to the viewer. Used to provide a realistic view of a solid object on a flat medium.

Pixel   A single picture element (dot) on the computer screen or in a bitmap.

Plumbing   The art of installing pipes, gutters, and toilets.

Quaternion   A mathematical representation for a rotation of N radians about a given axis. Used to represent object rotations in animated scenes.

Rasterizer   A device for translating a description of a picture into a series of horizontal lines of pixels.

Rendering Pipeline   A piece of hardware and/or software that processes graphical commands in sequence in order to create some sort of picture—usually in an image buffer.

Retained Mode   The Direct3D mode that allows a programmer to work with objects, lights, and 3D coordinates.

Scale Factor   A multiplying factor applied to make a thing bigger (to scale it up) or smaller (to scale it down).

Specular Reflection   Light reflected from a (typically) shiny object that is usually the color of the illuminating light source rather than the color of the object.

Texel   A single element from a texture map. Somewhat like a pixel but related to the map image rather than a screen.

Unit Vector   A vector whose length is unity (one unit), i.e., $x^2 + y^2 + z^2 = 1$.

Viewport   A mathematical representation of the bounding box of a scene as projected onto the viewing plane. The viewport describes what will be visible in the scene from the observer's viewpoint.

Wrap   A set of data that describes how a texture map is applied to a solid object, i.e., how the texture map is "wrapped" around the object.

Z Buffer   A buffer used to determine whether objects in a scene are in front of or behind the last pixel rendered to a given location. As pixels are rendered to the back buffer, their z value is set in the Z buffer.

Bibliography

I have referred to texts throughout this book, and to help you decide whether any of them would be of value to you, I've summarized here their value to me. I've also included one or two more books that I really like.

3D Computer Graphics: A User's Guide for Artists & Designers

By Andrew S. Glassner

Lyon & Burford. ISBN 1-55821-305-8

This book gives a great introduction to 3D computer graphics for the professional engineer or designer. It starts with some basic concepts, describes the computer hardware, and then moves on to cover shape generation, texture maps, and lighting—right up through animation. If you have no 3D background at all, this might be a good place to start.

Animation Techniques in Win32

By Nigel Thompson

Microsoft Press. ISBN 1-55615-669-3

Because I wrote this book, I'm just the tiniest bit biased as to its value. If you want to understand how bitmaps and especially palettes work in Windows, it's not bad. OK—it's the best.

C++ Component Patterns

By Dale Rogerson

Microsoft Press. ISBN 1-57231-349-8

To be published winter 1996. This book covers COM objects from top to bottom. Destined to become the standard on the subject.

Computer Graphics Principles and Practice

By Foley, vanDam, Feiner, and Hughes

Addison-Wesley. ISBN 0-201-12110-7

I love this book for its theoretical coverage of computer graphics in general. Its only drawback is that every time I want to see a piece of sample code, I find a student exercise instead! Not for the lazy code pasters among us.

Graphics Gems IV

Edited by Paul S. Heckbert

Academic Press. ISBN 0-12-336155-9

Actually, all of the *Graphics Gems* books are great for reference. I include this edition here because I happened to buy it recently and because it has some PointInPolygon routines that you could use to replace my rather feeble code.

Inside OLE 2

By Kraig Brockschmidt

Microsoft Press. ISBN 1-55615-618-9

This has been the reference text on COM objects and OLE programming for some time. I find it too long-winded and a little obscure in places, but it covers the subject of OLE programming in great depth. Not bedtime reading.

Microsoft Developer Network Development Library

By various authors, including Microsoft product groups, Rabbit's friends and relations, and me, too.

Microsoft Corporation

If you're already a Windows developer, then you'd have to have been hiding under a pretty big rock not to know about this CD-based programming reference. If you're new to the Windows experience, then you *must* subscribe to at least Level I, which gets you all the documentation on Windows programming you'll need for quite a while. Level II provides you with the SDKs for all of Microsoft's operating systems. The Level I CD includes my *Animation Techniques in Win32* and Brockschmidt's *Inside OLE 2*, to mention only two.

More Effective C++

By Scott Meyers

Addison-Wesley. ISBN 0-201-63371-X

If you've been writing C++ for a year or so, then I highly recommend this book. I learned so much on my first pass through that I wanted to rewrite every C++ class I'd ever created. I found the topics to be relevant, well explained, and extremely useful. My only regret is that I bought it after I wrote this book. How much more praise do you need? Not for the C++ novice, though.

Plumbing (Eighth Edition)

By William Paton Buchan

Crosby, Lockwood and Son, London.

First published in about 1850, this 1876 edition is an absolutely fabulous work for those with a passion for lead pipe, gutters, water closets, and all other aspects of plumbing. I found this book in a used book store in Gloucester, England, many years ago, and it is one of my favorite engineering books. William Buchan knew a thing or two about plumbing—he'd have made a great programmer.

Index

Page numbers in *italics* refer to figures and tables.

Numbers

I

J, K

L

M

macros, 45. *See also specific macros*
main window
  3D window as child of, 22–23
  creating, 20–22
  for tank application, 142–44
MakeCurrent function, 149, 159
material, 53–54
  adding to execute buffer, 303–4
  creating for D3DEval background, 298
  location of various parts of, *289*
  manipulating object in hardware, 289–90
  properties of, 169–71, *170, color insert*
matrices
  Immediate Mode, 291–92
    creating D3DEval, 297
    creating for D3DEval test, 300
  using for transformations, 104–6
maze
  building, 212
  floor plan of, *212*
memory
  frame capture and, 233
  transferring data from main, 32
  video, 30
    clippers, 262–63
    copying, 31–32
    surfaces, 260–61
mesh, 46
mesh builder interface, setting color and, 167
methods. *See specific method names*
MFC library, 4
Microsoft Video for Windows components, 245
m_ImageList member list object, 64
mode, setting, 269–70. *See also* windowed mode
MONO mode, 217
  capturing palettes in, 233
Mono rasterizer, 302
Motion Picture Expert Group. *See* MPEG
mouse axis mappings, *121*
mouse input devices. *See* input devices, mouse
movie, path to palette from, *234*. *See also* images

movie classes, 233
MPEG, 245
m_pScene = NULL, 28
m_ShapeList member list object, 64

N

NewScene function, 24–25, 144
Normalize function, 76
normals, 78–80, 82–83
  default, 86
  faces and, *79*
  for flat-faced cube, 86–87, *87*
  nonperpendicular
    and faces, *80*
    face with, *84*
  vertex
    and faces, *80*
    flat face showing, *82*
notification function, 147–48
  modified for blobs, 163–64
  use of in application, 148–49

O

OnCreate function, 22–24
OnDestroy message handler, 26
OnEditBkgndImg function, 172
OnEditDefcube function, 85
OnEditSolidr function, 91
OnIdle function, 4, 6, 9, 21
OnSelChange function, 148
OnUpdate function, 126–27, 142
OnUserEvent function, 121
OpenDocumentFile function, 21, 22
OpenFile function, 28
OpenGL rendering engine, 258
Optimize function, 242

P

palette
  captured, 242
  capturing, 233–35
  DirectDraw and, 261
  path from movie to, *234*

S

X

x-axis, 12–13, 72, *73*
  generating data value for, 118
    with joystick input devices, 123–24
    with keyboard input devices, 119–20
    with mouse input devices, 120–23
  relationship with other axes, *119*
  scale increase on, 109–10, *110*
  translation along, 107–8, *108*
    and rotation about y-axis, 110–12,
      111
XOF tag, 139

Y

y-axis, 12–13, 72, *73*
  creating solids of revolution and, 91
  generating data value for, 118
    with joystick input devices, 123–24
    with keyboard input devices, 119–20
    with mouse input devices, 120–23
  relationship with other axes, *119*
  rotation about, *108,* 108–9
    and translation along x-axis, 110–12,
      111
  scale increase on, *109, 110*

Z

z-axis, 12–13, 72, *73*
  creating solids of revolution and, 91
  generating data value for, 118
    with joystick input devices, 123–24
    with keyboard input devices, 119–20
    with mouse input devices, 120–23
  relationship with other axes, *119*
  scale increase on, *110*
Z buffer, 33
  enabling for D3DEval sample, 296

Nigel Thompson

Nigel Thompson was born in England on October 11, 1955, which makes him pretty old for a Microsoft developer.

At the Weymouth Grammar School in 1970, he learned to write computer programs in EGTRAN, a variant of FORTRAN IV, for an English Electric Leo-Marconi KDF9 computer. Nigel attended Southampton University in England, where he graduated in 1977 with an honors degree in electronics, specializing in semiconductor physics.

Nigel began his professional career as a diffusion engineer, working for the Mullard company in England manufacturing UHF bipolar transistors. He learned all about the Zilog Z80 one weekend while house-sitting a friend's cat. Armed with this experience, he got his first job as a microprocessor engineer for Sarasota Engineering, using RCA's 1802 to create traffic data-collection systems. While working for Sarasota, Nigel wrote a 1.802 assembler in BASIC, which he later ported to PL/Z, Zilog's high-level language for the Z80.

Many similar jobs later, Nigel founded his own company, Redwood Electronics. Redwood's first project was the building of a machine to convert data from 8-inch IBM diskettes to half-inch magnetic tape files using an 8088-based PC clone and some custom-designed interfaces.

Nigel also worked as a part-time contractor for QA Training in England, teaching Microsoft Windows 1.0 and later Windows 2.0 programming courses.

Nigel joined Microsoft in 1989 as a software design engineer in the Multimedia section of the Windows group. He went on to create the first Windows sound driver as a skunk-works project and later led the development of the system components of the Level I Multimedia Extensions to Windows. He spent a year porting the Multimedia Extensions to Windows NT before joining the Developer Network group, where he wrote technical articles for the Windows-challenged.

The manuscript for this book was prepared and submitted to Microsoft Press in electronic form. Text files were prepared using Microsoft Word 6.0 for Windows. Pages were composed by Microsoft Press using Aldus PageMaker 6.01 for Windows, with text in Stone Serif and display type in Univers. Composed pages were delivered to the printer as electronic prepress files.

Cover Graphic Designers
Greg Erickson, Robin Hjellen

Cover Illustrator
Glenn Mitsui

Interior Graphic Designer
Pam Hidaka

Illustrator
Michael Victor

Principal Compositor
Barbara Remmele

Principal Proofreader/Copy Editor
Richard Carey

Indexer
Leslie Leland Frank

IMPORTANT—READ CAREFULLY BEFORE OPENING SOFTWARE PACKET(S). By opening the sealed packet(s) containing the software, you indicate your acceptance of the following Microsoft License Agreement.

MICROSOFT LICENSE AGREEMENT
(Book Companion CD)

This is a legal agreement between you (either an individual or an entity) and Microsoft Corporation. By opening the sealed software packet(s) you are agreeing to be bound by the terms of this agreement. If you do not agree to the terms of this agreement, promptly return the unopened software packet(s) and any accompanying written materials to the place you obtained them for a full refund.

MICROSOFT SOFTWARE LICENSE

1. GRANT OF LICENSE. Microsoft grants to you the right to use one copy of the Microsoft software program included with this book (the "SOFTWARE") on a single terminal connected to a single computer. The SOFTWARE is in "use" on a computer when it is loaded into the temporary memory (i.e., RAM) or installed into the permanent memory (e.g., hard disk, CD-ROM, or other storage device) of that computer. You may not network the SOFTWARE or otherwise use it on more than one computer or computer terminal at the same time.

2. COPYRIGHT. The SOFTWARE is owned by Microsoft or its suppliers and is protected by United States copyright laws and international treaty provisions. Therefore, you must treat the SOFTWARE like any other copyrighted material (e.g., a book or musical recording) except that you may either (a) make one copy of the SOFTWARE solely for backup or archival purposes or (b) transfer the SOFTWARE to a single hard disk provided you keep the original solely for backup or archival purposes. You may not copy the written materials accompanying the SOFTWARE.

3. OTHER RESTRICTIONS. You may not rent or lease the SOFTWARE, but you may transfer the SOFTWARE and accompanying written materials on a permanent basis provided you retain no copies and the recipient agrees to the terms of this Agreement. You may not reverse engineer, decompile, or disassemble the SOFTWARE. If the SOFTWARE is an update or has been updated, any transfer must include the most recent update and all prior versions.

4. DUAL MEDIA SOFTWARE. If the SOFTWARE package contains more than one kind of disk (3.5", 5.25", and CD-ROM), then you may use only the disks appropriate for your single-user computer. You may not use the other disks on another computer or loan, rent, lease, or transfer them to another user except as part of the permanent transfer (as provided above) of all SOFTWARE and written materials.

5. SAMPLE CODE. If the SOFTWARE includes Sample Code, then Microsoft grants you a royalty-free right to reproduce and distribute the sample code of the SOFTWARE provided that you: (a) distribute the sample code only in conjunction with and as a part of your software product; (b) do not use Microsoft's or its authors' names, logos, or trademarks to market your software product; (c) include the copyright notice that appears on the SOFTWARE on your product label and as a part of the sign-on message for your software product; and (d) agree to indemnify, hold harmless, and defend Microsoft and its authors from and against any claims or lawsuits, including attorneys' fees, that arise or result from the use or distribution of your software product.

DISCLAIMER OF WARRANTY

The SOFTWARE (including instructions for its use) is provided "AS IS" WITHOUT WARRANTY OF ANY KIND. MICROSOFT FURTHER DISCLAIMS ALL IMPLIED WARRANTIES INCLUDING WITHOUT LIMITATION ANY IMPLIED WARRANTIES OF MERCHANTABILITY OR OF FITNESS FOR A PARTICULAR PURPOSE. THE ENTIRE RISK ARISING OUT OF THE USE OR PERFORMANCE OF THE SOFTWARE AND DOCUMENTATION REMAINS WITH YOU.

IN NO EVENT SHALL MICROSOFT, ITS AUTHORS, OR ANYONE ELSE INVOLVED IN THE CREATION, PRODUCTION, OR DELIVERY OF THE SOFTWARE BE LIABLE FOR ANY DAMAGES WHATSOEVER (INCLUDING, WITHOUT LIMITATION, DAMAGES FOR LOSS OF BUSINESS PROFITS, BUSINESS INTERRUPTION, LOSS OF BUSINESS INFORMATION, OR OTHER PECUNIARY LOSS) ARISING OUT OF THE USE OF OR INABILITY TO USE THE SOFTWARE OR DOCUMENTATION, EVEN IF MICROSOFT HAS BEEN ADVISED OF THE POSSIBILITY OF SUCH DAMAGES. BECAUSE SOME STATES/COUNTRIES DO NOT ALLOW THE EXCLUSION OR LIMITATION OF LIABILITY FOR CONSEQUENTIAL OR INCIDENTAL DAMAGES, THE ABOVE LIMITATION MAY NOT APPLY TO YOU.

U.S. GOVERNMENT RESTRICTED RIGHTS

The SOFTWARE and documentation are provided with RESTRICTED RIGHTS. Use, duplication, or disclosure by the Government is subject to restrictions as set forth in subparagraph (c)(1)(ii) of The Rights in Technical Data and Computer Software clause at DFARS 252.227-7013 or subparagraphs (c)(1) and (2) of the Commercial Computer Software — Restricted Rights 48 CFR 52.227-19, as applicable. Manufacturer is Microsoft Corporation, One Microsoft Way, Redmond, WA 98052-6399.

If you acquired this product in the United States, this Agreement is governed by the laws of the State of Washington. Should you have any questions concerning this Agreement, or if you desire to contact Microsoft Press for any reason, please write: Microsoft Press, One Microsoft Way, Redmond, WA 98052-6399.

Register Today!

Return this
3D Graphics Programming for Windows 95
registration card for a Microsoft Press catalog

1-57231-345-5A   ***3D GRAPHICS PROGRAMMING FOR WINDOWS* 95**   *Owner Registration Card*

NAME

INSTITUTION OR COMPANY NAME

ADDRESS

CITY   STATE   ZIP

Microsoft Press
Quality Computer Books

**For a free catalog of
Microsoft Press® products, call
1-800-MSPRESS**